# Teachers Under Pressure

Our education system has undergone a process of enormous and rapid change and, all too often, teachers have found that insufficient support has been offered to help them cope with this. As a result, most teachers now find that they experience stress of one sort or another at some point during their career.

As a direct reaction to this, the NASUWT have commissioned a comprehensive study of the issue of teacher stress. This book reports on the findings of that study, and the implications this has not only for teachers, but also for the pupils they teach.

Cheryl Travers and Cary Cooper's book:

- helps to identify which teachers are currently at risk of stress;
- explores how teachers' problems vary according to where they work, their grade, whether they are male or female, and the age range they teach;
- suggests ways in which the problems of teachers can be helped;
- suggests preventative action to minimise stress and maximise educational experience.

The result is an extensive survey of the current state of teachers' health, well-being and job satisfaction, combined with practical ways forward. As the major study in the UK of teachers' stress, this book provides teachers, heads, lecturers, governors and policy makers with invaluable empirical evidence on this crucial subject. Clearly, by helping the teacher, we also help the learning process and the children who depend on it.

**Cheryl Travers** is Lecturer in Organizational Behaviour and Human Resource Management at Loughborough University Business School. She has trained a great number of teachers in stress and time management. **Cary Cooper** is Professor of Organizational Psychology at the University of Manchester Institute of Science and Technology. He has published many books on the subject of stress in the workplace.

# Teachers Under Pressure
## Stress in the Teaching Profession

Cheryl J. Travers and Cary L. Cooper

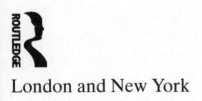

London and New York

First published 1996
by Routledge
11 New Fetter Lane, London EC4P 4EE

Simultaneously published in the USA and Canada
by Routledge
29 West 35th Street, New York, NY 10001

Typeset in Times by Keystroke, Jacaranda Lodge, Wolverhampton

Printed and bound in Great Britain by TJ Press (Padstow) Ltd, Padstow, Cornwall

*British Library Cataloguing in Publication Data*
A catalogue record for this book is available from the British Library

*Library of Congress Cataloguing in Publication Data*
A catalogue record for this book has been requested

ISBN 0–415–09484–4

*To Shirley (Mum)*
*and Kevin (Dad)*
*for the best teaching I've ever had.*

*To my closest teachers and mentors,*
*Fred Massarik and Peter B. Smith.*

# Contents

# Illustrations

**FIGURES**

**TABLES**

# Preface

In 1965, A. Kornhauser, an American professor, suggested in his acclaimed book, *The Mental Health of the Industrial Worker*, that:

> Mental health is not so much a freedom from specific frustrations as it is an overall balanced relationship to the world, which permits a person to maintain a realistic, positive belief in himself and his purposeful activities. Insofar as his entire job and life situation facilitate and support such feelings of adequacy, inner security, and meaningfulness of his existence, it can be presumed that his mental health will tend to be good. What is important in a negative way is not any single characteristic of his situation but everything that deprives the person of purpose and zest, that leaves him with negative feelings about himself, with anxieties, tensions, a sense of lostness, emptiness, and futility.

Unfortunately, this description aptly reflects what most teachers are currently experiencing in schools throughout the UK. Enormous change has taken place in teaching which most teachers find difficult to cope with. It is not that the majority of the changes are intrinsically flawed, but rather that the individual teachers have been unable to cope with the pace and extent of the change. Within a short period of time, a major restructuring of the teaching profession, schools and the educational establishment has taken place, from the National Curriculum to local management of schools to budget holding at school level to student assessment. Most of these changes have been introduced without piloting or adequate preparation. Many of them, teachers agree, were needed, but the way they were introduced and the way in which change was managed (or not managed) have created an environment ripe for stress and its nefarious consequences for the individual, students and education.

It was because of this concern that the second largest teachers union, the NASUWT, commissioned us to carry out a national study to assess the extent and sources of teachers stress throughout England, Wales, Scotland and Northern Ireland. The purpose of this research, which is reported in this book, was not to castigate government or win any political battles, but to help to identify which teachers are currently at risk of stress, and what can be done to help the individual teacher and the educational system deal with the problems. The problems of teachers were drawn to our attention over recent years by numerous letters, telephone calls, etc., particularly to our unit concerned with occupational stress, and finally culminating with a motion at the annual conference of the NASUWT to explore more systematically the issue of teacher stress. It was with the support and active help and encouragement of the union, therefore, that this work was undertaken.

This book will attempt to explore, therefore, the problems of teachers in all regions of the UK, focusing specifically on differences between various teaching grades, between male and female, and between different sectors (e.g. primary and secondary), all in an effort to provide a map of the current state of teachers' health, well-being and job satisfaction, and to suggest 'ways forward' in terms of remedial and preventative action to minimise stress and maximise the educational experience. If we can help the teacher, we can help the learning process and the children that depend on it. It is important to understand that teachers, like many other workers are                                                                                                         not driven by money in pursuit of their careers but by many other motives. As F. Terkel (1972) suggests in his book *Working*: 'It (work) is about a search, too, for daily meaning, as well as daily bread, for recognition as well as cash, for astonishment rather than torpor; in short, for a sort of life rather than a Monday through Friday sort of dying.' We hope this book will help to highlight the problems and joys of teaching, to minimise the former and maximise the latter.

# Acknowledgements

The authors would like to express their thanks to the NASUWT for all their help and support throughout the study, all the teachers who gave their time and opinions to make the study possible, and Jenny Ellison for much needed secretarial support.

# Part I
# Background to the study of teacher stress

*The proper study of mankind is books.*
(Aldous Huxley)

# 1 Introduction
## Why Teacher Stress?

> The end result [of teacher stress] is that many talented men and women with high expectations of achievement are dispirited and disillusioned. Some leave the profession, others stay but are plagued by a multitude of physical, emotional and behavioural stress-related manifestations.
>
> (Milstein and Golaszewski 1985)

The above comment outlines what happens as a response to teacher stress. The picture created is not a pleasant one but has to be taken seriously. In the last few years, the incidence of stress among teachers has received a considerable amount of attention, particularly by the press, teacher unions and academics (e.g. Phillips and Lee 1980). In an international review of teacher stress and burnout, Kyriacou (1987) refers to the occurrence and consequences of stress in the teaching profession in countries as widespread as Great Britain, the United States, Israel, Canada and New Zealand. The vast array of books, journal articles, newspaper reports and workshops has lead to a multiplicity of approaches and a wide variety of opinions with very little in the way of consensus. Due to the findings from these studies and the public display by teachers and their unions, teaching has recently become characterised as being among the league of traditionally viewed high-stress occupations (e.g. Milstein and Golaszewski 1985). Teachers are reported as being stressed by the workload, the behaviour of the pupils, lack of promotion prospects, unsatisfactory working conditions, poor relationships with colleagues, pupils and administrators and a host of other problems. There are a multitude of studies that draw attention to the prevalence of the perception of stress among school teachers (e.g. Kyriacou 1987).

Although there have been many attempts to investigate the real causes and symptoms of teacher stress, often the findings of such studies have not been consistent. A major problem has been the variety of ways in which people have studied the phenomena of teacher stress, and also the fact that teachers are often reluctant to admit the extent to which they experience stress due to the fear that it may be seen as a weakness. However, over the last 10 years there have been many changes that have resulted in disillusioned teachers expressing their concerns, and bringing the issue of teacher stress into the spotlight.

This book aims to explain and explore the causes and consequences of teacher stress in more detail, and to present the results of a major nation-wide UK study of stress among teachers. Comprising seven chapters, the book is divided into three parts. In this chapter of Part I we shall provide a backdrop to the study and outline the changes that teachers have been experiencing. This chapter will also provide a working definition of stress as used throughout the book and the research upon which it is based. Chapters 2 and 3 will explore the consequences and sources of stress in the teachers' environment. Part II will present the results of the study with Chapter 4 describing the sample, Chapter 5 documenting how Britain's teachers are responding to stress and Chapter 6 reporting on the sources of pressure and their effects. Finally, Part III will make recommendations as to some of the ways stress in Britain's schools may be alleviated.

## CHANGE AND ITS EFFECT ON TEACHER STRESS

Whatever the merits of such changes and their final outcomes, there is no doubt that radical change in itself, is a source of stress and its possible effects and consequences for schools need to be positively managed.

(HMSO 1990)

Cox *et al.* (1988) have identified change as a major factor among current sources of stress for teachers and adds that it is: 'not only change, but change-on-change beyond the control of most teachers that is a cause of stress.' Many of the pressures of change, associated with increased demands on time (e.g. changes in the curriculum), require teachers to assimilate proposed changes, examine their current practice and, in the light of new requirements, modify it. In addition, they are expected to evaluate the success of these modifications by assessing the progress of pupils, and to review their practice accordingly.

## A BRIEF HISTORY OF THE BACKGROUND TO THE CHANGES

By the late 1970's a number of LEA's began to appreciate the scale of the falling birth rate and the effect it would have upon their school rolls. For some, the prospect was that by 1990 they would not have enough pupils to fill half their existing schools. Change was inevitable, yet the issue of what to do with surplus capacity in schools generated a number of controversies.

(Ranson 1990)

Between 1955 and 1975, education was the fastest growing service whether in the public or the private sector (Cheshire 1976). This was in part due to: a rising birth rate, economic growth and political will. In addition, growing school populations after World War II led to a greater emphasis upon expanding educational programmes to provide equal opportunities for development for all pupils (James 1980). Many would argue that the 'widespread belief in the benefit of education to society and the economy' (Ranson 1990) does not exist at present.

As educational growth occurred, expectations of the standards of the service increased, and the 1970s brought concern as to whether the ambitions were being fulfilled, particularly in evaluation of achievement and behaviour, curriculum and preparation for transition from school to work. Also the question arose as to whether the teachers were properly accountable to parents and the community, as well as to the LEA. A major question leading to changes in the curriculum span was the desire to reduce the differences between schools and further education (DES 1980), i.e. redirect teaching towards the needs of industry and employment (cf. MSC 1984), or widen curricular choice and expand educational opportunity (Hargreaves Report 1984; Pring 1984; Ranson *et al.* 1986).

The reverse of these features were those which led to the contraction of education in the mid-1970s. Many changes taking place within education have been due to a dramatic fall in the birth rate between the years 1964 and 1977, and only a slight rise since then. This has had a dramatic effect on the number of pupils in school and the peak of 9 million in 1977 was expected to decline to below 7 million by 1990. Although subsequently it was expected to increase, it could not be expected to increase the school rolls automatically. This meant that LEAs could not anticipate filling the spare places in classes, as young people were also choosing to leave school to go on to further training.

In addition, after the Middle East war in 1973, many cuts in public expenditure and local authority spending were made and were designed to reduce education costs, which accounted for 60 per cent of local government budgets. Ranson (1990) states that Peston (1982) and Stewart (1983) revealed substantial cuts in allocated expenditure, when analysing the value of rate support grants in 'real' terms, and that constraints on expenditure have grown more severe in the 1980s. This has had serious implications for the working environment of teachers. The HM Inspectorate produced annual reports on effects of expenditure policies in education and concluded that:

> Many schools are finding it increasingly difficult to replace old books, equipment and furniture, to implement curricular change, and to respond to planned changes in assessment and examination procedures.
>
> (HMI 1986)

This is likely to have effects on the teachers and, inevitably, on the young people in schools (Hewton 1986), and will affect morale and the quality of teaching. Claims by the Conservative government that spending per pupil has risen since 1979, may indeed be accurate, but as LEAs have been reluctant to close schools and reduce teaching forces, cuts in other areas of expenditure have been inescapable.

The fact that there were a number of elements of transformation and challenge occurring simultaneously for teachers throughout this period, which required major changes in the operation of the service (i.e. 'No change was not an option' (Fiske 1978)) have had a number of implications, affecting the job of teaching, which will be briefly outlined in the following sections.

## CHANGES IN THE JOB OF THE TEACHER

The Education Reform Act (1988) introduced the following changes:

1 the introduction of the National Curriculum and testing and assessment;
2 new requirements for religious worship;
3 local financial management of schools;
4 changes in the membership, responsibilities, and powers of governing bodies;
5 granting schools the right to 'opt-out' of local authority control;
6 establishment of city technology colleges;
7 open enrolment.

One of the changes that has resulted in a great deal of disruption in the education sector, has been the introduction of the assessment and testing of seven year olds. Recently there have been many disagreements with regard to these changes. The NUT, for example, Britain's largest teaching union, attempted to boycott the tests, only to have their members vote against the boycott, in an effort to avoid another head-on collision with the government.

In addition, there have been other major governmental changes in the five years prior to the study which have also added 'fuel to the already simmering fire'.

1 Abolition of the teachers' Pay Review Body and its replacement by an 'Advisory Committee'.
2 Changes in conditions in service, in particular the introduction of the 'Directed time budget' and compulsory assumption of new responsibilities.
3 GRIST (Grant-Related-In-Service-Training) and five Baker Days for INSET training.
4 Technical and Vocational Educational Initiative (TVEI).
5 Abolition of the Inner London Education Authority (ILEA).

These changes have lead to extra pressures being imposed upon teachers, with greater levels of uncertainty, job insecurity and the restructuring of teaching itself. Local Management of Schools and new ways of working brought in by the Education Reform Act, have put enormous pressures on those working within schools. It is not just changes in governmental policies that have led to problems for teachers. As Esteve (1989) explains:

accelerated social changes have had a profound effect on the part played by teachers in the teaching process, without many teachers having known how to adapt themselves to these changes.

Naturally, with increasing change and new policies, added administration and information packages have been introduced. A teacher from the West Midlands was quoted as saying: 'They used to send us letters, now it's videos and books' (*The Independent on Sunday*, 24 March 1991).

This increased need for administration is reported to be a problem for teachers, and this may have subsequent effects on their job satisfaction and attitudes towards teaching as a whole. For example, a female primary teacher was reported in the same newspaper as saying:

> It's the sheer volume of new things we have to take on board. Look at this [she indicates a pile of fat booklets containing details of the tests and how to mark them] – it all has to be read and digested this week-end. A lot of teachers are getting to the stage when they feel, 'what about me and life beyond teaching?'.

The next chapter will look at the consequences of stress in teaching, and in particular teachers' intentions to leave the profession. This seems to be a way in which teachers are reflecting their discontent. Esteve (1989) explains that the major problems resulting from these changes described above are due to the fact that:

> administrators have come up with no strategies for coping with this new situation, above all, in the training of teachers, where no effort has been devoted to answering the demands created by the aforementioned changes.

He identified five recent major societal changes that have imposed pressure on teachers and have therefore created reasons as to why the study of teacher stress is growing increasingly important. These changes are those which Esteve refers to as 'secondary factors' (i.e. environmental-based, affecting the *situation* in which teaching takes place). 'Primary factors', on the other hand, are those which have a direct effect on the teacher in the classroom (e.g. pupil behaviour). The secondary changes Esteve refers to are:

- transformation of the role of the teacher and of the traditional agents of social integration;
- increasing contradictions in the role of the teacher;
- changes in the attitude of society towards the teacher;
- uncertainty about the objectives of the education system and the furthering of knowledge;
- the deterioration of the image of the teacher.

**Transformation of the role of the teacher and of the traditional agents of social integration**

The demands facing teachers have changed quite dramatically in the last 15–20 years, leading to greater responsibilities being imposed upon teachers. At the same time, the family and community in general have been accepting less responsibility for the educational well-being of the child. The major problems facing teachers, however, are due to the fact that these increases in responsibility have not necessarily or adequately been accompanied by appropriate changes in facilities and training to equip them to deal with these new demands. Therefore, the process of adaptation has not been an easy one and has led to confusion as to what the role of the teacher actually is (Goble and Porter 1980). This situation was summed up by a teacher when she said that teachers are now expected to be surrogate parents and social workers as well as educators:

> With some of the kids I feel that I'm bringing them up. The parents expect me to do their disciplinarian work.
>
> (*The Independent on Sunday*, 24 March 1991)

According to Claude Merazzi (1983), who is Director of a major Swiss training college, society expects teachers to fulfil the function of resolving conflicts. Training, therefore, needs to take this into account, but often fails to do so. He has outlined three fundamental features of this change, which are a result of the increase in 'dual career families' (Cooper and Lewis 1994): the amount of time parents can spend with their children; the size of families; and changes in the degree of involvement in the task of education from parents to other relatives (e.g. older brothers/sisters, aunts, uncles and grandparents). Therefore, these 'voids' have to be considered by teachers, as many parents believe that more should be done for their children while they are in school.

There have also been changes in the role of the teacher as a 'transmitter of knowledge' in the traditional sense. Teachers are often having to modify their traditional role in order to incorporate the style of powerful 'media' linked sources of information (e.g. TV, computers). This may not always be possible, if the resources within the school are not sufficient to meet the needs of all of the children within it.

Today's society has very clear views on the role of school, education and society; this means that whatever stance teachers may take, they face possible criticism. It might indeed be the case that if teachers do not clearly define the type of education they wish to encourage, then they may encounter problems. They need to be able to defend the model they incorporate. With schooling a reality for 100 per cent of the population, teachers need to be sufficiently equipped to cater for a wide variety of pupil beliefs and ideals. A 1981 International Labour Organisation (ILO) report stated that it is unfair to expect teachers to meet the challenges imposed by a world in rapid transformation if they do not have the adequate means at their disposal.

## Increasing contradictions in the role of the teacher

These vast changes mean that the various roles of teachers are often contradictory. They are required to fulfil the role of 'friend, colleague and helper', a role perhaps incompatible with that of 'evaluator, selector and disciplinarian'. Although these examples of role contradiction may be seen to be traditional, it must be accepted that the accelerated social changes have increased the number of contradictions. Faure (1973) has suggested that a major problem for teachers is the preparation of pupils for a future society that does not yet exist. Even a healthy individual, when faced with rapid change, may find stress unavoidable. The time schedule is also crucial (Toffler 1970).

## Changes in the attitude of society towards the teacher

> Teachers are persecuted by the development of a society which forces profound changes upon their profession.
>
> (Ranjard 1984)

Ranjard states that, with regard to work, teachers feel persecuted, as the expectations, support and judgement of teachers has changed in the social context within which they work. In recent years, attempts have been made to blame teachers for all types of ills (e.g. the Heysel Stadium disaster in Brussels (Cole 1985) and increasing vandalism). This belief that teachers are to blame for a vast number of deficiencies, and a general unease of the education system, has spread among politicians, the mass media and even pupils' parents.

In addition, there have been changes with regard to society's attitudes towards discipline in schools, often to the detriment of the teachers. They are often left with very little means of control and support from their immediate bosses. This can be seen in the following example:

> Teachers at the Bishop of Llandaff High School were on strike last week because of the governors' refusal to expel three boys who allegedly assaulted a girl. The governors suspended them for four weeks. The case brings echoes of Poundswick school in Manchester where, four years ago, the council overruled the expulsion of five pupils who had daubed obscene and racist graffiti on school walls. Staff who refused to teach the boys were suspended without pay for nine months.
>
> (*The Independent on Sunday*, 24 March 1991)

## Uncertainty about the objectives of the education system and the furthering of knowledge

It is absurd to maintain within mass education the objectives of a system designed for the education of an elite.

(Ranjard 1984)

With the implementation of 'mass education', qualifications no longer guarantee a student future employment. This change will have an effect on the level of motivation that a teacher can expect to encourage and instill in his or her students. This means that many teachers are facing the difficulty of aiming to work towards objectives that no longer correspond to existing societal circumstances.

Teachers also face the problem of trying to keep their knowledge up-to-date. For example, modern advances in new technologies mean that many teachers will have to incorporate new ideas and facts that did not exist when they began teaching, and they are not often given the chance to update their knowledge.

## The deterioration of the image of the teacher

The traditional 'stereotype' of the teacher has been one of friend and adviser, dedicated to helping and relating to students, one who, in or out of school, maintains an attitude of service. This is increasingly being replaced by the media-based stereotypes linking teachers with physical violence in the classroom, dismissals, ideological clashes, low salaries, lack of materials and facilities, and even poor heating (Esteve 1984)! It is becoming apparent that teacher training tends to over-promote the first stereotype and neglect the potential reality of the second. This may mean that inexperienced teachers may experience problems, as they are ill-equipped to deal with the range of varied difficulties they face (Martinez 1984).

## Conclusion

So, it would seem that the main reasons for a greater emphasis on the problems faced by the teaching profession and the resulting stress has been due to the changes in their role and ways of working, but how widespread is that stress?

## THE PREVALENCE OF TEACHER STRESS

Many researchers investigating teacher stress have attempted to estimate the percentage of teachers actually experiencing high levels of perceived stress. The results have varied considerably, such that reports have concluded the figure to be from 30 to 90 per cent (e.g. Hawkes and Dedrick 1983; Laughlin 1984). British research has indicated that between one-fifth and one-third of teachers experience a great deal of stress (e.g. Dunham 1983; Pratt 1978). More teachers than ever before are experiencing 'severe stress' according to Dunham (1983).

Teacher stress, however, is not just a British phenomenon. Teachers in American studies have been found to be showing slightly higher levels of perceived stress than those in British studies (Sparks 1983). In addition, a survey conducted by the National Education Association reported that 70 per cent of US teachers experience moderate to considerable levels of stress (Coates and Thoresen 1976).

A study by the Chicago Teachers' Union (1978) discovered that 56 per cent of the teachers reported suffering physical illness and 26 per cent were suffering mental illness which they related to stress on the job. A survey by the National Education Association also gave evidence of the major sources of teacher stress (McGuire 1979). Tunnelcliffe *et al.* (1986) revealed that teachers in Western Australia believed that they were working under considerable stress. The researchers claimed that 'the problem of teacher occupational stress and the search for effective ways of stress management remains chronic'.

However, there are a number of contrasting findings. For example, a recent survey of 3,300 Ohio public school teachers by Feitler and Tokar (1982) found that only 16 per cent of the sample reported their jobs to be 'very stressful' or 'extremely stressful'. In addition, Bentz *et al.* (1971) investigated a number of groups, including school teachers, and discovered that only one in three teachers reported even *mild* to *moderate* emotional symptoms, and that the overall mental health of teachers was slightly better than that of the general public. Hiebert and Farber (1984) emphasise the need for caution when proclaiming teaching a 'stressful' occupation, as it may set up an 'expectancy' to be stressed. This means that teachers may be more vulnerable to stress-induced disorders. Their questions were based on a review of 71 articles concerning teacher stress, and suggested that there was little empirical support for the claim that teaching is a stressful job.

Regardless of the contradictions, in some findings both in this country and the US, the overall results suggest that all teachers will experience some degree of occupational stress. Although, as Fimian (1982) explains: 'the frequency with which stressful incidents occur and the strength of their occurrence varies from teacher to teacher'.

Depending on the biographical characteristics of the individual (i.e. individual psychological characteristics), situational demands (i.e. intensity and duration) and past experiences, as well as differences in the appraisal process in the individual, a potential stressor may become an actual stressor. Subsequent chapters in this book will aim to examine the role of the individual teacher in terms of his or her own stress experience.

Consequently, the effects of stressful events on teachers' well-being will greatly depend on the mediating effect of differences in physiological, psychological and social responses (Krause and Stryker 1984). A UK study by Hiebert and Farber (1984) showed that although teacher stress did not vary much between schools, reported levels of stress varied widely within schools. The increase in concern regarding the issue of teacher stress arises mainly from the growing awareness of the negative aspects of prolonged occupational stress on both the teachers' mental and physical well-being, as well as on the working relationships of the teachers and their pupils. It also helps lead to an improvement in the quality of working life for teachers as well as the quality of their teaching (Kyriacou 1987). These costs and consequences of stress in teaching will be considered in more detail in the next chapter.

## THE NATURE OF STRESS: WHAT IS IT?

> Stress is ordinary and commonplace, but its clearly definable properties are elusive.
>
> (Goldberg 1983)

> This strange disease of modern life.
>
> (Matthew Arnold)

In order to study stress in teachers we need to be clear that we understand what we mean by the term 'stress'. The major problem for anyone attempting to read and understand about stress is that it has taken on many different meanings, which are sometimes contradictory and confusing. The word 'stress' has become largely a buzz word that is used in a variety of settings, and most people do not define what they mean by the word. Many of the criticisms of its usage have come down on the fact that we do not have a clear picture of current thinking about what stress actually is. Selye (1983) also makes the point that stress as a concept suffers 'from the mixed blessing of being too well known and too little understood'. This feature of stress as having an 'elusive' nature is enhanced by the fact that a single definition fails to be agreed upon, as Cox (1978) remarks:

> It is a concept which is familiar to both layman and professional alike; it is understood by all when used in a general context but by very few when a more precise account is required, and this seems to be a central problem.

We would like to present here a clear conceptualisation, and thus understanding, of the definition of stress, at a fundamental level, used throughout this book, both in the way our study was carried out and the interpretation of its findings.

### Definitions of stress

One area in which, it appears, people are in agreement is with regard to the definitions of the terms 'stressor' and 'strain' (Beehr and Franz 1986).

A 'stressor' is something in the environment that acts as a stimulus, and is either physical, psychological or behavioural in nature. A 'strain' response is used as an indicator of ill health and/or well-being of the individual. Of interest in this particular study are those *stressors* resulting from the job of the teacher, occurring in the teaching environment, that may cause *strain* to be subsequently experienced by the individual teacher.

When looking at the stress phenomenon, it can be seen that stress can have both positive and negative consequences for the individual. It can, up to a certain point, be a stimulant, and can have positive consequences (e.g. a new coping skill or resource may be developed) (Hoover-Dempsey and Kendall 1982), but it is important that individuals can find their optimal stress levels. The important point to note is that an event will not have the same stressful implications for all individuals. It may be a case of 'one man's meat is another man's poison'. Certain characteristics of the individual (e.g. age, sex, education, personality characteristics, social situations and past experiences) can all lead to variations as to what constitutes a stressful experience. This study therefore will aim to incorporate aspects of individuals which may exacerbate their responses and experience of stress.

Further confusion in conceptualising stress is derived from the multiplicity of methods employed to investigate its existence and nature. As Payne *et al.* (1982) have expressed:

> There have been problems in definitional and conceptual clarity, questionable causal inferences from self-report data correlating stress and strain, and often untested action recommended.

This means that an understanding of the stress phenomenon is still limited. Pearlin *et al.* (1981) claim that the methodology employed will dictate the particular manifestation of stress that may be observed (e.g. what is the focus), in the functioning of the individual, where the stress response is most clearly reflected (e.g. physiological, behavioural or psychological).

Additional criticisms of stress research result from its heavy reliance upon correlational data, which limits inferences about causality and does not consider the role of intervening variables, the lack of adequate control groups and the use of retrospective studies. Therefore, as Kasl (1983) concludes, four main approaches to stress have emerged:

- as present in the environment;
- as an appraisal of that environment;
- as a response to conditions in the environment;
- as some form of interaction between the environmental demands and the individual's ability to meet those demands.

The methodology which was employed in this particular study of stress aims to gather data along the lines of the views expressed by Kasl outlined above.

## WAYS OF CONCEPTUALISING STRESS

In studying occupational stress, researchers have focused on one of the following three approaches.

1 *Stress as the dependent variable, i.e. the response.* Here researchers have focused on stress as a response to stimuli that may be a disturbing situation or environment, e.g. shift work, noxious environments. Responses may be physiological, psychological or behavioural.
2 *Stress as the independent variable, i.e. the stimulus.* Researchers have concentrated on stress as the phenomenon which is extraneous to the individual, with no account taken of individual perceptions, experience, etc. Stress is a disruptive environmental agent.
3 *Stress as the intervening variable, i.e. the interactionist approach.* This approach emphasises the importance of the way individuals perceive and react to situations which are forced upon them; it reflects therefore a 'lack of fit' between the individual and the environment, its antecedents and effects – a stimulus–response approach (Fisher 1986).

The above three approaches do cover common ground, but mainly differ in the definition they propose, and the methodologies they employ to investigate the phenomena.

### Stress as a response

This view of stress as expressed in the response-based model is one of a dependent variable – that is, it is described in terms of the person's response to some threatening or disturbing stimuli. As Fisher (1986) suggests: 'A person can be deduced to have been exposed to stressful conditions if signs of strain are present.'

Most people can readily sympathise with the plea of being 'under pressure' as the most obvious tangible evidence we have of the effects on an individual of stress is the symptoms that are exhibited. Other adjectives that may be used synonymously with stress are tension, strain and pressure. This means that of most interest in this model of stress is the manifestation of stress. Stress responses may occur at three levels: the psychological, behavioural and physiological levels (see Figure 1.1). Although this model creates the impression that the three types of response are discrete elements, this is not so, as the three are interrelated, though the exact relationship between them is not clear (Schuler 1980).

### Stress as a stimulus

This is an approach to stress that links health and disease to certain conditions in the individual's external environment. In the fifth century BC, Hippocrates believed that the external environment conditioned characteristics of health and disease (Goodell *et al.* 1986). This early approach to

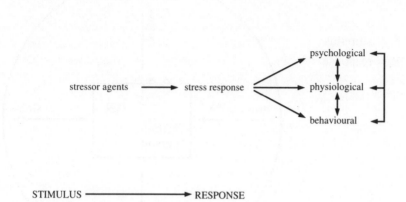

Figure 1.1 A response-based model of stress
*Source:* Sutherland and Cooper (1991)

stress perceives stress as an independent variable and employs a simple static model to explain its major proponents. It is a definition that is well established and widely used in the research literature, resting firmly on models based upon the physical sciences, in particular engineering.

The view is that various disturbing features in the environment impinge upon the individual in a disruptive way, and that this brings about changes in the individual. The observable strain level and type will depend upon the individual and the duration and severity of the pressure exerted. In 'people' terms, the pressure may be physical or emotional, and, if taking place over a period of time, may eventually lead to various anxiety reactions, which in turn may become stressful (see Figure 1.2). Therefore, as Fisher (1986) points out: 'Stress is assumed to be a condition of the environment. The environment could be physical or psychological.'

Methodology employed by this approach usually attempts to focus on the identification of potentially stressful stimuli: environmental stressors (e.g. noise), social stressors (e.g. racism), psychological stressors (e.g. depression), physical stressors (e.g. disability), economic stressors (e.g. poverty) and natural disasters (e.g. floods). Therefore, an attempt is being made to measure the toxicity of a stimulus (e.g. Holmes and Rahe 1967).

This approach has been given a tremendous amount of attention in the research of occupational stress, and studies have attempted to isolate features in the work environment that are detrimental to the individual's psychological and physiological well-being. One possible cause for its popularity is perhaps the 'scientific approach' that it utilises. It allows researchers in psychology to measure stress in a more mechanistic way; that is, in much the same way as we might observe stress imposed on a bridge and its effects. Inherent in this stress theory is that any individual has a

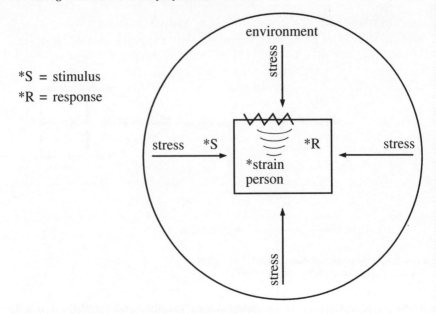

*S = stimulus
*R = response

*Figure 1.2* A stimulus-based model of stress
*Source:* Sutherland and Cooper (1991)

tolerance level that may be exceeded, and this 'over-stepping' may result in temporary or permanent damage. This also emphasises the fact that an individual is exposed to a multitude of stressors *all* of the time and may cope with these quite effectively, though it may just take a minor insignificant event to 'tip the balance' between coping behaviour and potential total breakdown.

A large emphasis on the approach was made with the rapid increase in industrialisation and its subsequent relevance to the physical, working environment (i.e. noise, heat) and to the task itself (e.g. work overload).

Selye (1980) has emphasised, importantly, that the word and concept 'stress' must not be assumed to be automatically negative, as it can be viewed as a stimulant and is a feature of living. He divides stress into the positive 'eustress' (i.e. a motivator for growth, development and change) and the negative 'distress', the unwanted, unmanageable and possibly damaging type of stress. This is the central theme of the stimulus-based model (i.e. the identification of potential sources of stress). He describes four types of stress that may be experienced by the individual: overstress or *Hyperstress*; under stress or *Hypostress*; bad stress or *Distress*; good stress or *Eustress*.

## Stress as an interaction

For the majority of those working in the area of stress research today, stress is no longer seen as a static phenomenon, as a response or a stimulus, but rather as a complex process, incorporating both of the previously mentioned models. Pearlin *et al.* (1981) suggested that: 'Stress is not a happening, instead it is a complex, varied and intellectually challenging process.' There has therefore been a shift from viewing psychological stress as either an environmental demand or as a response, to viewing it rather in relational terms (e.g. McGrath 1974; Cox 1978; Cooper *et al.* 1988).

A large number of researchers working in terms of these relational models conceptualise stress as an interaction or transaction between the person and the environment (e.g. Cooper *et al.* 1988). These theorists assume that people both influence and respond to their environments. Therefore, stress is essentially the degree of fit between the person and the environment. In other words, it is not the environment *per se* that is stressful, but it is the relationship between the person and the environment which may result in the experience of stress. Figure 1.3 provides a version of an interactive model of stress. Stressful transactions are therefore seen as a product of the two interacting systems. Stress occurs at the point at which the magnitude of the stress stimuli exceeds the individual's capacity to resist. In order to deal with the experience of stress, a person may attempt either to alter his or her environment or to learn ways of trying to change how he or she reacts to a particular situation. Therefore, coping occurs in order to try and reach a state of fit between the person and the environment. The transactional models have resulted in the increasing recognition of the importance of mental activity as a crucial factor in determining stress. For an event to be seen as a stress stimulus, it must be phenomenologically interpreted by an individual (Lazarus 1966). From a transactional perspective 'stress is defined as a cognitively mediated relational concept' (Meichenbaum 1985). The assumption is made that

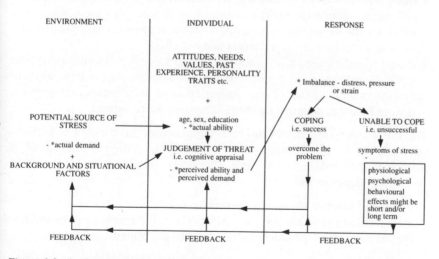

*Figure 1.3* An interactive model of stress
*Source:* Sutherland and Cooper (1991)

'mental states or structures determine the presence or absence of stress' (Fisher 1986). In other words, it is the individual's *perception* of the stress stimulus, rather than the objective existence of the stimulus, which is important.

The concepts of cognitive appraisal and coping responses are the essence of these models. The assumption is made that intervening structures, such as cognition, will influence whether a person will experience a situation as stressful or not (e.g. Lazarus 1978, 1981). These models view a person as an active agent in his or her environment; someone who actively appraises the importance of what is occurring to his or her well-being.

In summary, stress is not simply an environmental stimulus or a response to environmental demands, but a dynamic relational concept. There is constant interplay between the person and the environment, which is mediated by a complex set of ongoing cognitive processes. There are five major aspects of the interactive model that need to be considered in any study of stress.

1 *Cognitive appraisal* – the subjective perception of the situation leading to the experience.
2 *Experience* – the perception of the situation or event will depend on the individuals experience i.e. familiarity with the situation, previous exposure, learning training (i.e. actual ability). This also is determined by past success or failure (i.e. reinforcement of past response).
3 *Demand* – this comprises actual demand, perceived demand in addition to perceived ability and actual ability. The perception of the demand is further influenced by the individuals' needs, desires and immediate arousal level.
4 *Interpersonal influence* – the way a potential source of stress is perceived will largely depend upon the presence or absence of others which will influence the subjective experience of stress, response and coping behaviours and can be both detrimental and beneficial.
5 *A state of imbalance* – when a state of imbalance occurs between perceived demand and perceived ability to meet that demand, coping strategies are derived, with feedback of the consequences of these actions (i.e positive restore balance, negative further exacerbate the situation).

The ideas behind the above model originate from the concept of person–environment fit (e.g. Edwards and Cooper 1990). Within such a model, it is important therefore in our study of teacher stress to consider the three conceptual domains of:

1 sources of teacher stress, e.g. disruptive pupils;
2 mediators of the teacher-stress response, e.g. the teacher's personality;
3 the manifestations of teacher stress, e.g. psychosomatic symptoms.

A major limitation in the interactive model is with regard to 'person–environment fit' (e.g. Cooper 1981), in that it assumes that some sort of static situation exists, whereas in reality both stressful situations and individuals' responses to those situations are dynamic and ever changing. There are, however, certain characteristics that teachers may exhibit which are relatively stable over time (e.g. their behavioural style), and these will be examined in more detail in Chapter 3.

Having provided a background to and rationale for the study of teacher stress the rest of the book will, first, present previous findings with regard to costs and causes of stress in teaching; second, present the findings of our major nationwide study of teacher stress; and, third, from these findings, present our recommendations for managing stress in teachers.

It is clear that there is no turning back now that teaching has been acknowledged as a stressful occupation. We hope that this book will provide a positive stimulus for those who are involved in teaching in any shape or form, and that the open discussion of stress will not be seen as a weakness. As Dunham (1992) says:

The first step in tackling stress is to acknowledge its existence in teaching. Acceptance is difficult for people who associate stress with personal weakness and professional incompetence. For them, admitting to classroom difficulties is tantamount to admitting that they are bad teachers. They are afraid to disclose professional problems to colleagues who would regard them as signs of failure. They are unwilling to ask for help because that action would be seen as a form of weakness.

# 2 The costs and consequences of stress among teachers

In nature there are neither rewards nor punishments – there are consequences.
(R.G. Ingersoll)

Increasingly it is becoming apparent that the stress that teachers are facing is having adverse effects. The purpose of this chapter is to explain the costs and consequences of teacher stress in terms of the individual teacher, the school in which he or she teaches (including the effects on the pupils) and at the national level (i.e. costs to the educational system and society as a whole).

When examining the effects of stress it needs to be acknowledged that some demands that are seen as potentially stressful may have positive outcomes (i.e. increased challenge). In this study, the focus will be on the stress which is perceived as being negative in terms of its impact, i.e. those which result in '*distress*' rather than positive '*eustress*' (Selye 1983) (see Chapter 1). In general terms, research into the experience of stress in teachers, as with any occupational group, is justified for two main reasons.

1 Stress has serious implications for particular attitudes and behaviours.
2 There are many costs incurred by the presence of negative stress at an individual, organisational and national level.

The relationship between sources of stress at work and the symptoms of stress will be more thoroughly investigated in Chapter 3, but it is safe to say that research evidence supports the view that sources of stress in a particular job, coupled with individual characteristics, can be predictive of stress symptoms, which may reveal themselves in the form of job dissatisfaction, mental ill health, accidents, intention to leave, absenteeism, excessive drinking and smoking, family problems and a whole range of physiological symptoms (Cooper 1985). Cox (1978) has suggested, for example, that 'stress is a threat to the quality of life and to physical and psychological well-being'.

Physical responses to stress can have fatal consequences (e.g. coronary heart disease), as well as more minor symptoms such as headaches and migraines, ulcers and indigestion, back/neck problems, exhaustion and fatigue (Quick *et al.* 1986). Although it must be acknowledged that one's mere existence may itself be stressful, we spend a large proportion of our life in work, and so occupational stress merits detailed examination. When examining the effects of stress, it must be noted that we cannot clearly refer to causes and costs as discrete entities. A major problem in stress research is the fact that often a symptom of stress may actually begin to be the source of the stress. As Sutherland and Cooper (1991) explain:

> One of the main issues in health psychology is the identification of causal pathways and the mechanisms of internal function. The situation is complex because little is known about the temporal sequencing of the effects of stress and the relationships that exist between the variables involved.

Sutherland and Cooper (1991) provide a model to show the complexity of this issue, with examples of how exposure to stress may wield indirect negative consequences (see Figure 2.1) An example of how this might apply to the outcomes of stress in teachers is shown in Figure 2.2.

There are many examples and data available which illustrate the impact that stress is having on the teaching profession, and these will now be explored.

## COSTS OF TEACHER STRESS FOR THE INDIVIDUAL TEACHER

At a general level, there has been a great deal of investigation of the association between the various sources of occupational stress and the resulting manifestations of stress (i.e. psychological, physiological and behavioural). The long-term effects of these stressors have also been well documented (Cooper and Payne 1988). Individuals who are unable to cope effectively with environmental demands which they perceive to be threatening, soon begin to show manifestations of distress. Depending on the nature of the stress, the individual teacher and various mediating variables, the consequences of stress may reveal themselves in: *emotional manifestations* – feelings of undefined anxiety, dissatisfaction, depression, fear and frustration and low self-esteem with a possible extreme result being burnout; *behavioural manifestations* – behavioural problems such as appetite disorders, excessive smoking and alcohol and/or drug abuse, violence or inability to sleep, plus possible displays of withdrawal symptoms (i.e. absence and resignations from the profession); *physiological manifestations* – heart disease, psychosomatic illness, fatigue and depleted energy reserves (Milstein and Golaszewski 1985). Fimian and Santoro (1981) claim that emotional manifestations are often precursors for behavioural and physiological manifestations of stress in teachers, and so these should never be seen as discrete in nature.

When identifying manifestations of teacher stress, it is important to note that in some circumstances, the feature of the work environment may be

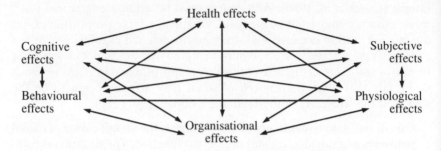

*Figure 2.1* The interactive nature of the symptoms of stress
*Source:* Sutherland and Cooper (1991)

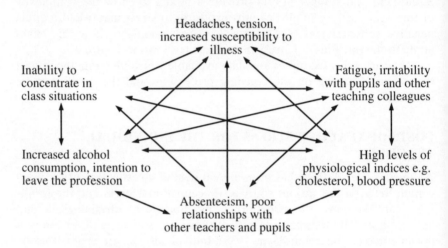

*Figure 2.2* The interactive nature of the symptoms of stress: an example related to teachers

the source of stress (i.e. poor relationships with work colleagues) or the manifestations of some other stressor (i.e. increased workload leading to poor relationships). In addition, if an individual fails to deal with one source of stress adequately, this may have a 'knock-on' effect and can result in other stressors being created. Outside of work stressors may also be evident and may interact with, and consequently influence, the levels of stress experienced at work. It is also important to recognise the importance of individual differences in terms of perception, nature and intensity of reactions to stressors, as the same stressor may evoke a variety of responses in different people.

The following sections present research evidence, where it is available, relating specifically to teachers, both inside and outside of the UK. Also, in some cases, evidence relating to other occupational groups will be presented where data on teachers has not yet been collected.

## Mental ill-health and teachers

On a general level, Tinning and Spry (1981) suggest that in excess of 40 million days are lost per year due to psychological disorder (poor mental well-being, nervous debility, tension, headaches, etc.). Poor mental well-being can be directly related to unpleasant working conditions, the necessity to work fast, expenditure of physical effort and inconvenient hours (Argyris 1964; Kornhauser 1965). A review by Miner and Brewer (1976) suggests that 'certain stresses in the occupational sphere can be a source of emotional disorder'.

A number of studies have highlighted a positive relationship between self-reported teacher stress and overall measures of mental ill health (e.g. Pratt 1978; Galloway *et al.* 1982b; Tellenbeck *et al.* 1983). Kyriacou and Pratt (1985) emphasise, however, that it may be more beneficial to examine more specific mental symptoms in order to consider appropriate coping strategies, as a purely 'overall' indicator may not be precise enough (e.g. Beech *et al.* 1982; Fletcher and Payne 1982). Emotional reactions may take the form of depression, anxiety, helplessness, insecurity, vulnerability and inadequacy, general uneasiness, irritability, emotional fatigue, resentment towards administration, negative self-concept and low self-esteem.

Dunham (1976a) has identified the two most common types: (a) frustration and (b) anxiety. Frustration can be seen to be associated with the physiological symptoms of headaches, sleep disturbances, stomach upsets, hypertension and body rashes and, in severe cases, depressive illness, whereas anxiety can be linked to loss of confidence, feelings of inadequacy, confusion in thinking and sometimes panic. In severe cases, anxiety can lead to the physiological psychosomatic symptoms of a nervous rash, twitchy eye, loss of voice and weight loss. In prolonged cases, a nervous breakdown may result.

### Burnout in teachers – an extreme reaction to stress

A more extreme result of long-term effects of teacher stress is total emotional exhaustion (Hargreaves 1978). This state of 'burnout' may lead to out-of-school apathy, alienation from work and withdrawal into a number of defensive strategies. Burnout may be identified as a type of chronic response to the cumulative long-term negative impact of work stress (Blase 1982). This is different to short-term acute stress, is far more intense and refers to the negative working conditions, when job stress seems unavoidable to an individual, and sources of satisfaction or relief appear unavailable (Moss 1981). Since it was first identified by Freudenberger in 1974, it has been identified as a separate phenomenon to stress. Burnout research has attracted an increasing amount of attention since the mid-1970s (Gillespie 1983), but stress and burnout research have progressively overlapped.

Burnout may be defined as a reaction to job-related stress that varies in nature with the intensity and duration of the stress itself, resulting in workers becoming emotionally detached from their jobs altogether (Daley 1979). Certain studies have identified the conditions that precipitate burnout. It would appear that it is experienced mainly by those professionals who deal with other people (e.g. lawyers, accountants, managers, nurses, police officers, social workers and, in particular, teachers). Another view expressed by Harvey and Brown (1988) is that those who experience job burnout as a result of job-related stress are those who are professionals and/or self-motivating achievers seeking unrealistic or unattainable goals. As a consequence of this, they cannot cope with the demands of their job and their willingness to try drops dramatically.

Studies into burnout in teachers have shown that it is largely a result of excessive work stress over extended periods of time (Blase 1982), and relentless work demands (Begley 1982). A study of 33 teachers of emotionally disturbed children by Lawrenson and McKinnon (1982) revealed that a way of preventing burnout was to be aware of the stressful nature of the job. Nagy (1982) found that Type A personality, workaholism and perceptions of working environment were individual factors that contributed to burnout. However, none of these was a good predictor of its occurrence.

A relationship between a teacher's personality and burnout has also been identified by research. Teachers with a negative attitude towards students, external locus of control (see explanation in Chapter 3) and intolerance of ambiguity were reported to have higher levels of burnout than other teachers in Fielding's study (1982). A further finding was that a school with a negative work climate exhibited a greater 'burnout–personality' relationship, than one with a positive work climate. A study of 100 teachers in the USA by Zabel and Zabel (1982) revealed that young, less experienced teachers exhibited higher levels of burnout. A clue to the prevention of burnout was also revealed in this study, as it was found that less burnout was experienced by those receiving more support from administrators, fellow teachers and parents.

It is not only individual features that can precipitate burnout. Pines and Aronson (1981) have discovered that different organisational environments can significantly affect burnout rates within an organisation. Very similar organisations have been found to have significantly different levels of burnout. In a further study, Pines (1982b) identified four dimensions of the environment which could prevent or promote burnout:

(a) the psychological, i.e. autonomy and activation;
(b) the physical;
(c) the social;
(d) work environment.

Studies by Westerhouse (1979) and Schwab (1981) have shown that role conflict and role ambiguity were significantly related to teacher burnout. A study of 40 American teachers by Cooley and Laviki (1981) concluded that individual, social-psychological and organisational factors were all strongly associated with burnout, and that it was important, therefore, to study all of these factors together rather than individually.

Lowenstein (1991) carried out a study into teacher stress and burnout and found that it was caused by a lack of social recognition of teachers, large class sizes, lack of resources, isolation, fear of violence, lack of classroom control, role ambiguity, limited professional opportunities, and a lack of support.

This previous research suggests, therefore, that, as it is such a complex issue, an interactionist approach must be taken in order to study burnout. The major symptoms of burnout as defined by Pines (1982a) are:

(i) high emotional exhaustion;
(ii) high depersonalisation;
(iii) low personal accomplishment.

Of major concern to the teaching profession is that 'burnout' can detract from the quality of teaching. Mancini *et al.* (1982, 1984) have shown that 'burned-out' teachers give significantly less information and less praise, show less acceptance of their pupils' ideas and interact less frequently with them.

## Job dissatisfaction

One of the major significant behavioural manifestations of the experience of stress at work is low job satisfaction. There has been a vast amount of research regarding the degree of satisfaction that teachers express regarding their work, but this has led to a discrepancy in the findings.

A study of UK teachers by Fletcher and Payne (1982) of 148 teachers found that the majority of this sample actually liked their job, but at the same time felt a considerable amount of pressure. However, a comparison of teachers' experience compared with participants in the University of Michigan's (Institute for Social Research) Quality of Employment Survey revealed that teachers were less satisfied with their jobs (cited in Cooke and Kornbluh 1980) than other professionals. This study did show that levels of job satisfaction varied from school to school. A study by Moracco *et al.* (1983) discovered a high level of dissatisfaction with teaching as a career, with stress being seen as a major contributory factor.

More detailed analysis of the issues relating to this job dissatisfaction reveals that factors such as salary, career structure, promotion opportunities and occupational status are involved (Tellenbeck *et al.* 1983). Kyriacou and Sutcliffe (1979a), in a study of 218 teachers from mixed comprehensive schools in England, found that self-reported teacher stress was negatively correlated with job satisfaction. However, they found that there was no significant difference in terms of age, length of experience and position held in school.

Needle *et al.* (1980) also found that teachers reporting higher levels of job stress reported greater job dissatisfaction. More specifically, Kyriacou and Sutcliffe (1979a) found that job satisfaction was significantly negatively correlated to the following job stressors:

- poor career structure;
- individual misbehaving pupils;
- inadequate salary;
- inadequate disciplinary policy of school;
- noisy pupils;
- difficult classes;
- trying to uphold/maintain standards;
- too much work to do.

Contrary to these findings, Feitler and Tokar (1981) have found biographical differences in reported levels of job satisfaction in American teachers. They found that elementary and urban teachers, and teachers with few years' experience, reported highest levels of job dissatisfaction. There are also contradictions in terms of sex differences, in that some studies have found no differences, whereas others have found that there is higher satisfaction among female teachers. It is important to recognise that satisfaction can be both a result of stress, a cause or a moderator, playing therefore a very complicated role in the work experience. In Chapter 5 we shall examine teacher job satisfaction as compared to other occupational groups, and explore the major predictors of this stress outcome in Chapter 6.

## BEHAVIOURAL RESPONSES TO STRESS

Many changes in behaviour may result from stress: impulsive behaviour, excitability, restlessness, emotional outburst, excessive eating or loss of appetite, drug taking, including excessive drinking and smoking, absence from work and unstable employment history (Cox 1985a, b). Many of these have direct and indirect consequences for the health and well-being of the individual.

Though there is little evidence on the teaching population with regard to stress and smoking and drinking, we may suppose that teachers will be as vulnerable to these responses to stress as any other occupational group. Examples of evidence on a more general level suggest that the level of smoking displayed by an individual does largely depend upon the working environment and social acceptability. In addition to social pressures and personality, work environment and exposure to stress is also an important factor which influences smoking behaviour. Russek (1965) found that 46 per cent of men in high-stress occupations were smokers, compared to only 32 per cent in low-stress jobs.

Caplan *et al.* (1975) found that an inability to stop smoking was linked to high demand (i.e. quantitative overload, too much to do, time urgency, etc.). In addition, it is also linked to tension and anxiety (McCrae *et al.* 1978), and it appears that increased smoking under stress is proportional to the number of stressors within a given period of time (Lindenthal *et al.* 1972). O'Connor (1985) suggests that perhaps it is important to understand why an individual smokes. For example, under high stress it may be secondary activity and a minor distraction from the task; in a low-activity, low-stimulation situation, it might be associated with changing affective states to escape unpleasant situations, or to help overcome distraction and maintain a state of relaxation.

With regard to alcohol consumption, it is generally believed that alcohol is consumed in order to help relieve stress and 'help' the individual to manage a crisis, but in reality, alcohol renders the distressed person less able to cope. Social influence and social pressure are strong influences in alcohol use and abuse. Plant (1979) suggests that one's 'occupation' may be the most influential factor in determining drinking habits. Margolis *et al.* (1974) and Hurrell and Kroes (1975) found that those individuals experiencing high job stress drank more than those in low-stress occupations, although it is not understood why some individuals under stress control their alcohol intake, whereas others become alcoholics. There is no reason to doubt that Britain's teachers are just as vulnerable to turning to alcohol to manage stress.

## WITHDRAWAL FROM TEACHING AS A RESPONSE TO STRESS

Another set of symptoms associated with teacher stress are those of absenteeism, intention to leave and early retirement, all forms of withdrawal (Dunham 1976a). These are perhaps the options teachers take when they find themselves in intolerably stressful situations.

In general terms, behavioural responses to stress in the form of alcohol abuse and cigarette smoking are, in part, responsible for high levels of absenteeism in industry, although there are a host of other causes. Miner and Brewer (1976) found that poor health, especially poor mental well-being, is a major cause of absenteeism. Research in a more general sense has suggested that there is a positive relationship between stress levels at work and frequency and duration of absenteeism, and the tendency for progression from absenteeism to labour turnover (Muchinsky 1977). Job satisfaction, job context and personality factors have been shown to relate to turnover (Gruneberg and Oborne 1982).

More specific findings reveal that dissatisfaction with pay, failed expectations, inconsiderate leadership, lack of autonomy and poor social support from colleagues leads to high turnover. Also certain personality variables (e.g. high anxiety, ambition, aggression and emotional insecurity) are related to high turnover, along with age and tenure (i.e. the young and job hoppers) (Porter and Steers 1973).

So how are teachers responding to stress in terms of withdrawal behaviours?

## Methods of escape as ways of dealing with stress

Turnover of teachers is increasing, the profession is failing to attract young people and most resignations are in key subjects, according to a survey published today. The survey by local authority employees and teacher unions shows that in one Greater London borough, about a third of staff resigned last year. A spokesman for the National Union of Teachers said that the survey showed a picture of a profession under stress.

(The *Independent*, 18 September 1990a)

On a national level, the effects of teacher stress are considerable in terms of staff turnover which results in a host of problems.

## Absenteeism and turnover in teaching

The Health and Safety Commission yesterday urged every education authority to draw up a policy for dealing with stress among teachers. It is seeking to reduce absenteeism and cut staff turnover in schools. The costs of reduced productivity and loss of trained teachers add up nationally to several million pounds each year.

(*Financial Times*, 17 November 1990)

The last few years have witnessed a problem with regard to absenteeism, turnover and early retirement in teaching, and this has led, in some areas of the country, to the phenomenon of 'teacher-less classes'. As the above comment implies, the loss of well-trained teachers by whatever source is far too costly to be neglected. Many experts believe that the problem is a direct manifestation of teacher stress. A turnover rate in any profession of between 7 and 8 per cent may be seen as healthy, but in teaching this has been seen to be far greater:

According to the survey of 8,500 schools in England and Wales, the largest of its kind, the resignations rate went from 9.4 per cent in 1987 to 13 per cent in 1989.

(The *Independent*, 18 September 1990a)

The resignations would appear to be affected by both the subject area in which teachers teach, the type of school and the sector. In a study by local authority employers and teacher unions (cited in The *Independent*, 18 September 1990a), it revealed that higher rates were found in foreign language, business, commercial and music teachers. Other findings suggest that Greater London has been worse hit, and evidence reveals that teachers within the primary sector may be the most likely to 'escape' from the profession:

Greater London has a higher regional rate of resignations (in primary 17.1 per cent in 1985 compared to 23.5 per cent in 1989) and other regions show a dramatic increase (in primary in the West Midlands 6.7 per cent in 1985 compared with 12.1 per cent in 1989).

(The *Independent*, 18 September 1990a)

This results in an unexpectedly older workforce in primary schools. The same survey discovered that half of all primary teachers were over 40 and very few were under 30.

## Early retirement and teachers

The number of retirements due to ill health increased from 1,617 in 1979/80 to 4,123 in 1989/90, with a large jump in 1988 when the Education Reform Act brought in the National Curriculum.

(The *Independent*, 25 January 1991)

A large number of teachers are looking for early retirement as a way out of teaching. This is not to say that for the vast majority this is not legitimate on the grounds of ill health, but for many this is the only way they see to get away from the job that is causing them excessive pressure. This means the education system and society as a whole are losing a large proportion of its experienced workforce. Many have explained that this desire to leave early is indeed a reaction to the stress of the job. While estimating that about one-third of headteachers are retiring early due to stress, David Hart, The National Association of Headteachers, remarked:

There is an urgent need to raise the morale of and to provide motivation for the most senior members of the profession. Better training, more administrative support for heads and more resources are essential.

(*The Times*, 16 November 1990)

Action needs to be taken because the education system cannot afford to train teachers only to lose them, very early on in their career. A report in *The Times* recalled:

A younger primary school teacher said he was leaving teaching after only three years because of the amount of work he had to take home with him, which he said, left him without a life of his own.

(*The Times*, 16 November 1990)

It has been suggested that the shortage of teachers in Britain's classrooms is being exacerbated by the government's inability to control a surge of these early retirements among staff (Hughes 1990). Financially, the costs of such early retirements were outlined by John Bown the Comptroller and Auditor General in a report to Parliament on the superannuation accounts for teachers for England and Wales, published by the National Audit Office in October 1990. This showed that the DES were urgently looking for a reduction in early retirement seekers, due to the excessive costs incurred. The DES had set aside £287 million, but this was insufficient to meet demand:

> Between 1987/88 and 1989/90 the numbers of teachers taking early retirement rose from 7,594 to 12,343 at a time when pupil numbers were rising, and shortages becoming more intense. Meanwhile, the department had to dip into its contingencies fund, and a supplementary £170 million was raised to meet the shortfall. By the end of last March there were 40,000 teachers still under the normal retiring age receiving pensions accounting for a little more than one fifth of the pension sums being paid out.
>
> (The *Independent*, 5 November 1990c)

Not only is this costly on a national level, but it affects the local authorities in that they incur additional costs of recruitment and training.

**Sickness absence in teachers**

Simpson (1976) has suggested that sickness absence is a way that teachers can allow themselves time to temporarily withdraw from stress at work, without having to make a definite break. It is believed that this then allows teachers to continually readjust to stressful work situations by such occasional withdrawals, and at the same time, develop skills necessary to deal with the sources of stress that they face. A problem with this interpretation, however, lies with the fact that it is difficult to distinguish between somewhat 'voluntary' absenteeism related to psychological causes (e.g. depression) and stress-related physical illness.

In a study of 218 secondary school teachers, Kyriacou and Sutcliffe (1979a), investigating an association between self-reported teacher stress, job satisfaction, absenteeism and intention to leave the teaching profession, found that significant associations existed between stress and satisfaction, total days absent and intention to leave teaching. But as the level of correlation suggests, the size of these relationships are not as large as has been implied in previous discussion.

**Intention to leave the profession**

Turning more specifically to the intention to leave the profession, most models describing the psychological process leading to resignation, or the intention to resign, assume a sequence from the work environment, through employees' affective reactions, to the decision to remain or leave the organisation (Lachman and Diamant 1987). The models go on to explain that employees will then appraise the various dimensions of their work environment, which leads to the development of positive or negative affective reactions to them. The positive reactions will induce them to stay, negative ones induce them to leave (e.g. Hendrix *et al.* 1985). In order to look at teacher turnover intentions, we need to look at a model of intention to leave and the study needs to examine why teachers are leaving.

It is not always possible to make turnover predictions unless factors from the outside of the immediate work environment are considered, because negative affective reactions do not always result in quitting. Other factors (e.g. education, availability of alternative employment) can also affect intention to leave (e.g. Martin 1979), or actual quitting itself (Spencer *et al.* 1983). In addition, other factors affecting the decision to leave will be those associated with the immediate job context or organisation (e.g. valuable investment outcomes or accumulated gains). Research has often neglected these factors or only paid partial attention to them (Mowday *et al.* 1984). This means that even if teachers are very job dissatisfied, they might still endure their jobs if they weigh up the 'pros and cons' and believe that they have too much to lose. It is not always possible to transfer such accumulated gains from one organisation to another (e.g. Steers and Mowday 1981).

Although studies have looked at the restraining effects of employee commitment and loyalty (e.g. Mowday *et al.* 1984), self-interest in the form of employees themselves has not been fully employed. Another problem in assessing the effect of withdrawal inducing and restraining factors is that the association between intentions to quit and actual quitting is not clear cut. Some intentions do not come to fruition and some resignations are of an impulsive nature (Mobley 1982). However, as teacher turnover intentions appear to be on the increase, a study of teachers' intentions to quit might help us understand more about the psychological process of withdrawal – an important feature in employee turnover (e.g. Mowday *et al.* 1984).

**Withdrawal factors: factors inducing the intention to leave the profession**

Withdrawal factors are the focus of most studies concerning the withdrawal process, and they are features of the work environment that induce the intention to leave (e.g. Lachman and Aranya 1986). Features affecting intention to withdraw have been found to be both consistent and inconsistent across work environments, therefore it is important to consider both general and specific work factors in relation to teacher withdrawal (Lachman and Aranya 1986).

The most frequently cited predictors of withdrawal have been those of intrinsic and extrinsic rewards (Bridges 1980). The studies regarding teachers' intention to leave have come to different conclusions regarding the effects of these two features of the working environment. Intrinsic rewards (i.e. recognition, sense of accomplishment, fulfilment, advancement) have been found by some to play a more important role than extrinsic rewards (i.e. working conditions, management policies) in the process of withdrawal. As teachers are in the service sector, motivation is assumed to be linked with intrinsic rather than extrinsic rewards (Spuck 1977). Other studies highlight the equal effect of extrinsic and intrinsic rewards, with the absence of extrinsic rewards leading to frustration, intrinsic leading to low job satisfaction, and job dissatisfaction in turn leading to absenteeism, lateness and quitting (Miskel and Heller 1973). Other areas have been studied less extensively, but other features of the environment have been found to affect their withdrawal. Size of classes, administrative and teaching loads, availability of teaching aids, social and work relations have all been found to be related to teachers affective reactions, stress and turnover intentions (D'Arienzo *et al.* 1982).

In a study by Coughlan (1969), a factor analysis produced characteristics seen to affect teachers' withdrawal. Four main dimensions were distinguished:

1 Management (including policy, procedures, administration, conditions)
2 Interpersonal relations (staff and students)
3 School functioning (e.g. curriculum, student development, teaching load)
4 Teachers' self-actualisation (professional autonomy and recognition).

A study by Lachman and Diamont (1987) proposed that:

> Teachers' perceptions of their work environment lead to an affective reaction to the job, which in turn influences their intentions to leave. Specifically, it is hypothesised that self-actualisation, interpersonal relations, management and school functioning directly influence teachers' affective reactions to their job, which in turn influences their turnover intentions.

### Burnout: a mediating factor in the intention to leave

When using affective reactions as predictors in the withdrawal process, the difficulty lies in deciding which reaction to use, so a number of reactions have been focused in predicting turnover intentions (e.g. Lachman and Aranya 1986). Burnout, as mentioned previously, is:

> A feeling of physical emotional and mental exhaustion that results from a chronic state of cumulative pressure or stress at work, rather than the outcome of isolated, critical, or intermittent events.
>
> (Etzion 1984)

Studies have identified burnout as separate from job satisfaction and acute stress, and have suggested that it is rather a reaction, brought about by exposure to daily pressures constantly and continuously (Etzion 1984). It has been found to be *exacerbated* by structural characteristics of the job, lack of extrinsic and intrinsic rewards but *reduced* by group support, social cooperation and good work relations (e.g. Golembiewski *et al.* 1983).

Studies have suggested that burnout leads to turnover intentions and affects withdrawal behaviours (e.g. Burke *et al.* 1984). It is crucial to consider burnout when understanding teachers' affective reactions as a viable predictor of their turnover intentions, as it is more prevalent among those requiring control and high emotional involvement with other people (e.g. Parber 1983).

**Factors which restrain the intention to leave**

The longer a teacher holds a particular job or is employed within a particular school, the more benefits and privileges he or she accrues which are not transferable. Because of this, some individuals will be psychologically constrained from leaving by some of the following (Steers and Mowday 1981):

- individually tailored work conditions;
- financial rewards, e.g. pension plans;
- specialised information and skills;
- familiarity with organisational work procedures;
- seniority privileges;
- personal reputation, social standing or power.

These may well mean that teachers may feel that the prospect of losing these benefits and privileges outweigh the intensity of how they feel about the job of teaching itself.

In addition, studies of teachers' turnover intentions have shown that job investments and the gain derived have a restraining effect; that is, the greater personal investment in the job, the more likely is the teacher to view quitting as a 'penalty', and the more reluctant he or she is to leave (Dworkin 1980). Specific restraining factors in the school environment are:

- status within the particular school;
- specificity of teacher-training.

Teachers frequently complain about the limitations in terms of opportunities for hierarchical or horizontal mobility. Advancement is limited and, consequently, social standing is important and valued, whether this be formal or informal.

**The influence of gender on the intention to leave**

It has been suggested that there may be gender differences in the psychological process of withdrawal (Mowday *et al.* 1984), but this proposition has not been fully investigated by researchers. A major theoretical argument suggests that males and females perceive their careers differently (Maccoby and Jacklin 1974), and it is these differences that may result in the different psychological withdrawal processes. It has been suggested that the benefits that teaching as a career offers to women (i.e. shorter working hours and conditions suitable to the traditional female family role), are those which attract large numbers of women into the profession (Lortie 1975). Men who choose teaching, on the other hand, do so as a first career choice, and see it as a way of having social mobility (Dworkin 1980). As teaching consists of almost equal numbers of men and women, it gives us the chance to examine these claims, and discover whether differences exist in terms of perceptions of organisational rewards, affective reactions, and overall frequency of withdrawal behaviours.

Lachman and Diamont (1987) produced a study model to examine the influences of withdrawal and restraining factors on turnover intentions in teachers (see Figure 2.3). They claim that the direction of influence, from withdrawal factors through work reactions to behavioural intention, has been supported by studies on turnover intentions (e.g. Lachman and Aranya 1986) or actual turnover (Mowday *et al.* 1984). In addition, the same directional influence has been found with regard to burnout, which is influenced by the work environment (e.g. Cherniss 1980), and has been found to affect intention to leave rather than the reverse (e.g. Burke *et al.* 1984). Inherent is the assumption that restraining factors have an unmeditated effect on turnover.

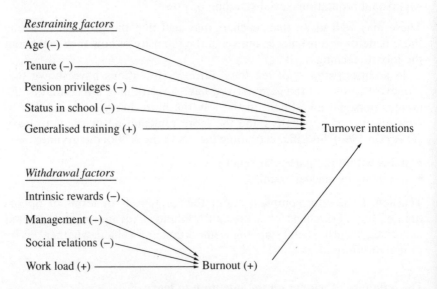

*Figure 2.3* Path model of teacher turnover intentions
*Source:* Lachman and Diamont (1987). Reprinted by permission, John Wiley & Sons Ltd.

Lachman and Diamont (1987) tested this model on a sample of 239 high school teachers in Israel and found differences between male and female teachers, and some restraining effects on the intention to resign in both groups. However, the assumption that affective work reactions mediate between the work environment and the intention to leave were found for male teachers only. Other findings suggested that when examining withdrawal behaviours, gender adjustments need to be made.

## COSTS TO SCHOOLS AND SOCIETY AS A WHOLE

So what impact is teacher stress having on the schools in which they teach, and indeed on education as a whole? It is hard to measure and needs longitudinal analysis, but it must be seen that all of the above problems will have an indirect or direct effect on the way the school runs (e.g. in the form of lower funding). In addition, a further cost to schools of high teacher turnover is that many are consequently struggling to fill their classes.

> On average a school is having to recruit 10 new teachers a year. In one borough in Greater London 25 or more teachers are changing in one year.
>
> (The *Independent*, 18 September 1990b)

This turnover will have an effect on the climate of the school, affecting relationships between staff and between staff and pupils, as Nigel De Gruchy, General Secretary of the NASUWT said of a survey by the Local Authority and Teacher Unions:

> This is a survey of 361,000 teachers, about 46,950 teachers in any one year are changing jobs. This is a remarkable amount of turbulence which must damage the stability of schools.
>
> (The *Independent*, 18 September 1990b)

Other problems facing schools are the decisions involved with losing staff through the introduction of school-based budgeting, as many schools are having to shed posts to match their budgets.

In terms of the effects of teacher stress on the pupils within schools, this has not been studied at great length, mainly due to the difficulty of gathering such information. However, the effects may be apparent when we consider the need for children to have consistency in their education, i.e. if a teacher is constantly absent from school due to ill health, or pupils have to have a number of different teachers throughout the course of the school year, their education may suffer. This may mean that they lose confidence in their own ability and that of their teachers, and they may also fail to reach examination standard. In addition, it is important for children to be able to form trusting relationships with their teachers, and this may not be possible if (a) teachers are not as approachable due to the levels of stress and fatigue they are experiencing, and (b) if turnover is high and the school is constantly recruiting new, and often temporary, staff.

Whatever the costs, in order to be able to reduce these effects and symptoms we need to obtain a clear understanding of what causes teacher stress – and this will be explored in the following chapter.

# 3 Sources of stress in teaching

I believe in work, hard work and long hours of work. Men do not break down from overwork but from worry and dissipation.

(Charles E. Hughes)

In this chapter we look at the potential causes of stress in teachers working in Britain's schools, which may result in the symptoms outlined in the previous chapter of mental ill health, job dissatisfaction, increased alcohol consumption, sickness absence and intention to leave the profession. The underlying premise of our approach to stress is that undesirable responses to the pressure in the working environment result from a 'mismatch' between the individual teacher and the job that he or she does (Sloan and Cooper 1987). The lack of 'fit' will lead to the individual and organisational consequences mentioned previously. A crucial element of this model is the role of the teacher's personality, behavioural style, biographical features (e.g. age and sex), and the social support that the teacher seeks. In order to address the potential stressors in any work environment and design methods for alleviating them, it is necessary to understand them. If we want to alleviate the stress at the teacher level (i.e. help cope with existing individual stress), or at the level of the school, we need to understand both the aspects of the individual teacher that have an effect on the response to stress, and the aspects of the school that may exacerbate stress (i.e. following the interactive model of stress outlined in Chapter 1).

We shall use the six-factor theory outlined in the work and model of Cooper *et al.* (1988) to examine the potential sources of stress for teachers along with findings from researchers working in the area of teacher stress. Needle *et al.* (1980) highlighted the stressors from job content, conditions of work, relationships with co-workers, promotional opportunities, financial rewards, resource adequacy and role in the organisation as categories of stress. Four categories identified by Kyriacou and Sutcliffe (1978a) were: pupil misbehaviour, poor working conditions, time pressure and poor school ethos. Cox (1977) referred to stress resulting from training and career development, the nature of the work and the physical work environment, subsystems in the school organisation, and relationship between the

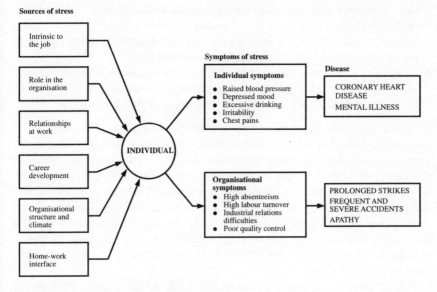

*Figure 3.1* A model of occupational stress
*Source:* Cooper *et al.* (1988). Reproduced by permission of Penguin Books Ltd.

school and the community. On a broader level, Wanberg (1984) presented the categories consisting of societal, institutional, and personal sources of stress.

## Sources of stress and the stress response

On a general level, a review of the literature by Fletcher and Payne (1980a) estimated that between 8 and 10 per cent of the working population are experiencing high levels of stress. Here they are referring to 'distress' as opposed to the more positive 'eustress' (Selye 1980). Concentrating on 'distress', Cooper and Marshall (1976) define occupational stress as: 'Negative environmental factors or stressors (e.g. work overload, role conflict, role ambiguity, poor working conditions) associated with a particular job.'

The stressors may be both outside and inside work, and can therefore have an effect on the whole family. The Cooper (1986b) model lists the following as causes of stress:

1 *stressors intrinsic to the actual job* – i.e. physical working conditions, level of participation and decision-making latitude and workload;
2 *role in the organisation* – i.e. role ambiguity and role conflict and levels and type of responsibility;
3 *relationships at work* – i.e. superiors, colleagues and subordinates and the demands made interpersonally;
4 *career development* – i.e. the presence of over- or under-promotion, possible lack of job security;

5  *organisational structure and climate* – these stressors may be those that restrict behaviours, i.e. the politics and culture of the organisation and how individuals interact with these. Specific features include, level of participation and involvement in decision making;
6  *home and work interface* – this refers to the stressors resulting from a mismatch in the relationship between work demands and family or social demands, which may be viewed as 'overspill' of one life into the other.

The last category (i.e. 'home–work interface') may be regarded as an extra-organisational factor (Sutherland and Cooper 1988). In addition, the extra stressor of being made redundant has been added to the model by Cooper *et al.* (1988). When investigating the six categories, it is important to recognise that they are artificially discrete and that there is an overlap between them, so they must not be seen as discrete entities. Individuals are dynamic in their behaviour and the whole process must be seen as being interactive (i.e. *'lack of job security'* included in the category of *'career development'* could also be included in the category of *'organisational structure and climate'*).

There have been many attempts to reach an adequate definition of teacher stress by a number of theorists and researchers. The one employed in this study is that of Kyriacou and Sutcliffe (1979a) who, in a revised version of their definition, describe teacher stress as:

> a response syndrome of negative affect (such as anger and depression), usually accompanied by potentially pathogenic physiological changes (such as increased heart rate) resulting from aspects of the teacher's job and mediated by the perception that the demands made upon the teacher constitutes a threat to his (or her) self-esteem or well-being and by coping mechanisms activated to reduce threat.

This is perhaps one of the most well-cited and influential of the contemporary definitions of teacher stress. The definition reveals that the issue of teacher stress is one of a complex 'interaction' of factors, whose result may well be the negative feelings that are associated with stress. A vital assumption inherent in the above definition is that an important contributory factor in the experience of stress in teachers is not only the aspects of the job, but also elements of the individual teacher – emphasising the individual subjective perception of work experience and supporting the 'transactional approach' (Laughlin 1984). They explain that the extent and type of stress experienced will largely depend upon:

(a) whether or not teachers feel threatened by particular demands facing them;
(b) whether or not the individual teachers, may, after facing initial threat, be able to modify or ameliorate the threat by particular actions.

An understanding of the contribution of the above two features would explain why the level of stress may vary from one teacher to another.

Kyriacou and Sutcliffe explain that:

> Teacher stress is conceptualized as being directly related to the degree to which the coping mechanisms are unable to deal with the actual stressors and the degree to which the teacher appraises the threat.
>
> (Kyriacou and Sutcliffe 1978b)

A model by Kyriacou and Sutcliffe (1978b) may be seen alongside that of Cooper and Marshall. Their model results in eight component parts.

1 *Potential occupational stressors* – these are the objective aspects of the teachers job that could cause excessive stress, for example, noise levels, heavy workload, inadequate buildings and physical working conditions.
2 *Appraisal* – this refers to how potential stressors in the teacher's working environment are perceived. This perception will largely depend upon the personal characteristics of the individual teacher and this 'interaction' will then determine the consequences of the potential stressor becoming an actual stressor.
3 *Actual stressors* – these are the potential occupational stressors that an individual teacher has seen as being a threat to his or her well-being or self-esteem.
4 *Coping strategies* – these are the attempts that an individual teacher makes in order to reduce a perceived threat. These strategies can range from 'denial', i.e. 'the problem does not exist' or 'direct action', i.e. 'I will do it now'.
5 *Teacher stress* – this describes an individual teacher's response to negative affect that has corresponding psychological, physiological and behavioural reactions.
6 *Chronic symptoms* – these are the feelings of negative effect that are both persistent and prolonged and have extreme psychological, physiological and behavioural reactions.
7 *Characteristics of the individual teacher* – these essential components in the experience of the teacher stress 'interaction' include demographics, personality attitudes, value systems and an individual teacher's ability to cope with any demands encountered in the workplace.
8 *Potential non-occupational stressors* – these are those 'negative' aspects of the teacher's life outside of school that may enhance or exacerbate the 'vicious circle' scenario of teacher stress, e.g. ill health, family crises, etc. These can become first-order stressors on their own, or indeed may be reactions to work stress.

For the purpose of this study, a suitable model of teacher stress is one which incorporates aspects of both the Cooper *et al.* (1988) model and that of Kyriacou and Sutcliffe (1978a). We shall now present each of these potential sources of stress in turn (outcomes of stress have already been identified in Chapter 2). Findings will be presented from studies carried out with teachers both inside and outside the UK.

## STRESSORS INTRINSIC TO THE JOB

A big rise in teachers' pay, a significant increase in teacher numbers and urgent action to bring every school in England and Wales up to a standard of good repair, were among the far-reaching recommendations of a report published yesterday . . .

(The *Daily Telegraph*, 10 May 1990)

Research indicates that there is a set of unique factors for every job that employees identify as being sources of pressure for them. Overall, there are a number of major recurring themes, concerned with physical working conditions, shift working, work overload/underload, occupational level, repetition and boredom, and the 'person–environment' fit (Sloan and Cooper 1987).

### Physical working conditions

General studies researching the relationship between the physical environment and occupational stress have been many (e.g. Kornhauser 1965). A large number of teachers in our society today find themselves faced by circumstances which, they believe, force them to do their job badly (Esteve 1989), in particular poor physical working conditions (e.g. Wanberg 1984). These poor conditions are largely reinforced by a lack of resources. The issues of conditions and lack of materials within the teaching profession are almost synonymous. Esteve (1989) refers to these as 'primary factors', because they directly affect teaching, create limitations or produce tension in the teacher's day-to-day practice. However, the anecdotal nature of the evidence available in the study of teacher's working environments creates a problem.

Aspects of working conditions that have received attention in the past include such things as class sizes, unsuitable buildings, noise level and inadequate resources (e.g. Connors 1983; Kyriacou and Sutcliffe 1978b). The significance of each of these factors does vary in importance depending on the specific circumstances of the schools themselves. This might be due to the fact that some schools have support from parents and perhaps local industry. A list of potential causes of poor conditions is as follows:

1 cuts in LEA information which means that schools cannot accommodate changes by reorganisation of budget;
2 children often have up-to-date technologies at home and schools cannot afford to provide these at the capacity that is required;
3 often schools are designed for different school populations/sizes. Amalgamation can therefore cause problems;
4 these can also lead to overheating and overcrowding in shared rooms;
5 there is limited space for storage;
6 sometimes no base classrooms are available;

7 inadequate staff facilities, e.g. coffee room, quiet places in which to work;

8 problems with travel to and from work.

In a study of stress and depressive symptoms in 255 female newly appointed teachers in the US, Schonfeld (1992) found that teachers who worked in the most adverse school environments showed the most depressive symptoms, while those in the best conditions showed the fewest symptoms of depression. These effects on depression were also found to be relatively immediate. However, the limitations in this study were that both measures of stress and depression were self-administered and so subject to bias.

Another US study by French (1993) examined the relationship between 223 elementary teachers' perceptions of class size as stressful and the pupil–teacher ratios in their schools. The study found that those teaching in schools with smaller ratios were more likely to see class sizes as creating little or no stress and were less likely to use ineffective and undesirable teaching methods (e.g. rote repetition).

Much research into teacher stress has revealed a general lack of resources as one of the most important factors (e.g. Laughlin 1984) – more specifically, inadequate school buildings and equipment (Smith and Cline 1980) and an unpleasant work environment (Fimian and Santoro 1983).

The lack of materials or the means by which to obtain them can be a great source of frustration or disillusionment for a teacher. The general feeling among many teachers is that there is an apparent contradiction imposed upon them by outside bodies (i.e. the demand for modern methods but without the adequate equipment to do the job). This situation is exacerbated by reduced expenditure on equipment due to a worsening financial situation in a number of schools (Fimian and Santoro 1983). An ILO report (1981) and the Breuse report (1984) have revealed that the lack of resources in teaching does not necessarily imply just a lack of teaching materials but also a problem of space, poorly preserved and dilapidated buildings, poor quality furniture, inadequate heating and lack of suitable premises, among other things. Poor staffroom facilities and the more modern problem of teaching at a split-site school are other reasons given for both dissatisfaction and stress at work (e.g. Dewe 1986). With reorganisation in education and the resulting school closures, a large number of schools are experiencing the 'split-site' phenomenon – this often means that teachers have to travel between two sites, which can have many time and practical implications.

Limitations in the environment in which teachers work need not be physical ones. Often institutional limitations are imposed upon their work. For example, Goble and Porter (1980) and Bayer and Chauvet (1980) emphasise that the institutional framework within which they work often dictates what teachers can do (e.g. timetable problems, internal rules, standards that have been laid down by the inspecting bodies or teaching institutions). They are also often required to set time aside for staff meetings, students, governing bodies, examination meetings, parents' evenings, etc.

**Work overload and work underload**

Many studies (Cooper and Payne 1988), in a variety of research settings and in various occupations, have consistently concluded that the particular characteristics of the job, particularly work overload and underload, are related to the experience of worker stress (Shaw and Riskind 1983). This curvilinear relationship between amount of work and health and performance is explained in terms of the Yerkes–Dodson law (Yerkes and Dodson 1908) or the inverted 'U' hypothesis (see Figure 3.2).

It is possible to make a further distinction between *quantitative* over- and underload (i.e. resulting from the employee being given too many or too few tasks to complete in a given time), and *qualitative* over- and underload (i.e. when the individual does not feel able or capable of doing the given task or the task does not utilise the skills and/or potential of the worker) (French and Caplan 1973). Both quantitative and qualitative underload lead to stress:

> Quantitative underload refers to the boredom that results when employees have so little to do that they find themselves sitting around much of the time. . . . Qualitative underload refers to the lack of mental stimulation that accompanies many routine repetitive jobs.
>
> (Baron 1986)

There are a great number of studies that have investigated the role of workload in teacher stress and the types of overload and underload that can occur are widespread, e.g. job overload may result from a poor teacher–pupil ratio (e.g. Kalker 1984; Russell *et al.* 1987).

Another aspect of the teaching profession which can be seen to be directly related to work overload is the problem of having a wide range of pupil abilities in one class. This may require more lesson planning and more detailed and lengthy assessment (e.g. Dunham 1980; Fimian and Santoro 1983; Hawkes and Dedrick 1983). Work overload is also heavily linked to time pressures not only in terms of the amount of work teachers have to fit in during the day, but also the amount that they have to take home at night, intruding into their personal life (e.g. Smith and Cline 1980; Fimian and Santoro 1983).

**Working long hours**

Research has suggested that the need to work long hours is a source of stress for teachers (Austin 1981; ILO 1981). Although many people outside of the profession believe that teachers have a short working day, in reality, many teachers, in particular those in senior managerial positions, work longer hours than expected. Many teachers claim to put in excessive hours at home not only marking, but also preparing and assessing work. This has been a major problem for primary teachers since the introduction of compulsory testing for seven year olds.

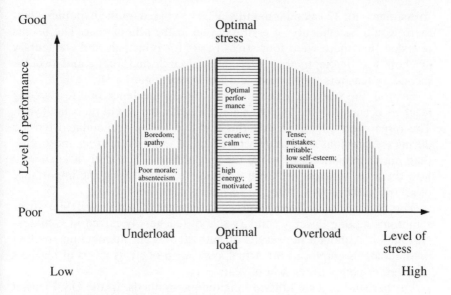

*Figure 3.2* The underload/overload inverted 'U' hypothesis
*Source:* Sutherland and Cooper (1991)

### The school day

Researchers have discussed the actual stress of the school day in terms of the constant workload that it imposes upon the teacher. It may also be the case that tension and stress among teachers arises partly from the fact that they have timetables that permit few or no breaks. In addition, Kyriacou (1987) has suggested that one of the main sources of stress for teachers may be the 'general level of alertness and vigilance required' of them. This 'pace' of the school day is perhaps more of a problem, because of the 'rigid' nature of the way the day is structured and the fact that teachers spend so much of their day in direct contact with pupils.

### Is there a teacher-stress cycle throughout the school year?

Although there has been a considerable amount of research concerning workload and teacher stress, there has been little with regard to attempts to trace the dynamics of teacher stress over a period of time (i.e. throughout the course of the school year (e.g. Kinnuen and Leskinen 1989)). The teaching workload is very much dependent upon the time of year (e.g. end of term/year examinations). It is important, therefore, to see what effects this may have on the teachers.

In a Canadian study, Hembling and Gilliland (1981) investigated the experience of teachers from one British Columbia school district by asking school principals, elementary and secondary school teachers to rate the stressfulness for 12 calendar months. This was based on the hypothesis that there would be evidence of a stress cycle in the school year. The results revealed that there were four stress peaks for principals and elementary teachers (i.e. in September, December, March and June) and two for secondary teachers (September and June) (see Figure 3.3).

Overall, the study revealed that the highest incidence of stress among teachers occurred at the end of each term and at the end of the school year. The researchers explained that this was due to the accumulated tension during the previous term and specific 'end of term' events (e.g. most often than not examinations are set at the end of term). The study also showed how the level of stress itself can accumulate, emphasising the importance of school holidays as a means of regaining personal stability.

The findings of a Finnish survey (Ojanen 1982) revealed that stress symptoms among lower secondary school teachers occurred in October–November. Although the results of both studies are illuminating, neither methodologies employed the actual *assessment* of stress levels of teachers at different points of the school year.

Further studies have utilised longitudinal methods. In the US, Fleishut (1985) studied stress patterns in elementary school teachers in Pennsylvania in a one-year study. The aim was to investigate the origins and intensity of job-related stress in 81 elementary school teachers, at five selected intervals during the course of one school year. These findings revealed that the

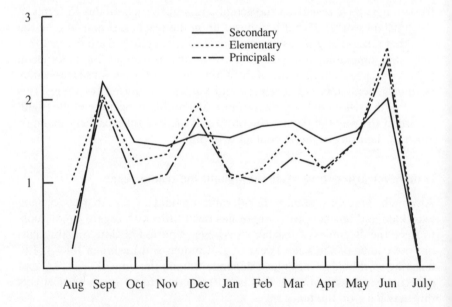

*Figure 3.3* Mean monthly stress perceived by secondary and elementary teachers and principals in Kamloops
*Source:* Hembling and Gilliland (1981)

teacher stress was highest at the start of the school year (September) and after the Christmas holidays (January), as opposed to November, March and May. The study also revealed that actual stress increased during the first part of the school year (September to November), and decreased after the Christmas holidays (January), with a steady increase throughout March, with another high point experienced in May. A study by the New York State United Teachers (NYSUT 1980) found that the opening week of school was the most stressful time.

In a Spanish study, Franco and Esteve (1987) gathered data between the years 1985 and 1986 in order to corroborate the relationship between teachers' stress and sick leave or absenteeism. Data were obtained from records of the Medical Inspection of the Regional Education and Science Authority in Malaga, covering all primary and secondary teachers in the city of Malaga and its province for that year. One regulation of this department concerns teachers that take more than three days 'sickness absence'. These teachers have to register their medical condition formally with their local education authority. The ensuing official statistics for Malaga (1985–6) show that teachers' sickness, with regard to symptoms of pathological or medically specific illness, are heavily represented in stress-related conditions. The results reveal that:

- 12.5 per cent of the 7,321 teachers took sick leave during the year for an average of 34 days each;
- of the 899 taking sick leave, 11 per cent were diagnosed as suffering from neuropsychiatric conditions, 15 per cent from respiratory or cardiovascular problems, and 9 per cent had complaints effecting the digestive system.

A study by Kinnuen (1988) aimed to examine how stress manifests itself and to describe any observed differences in the teachers background, personality and coping variables. This employed a longitudinal design of 153 teachers, with six repeated questionnaire assessments of indicators of stress (subjective mood ratings) during the autumn term of 1983. They discovered that four different groups emerged according to their experience of stress:

1 Teachers exhausted throughout the term.
2 Those who recovered from stress on the first weekends of term but not later.
3 Those not at all stressed.
4 Teachers feeling tired and anxious at the beginning and at the end of the term.

They found that these differences were determined by the personality of the teachers and the coping strategies they employed.

Research by the authors has attempted to shed further light on this topic (Travers and Cooper 1994). We studied 56 teachers from inner city schools in London by taking blood samples and using questionnaires at two time periods – the beginning and end of the autumn term – and found that almost half of the teachers had abnormally low levels of the chemical cortisol at the first measurement phase. The consultant pathologist involved in the research suggested that this showed a high level of fatigue among the teachers, even though this was after the long school holidays.

## TEACHERS' ROLE IN THE SCHOOL AS A SOURCE OF STRESS

Research evidence suggests that structural factors such as role conflict (conflicting demands) and role ambiguity (lack of clarity about the task) can be potential causes of stress (Kahn *et al.* 1964). On a more general point, change may lead to stress as it can introduce conflict or ambiguity into what was originally a stable teaching role (Kelly 1974). However, Dunham (1984b) has pointed out that change might equally be welcomed as an alleviation of stress, depending upon circumstances and participants. Dunham (1978, 1984b) studied the stress imposed by the demands of specific managerial roles and found that tension was created by role conflict and role ambiguity. A descriptive article was produced by Blackie (1977) who discussed the effect of role conflict on teachers as predictive of stress.

### Role ambiguity

This may exist in the workplace when an employee does not have adequate information in order to carry out the task or does not fully understand the requirements. The outcomes of this can be job dissatisfaction, lack of self-confidence, feelings of futility, lack of self-esteem, depression, low motivation and the behavioural outcomes of increased intention to leave the job. Other manifestations may be physiological (e.g. increased blood pressure and pulse rate) (Kahn *et al.* 1964; French and Caplan 1970; Margolis *et al.* 1974).

There are a number of situations that may lead to role ambiguity and these are contemporary issues in teaching (i.e. job relocation, changes in the method of working, new organisational structure and changes in actual requirements of the job). Role ambiguity is a pervasive part of the teachers' experience due to the endemic uncertainty regarding the teachers' role in the school (Schwab and Iwanicki 1982). A feature that perhaps exacerbates the problem is teachers' apparent lack of knowledge of how to cope with the insecurity resulting from the unpredictability of, and confrontations in, their occupation (Dunham 1981).

Bacharach *et al.* (1986), in an American study, made an attempt to investigate those characteristics of the organisation which lead to stress. They gathered data via questionnaires from over 2,000 teachers in 42 elementary (primary schools) and 45 secondary schools. Data were in the form of self-reports of both the nature and levels of stress and the characteristics of the organisation. Results revealed that organisational characteristics such as 'bureaucratised work process' or 'routinised organisations' were not clear predictors of stress, but 'role ambiguity', the 'rationality of promotion' and 'supervisory behaviour' were important stress factors.

A large-scale American study by Crane and Iwanicki (1986) investigated 443 urban, remedial education teachers in an attempt to discover a possible relationship between 'burnout', role conflict and role ambiguity. The picture they found was confusing with regard to the 'overall' moderating effect of burnout, which varied according to a complex interaction of age, sex, experience and setting.

## Role conflict

Role conflict may be seen to exist when an individual is torn between conflicting demands placed upon them by others in the organisation (e.g. being required to do things that they do not perceive to be part of their job), or when conflict exists between their job and their personal beliefs. Therefore, stress may result from the inability to meet these various expectations or demands. The results of this conflict have been found to result in lower job satisfaction and higher job tension. Four different types of role conflict have been identified by Miles and Perreault (1976) which may be appropriate for teachers.

1 *Person–role conflict*, e.g. the teacher wants to perform the job differently to that on the job description.
2 *Intrasender conflict*, e.g. the headteacher may ask the teacher to cover for maths when they have no maths training.
3 *Intersender conflict*, e.g. a teacher may be asked by the headteacher to assess a fellow teacher, which will please the head but not the fellow teacher.
4 *Role overload*, e.g. the teacher may be assigned a pastoral role in addition to one of head of department, meaning that neither role is sufficiently fulfilled.

The issue of role conflict may be seen to be very relevant to teachers as it may include both intra-role conflict due to contradictory expectations from parents, pupils, principals, etc., and inter-role conflict due to teachers having to assume several roles within the school setting. The multiplicity of roles that the teacher may have to fulfil can include that of a diagnostician, guidance counsellor, remediator, parent record keeper, evaluator and finally teacher. Increasingly, the role of 'social worker' is becoming part of the teacher's role (e.g. Phillips and Lee 1980; Austin 1981; Sparks and Hammond 1981).

Sometimes role conflict may require teachers to reject their own principles and better judgements (Dunham 1980). For example, due to staff shortages, they may be forced to teach a subject outside of their own speciality area and for which they have no desire or skill (Burke and Dunham 1982; Schwab and Iwanicki 1982; Kalker 1984). They may also have to spend a considerable amount of time controlling pupils and dealing with discipline problems at the cost of time spent on actual teaching (Kalker 1984). Other problems that may create role conflict day-to-day are: maintaining self-control when angry (New York State United Teachers 1980) and finding it difficult to accept the limits of what teaching can achieve (*Instructor* 1979).

The problems resulting from the occurrence of role conflict can be enhanced when certain psychological processes of individuals come into play. For example, if their belief system emphasises perfectionism and compulsive behaviour, this may result in excessive worrying about the situation and anticipation of the problems that result if they do not meet expectations (Moracco *et al.* 1981). Claggett (1980) also emphasises the problem of conflicting values as a source of role conflict. This may be very important for teachers at present as they may not agree with a number of changes that are taking place within education (e.g. the content of the National Curriculum).

## Role overload and underload

When referring to role underload one is portraying a situation where too little time is available to devote to the teaching function (Needle *et al.* 1981). This may be a concern of many contemporary teachers as more and more time is required to be spent on administrative and pastoral tasks and responsibilities. Problems connected with role overload may include: constant interaction with pupils which allows little time for relaxation, lunch, etc. (Weiskopf 1980); constant interaction with others (Schwab 1983); too many roles altogether (Austin 1981); and the problem of being physically and emotionally drained (Sparks 1979).

## Responsibility for others

When examining one's role in an organisation it is important to consider levels of responsibility. Research has discovered the necessity to distinguish between responsibility for people and responsibility for things, as the former is significantly more likely to lead to cardiovascular disease (French and Caplan 1970). However, it is also the case that a lack of responsibility can result in stress outcomes, if, for instance, it is perceived as being due to work underload.

One of the most potentially exhausting aspects of teaching must surely be the fact that teachers are, in most cases, constantly responsible for others (Weiskopf 1980; Brenner *et al.* 1985). Caspari (1976) has argued that:

> The exhaustion felt by most teachers at the end of the term is more closely linked to the demands made on the skills and personality of the teacher in keeping discipline over the children he/she teaches than to any other aspect of his/her work.

Dealing with pupils is the major aspect of their job, and many problems and potential sources of stress can result from this as pupils can be disruptive and undisciplined in their behaviour. This means that teachers can, depending on the nature of the pupils, spend vast amounts of time controlling this poor behaviour (e.g. Mykletun 1984; Wanberg 1984; Russell *et al.* 1987).

The behaviour of children may be very unpredictable and this noisy, rowdy, often abusive and insolent behaviour may lead to teachers feeling vulnerable, making them doubt their teaching methods and skills or their ability to cope (Dunham 1981). It may be that the contribution of discipline to stress is very subtle, e.g. a teacher may have to undertake constant monitoring of apathetic pupils (e.g. Hawkes and Dedrick 1983; Kalker 1984; Laughlin 1984). According to Claggett (1980), many teachers try to live up to the 'Good Shepherd' ethic, whereby each teacher tries to ensure that each child is successful in school by providing for individual needs.

## Role preparedness

Another potential stressor is that of being inadequately prepared for the role of a teacher, i.e. by inadequate training (Fimian and Santoro 1983). This can also be seen to be an example of 'role shock', which is explained by Minkler and Biller (1979) as ' . . . the stresses and tensions manifested as discontinuity are encountered when moving from familiar to unfamiliar roles. These unfamiliar roles may constitute totally new roles, or familiar old roles which are played differently in a new situation'. With the amount of rapid changes that have taken place within teaching in the last five years, it is very possible that a teacher's training may well be out of date by the time he or she actually starts to teach. Also it might well be that the 'teacher of today' has a very different role to that of a teacher starting a career ten years ago, and many teachers may find that it is not the job they expected. This may also apply to teachers who have been in the profession for a great many years.

Examining the effects of role overall it can be seen that these features may interact together to result in stress being experienced; for example, Kotlarska *et al.* (1956; cited by ILO 1986) found a much higher incidence of hypertension among elementary school teachers, exposed to conflicting situations and overload of responsibility, compared to groups such as miners.

## The role of senior managers in teaching

A number of characteristics of managers in the private sector have been identified by Cooper and Melhuish (1980) that make them prime candidates for heart attack:

(a) personalities that are extremely competitive, aggressive, and impatient, with the belief that they are under constant time pressure (i.e. type A personality which will be looked at in more detail later);
(b) a recent change in the job which makes greater demands on time and relationships;
(c) working in a job within a poor organisational climate with little social support;
(d) involved in a situation where personal values are in conflict with those of the organisation.

More recently studies have addressed in more detail the effects on the headteachers, who are finding themselves in the dual position of being both a manager of people and a financial manager.

> Britain's headteachers are becoming nervous wrecks because of school stress. . . . Hundreds are suffering break-downs and are turning to the bottle, cigarettes and drugs, as they try to cope with educational changes.
>
> (The *Daily Express*, 20 April 1991)

Sickness absence is also a problem owing to a variety of reasons, e.g.

> In Somerset, 30 head teachers, 10 per cent of the total, are on sick leave due to the pressures of trying to cope with juggling the purse strings and teaching the new G.C.S.E.'s.
>
> (The *Daily Express*, 20 April 1991)

A recent study by Cooper and Kelly (1993) assessed occupational stress among 2,638 headteachers of primary and secondary schools, together with principals/directors of further and higher education establishments, throughout the United Kingdom. Data were collected on personal/job demographics, sources of job stress, mental health, job satisfaction and coping strategies. These data were analysed by the 'Statistical Package for the Social Sciences' (SPSS), producing univariate, bivariate and multivariate techniques (see Chapters 4 to 6 for more details on these methods).

Cooper and Kelly found that as they moved from the further/higher education level to secondary and primary sectors, the levels of job dissatisfaction and mental ill health rose. In addition it was found that, with the exception of primary schools, female headteachers in secondary and F/HE seemed to be suffering from significantly greater job dissatisfaction than their male counterparts, though this does not necessarily translate itself into mental ill health. Male headteachers, on the other hand, seemed to suffer from poorer mental health than their female counterparts. And finally, the two main sources of occupational stress that were found to be the major predictors of job dissatisfaction and mental ill health were 'work overload' and 'handling relationships with staff'.

## RELATIONSHIPS AT WORK AS A SOURCE OF TEACHER STRESS

Past research has revealed that the pressure of relationships at work can be both a source of stress and a source of support, though there is a great deal of inconsistency in the literature with regard to the effect of relationships with colleagues (Sloan and Cooper 1987). A review of the literature reveals that, with regard to interpersonal relationships, the major aspects that may be deemed stressful are those concerned with: status incongruence, social density, abrasive personalities, leadership style and group pressure (Quick and Quick 1984a). When attempting to understand the link between stress and relationships at work it is also important to regard the effect of hierarchies (e.g. relationships with headteacher, fellow teachers), and in the case of teachers, relationships with the pupils they teach. Social support will be considered later in this chapter – as a moderator of stress, though its role as both a stressor and a support will be considered.

A review of the research literature with regard to teacher stress reveals that teachers are experiencing stress from their relationships with: *fellow teaching colleagues* (Wanberg 1984; Brenner *et al.* 1985), *headteachers* (Clark 1980; Needle *et al.* 1980; Tellenbeck *et al.* 1983), *administrators/ education authorities* (Hawkes and Dedrick 1983; Kalker 1984; Wanberg 1984; Russell *et al.* 1987), *parents* (Kalker 1984; Mykletun 1984; Wanberg 1984), *the community* (Cox 1977; Needle *et al.* 1980) and *pupils* (Tellenbeck *et al.* 1983; Brenner *et al.* 1985). The following sections will present available data on these relationships.

### Relationships with colleagues

Dunham (1977b) found that working relationships with colleagues were reported as a source of stress by teachers, and this finding has been replicated elsewhere. It has been argued that the dominant source of stress is the *quality* of these interpersonal relationships, and that good social relationships are of great value when providing support which may alleviate stress (Brenner *et al.* 1985).

Kyriacou (1981a) has suggested that schools should attempt to improve the social support received by staff, and that a great deal of the responsibility for doing this must lie with the headteacher. It must be noted at this point, however, that good working relationships may only flourish if the organisational structure is designed in such a way that it facilitates good working relationships between individuals. If a formal structure exists (i.e. with regard to responsibility and communication), then this can reduce the opportunities for these relationships.

Another problem that may face teachers in our schools is that they may fear protesting about their problems, when they are overburdened, because they do not want to let fellow teachers down. For example, although the only way to cope with stress might be absenteeism, they fearthe resulting overload this may impose on other teachers in the school. Kyriacou (1987) explains that although absenteeism may enable some teachers to cope, it may have a resulting negative impact, as it can worsen relationships when the classes of an absent teacher have to be covered by others on the staff.

It might be possible to witness the development of 'factions' within schools. According to Claxton (1988), this may be one way in which the breakdown of relationships manifests itself in stressed organisations. In addition, Spanoil and Caputo (1979) emphasise the development of a lack of trust in stressed organisations. The problem is that these 'divisions', though a *manifestation* of stress, can subsequently become a *cause* of stress themselves. A particular piece of evidence that may indicate their presence is the turnover of staff in less than satisfactory circumstances.

## Relationships with pupils

One of the potential stressors facing teachers is that of the pupils' attitudes and behaviour. Although this has been borne out in some of the literature, there are contradictions. A study by Litt and Turk (1985) concluded that pupil misbehaviour and discipline problems were *not* major sources of teacher stress, whereas a study by Cichon and Koff (1978) had suggested that the threat of personal injury and verbal abuse from problem children had a greater impact than other aspects of the teacher's experience, such as management and teaching methods. There are various possible explanations as to why these contradictions exist. Teachers may actually differ in their willingness to admit to experiencing problems with pupils, as this is seen by many to be a major feature of the teacher's job. In addition, there are many different types and levels of misbehaviour, from minor examples of restlessness to serious physical attacks. When pupil misbehaviour has been examined in relation to stress, some studies have made no distinction between different types of behaviour problem, while others have con-centrated solely on major stressful events (e.g. Comber and Whitfield 1979). Whatever the findings, it has been suggested that single, serious disruptive incidents may be a lesser cause of stress than the cumulative effect of constant or repeated 'low level' disruption (Kyriacou 1987). In addition, teachers have differing perspectives as to what constitutes a discipline problem. Freeman (1987) has observed that expectations may differ accord-ing to the particular nature of a situation, and the level of stress associated with a disruptive incident may also vary.

Pupil attitudes and behaviour have been identified as causing teacher stress. Those mentioned frequently include reference to a lack of moti-vation, and Kyriacou and Roe (1988) found that 'under-achieving' was rated as the most serious behaviour problem among first-year pupils, and the fifth most serious problem among pupils in their fifth year of school. This echoes previous work by Kyriacou and Sutcliffe (1978a) that the highest-rated source of stress was 'pupils' poor attitudes to work'. Other studies in this area refer to teachers' concerns to maintain high standards, or concerns for pupils' learning (Pratt 1976). If an examination is made of all of these problems resulting from pupils' behaviour, it seems to point to the fact that the underlying source of pressure begins with the teachers' desires to perform effectively in their work as teachers (i.e. they want to motivate pupils to achieve and fulfil their potential). The stress may result from the frustration at not being able to meet these standards and goals.

Teachers' concern with pupils' behaviour may also be seen to contribute towards job satisfaction. Freeman (1987) has argued that, for most teachers, job satisfaction lies in the experience of teaching itself and in the 'positive feedback' that comes from a successful lesson or series of lessons. Therefore, events that may interfere with this feedback (e.g. poor attitudes and behaviour of pupils), could be a cause of job dissatisfaction. In addition, Mancini *et al.* (1982, 1984) have suggested that 'burnout' may be associated with the breakdown in the teacher–pupil relationship, as they found that 'burned out' teachers gave significantly less praise and information and showed less acceptance of their students. A further problem leading to undesirable stress outcomes in teachers is the threat of actual violence. By examining medical records of teachers in the United States who had been subjected to physical or threatened assault, Bloch (1978) found that they had suffered symptoms similar to 'post-traumatic combat neurosis'. Much research has documented violence as a source of stress in school settings (e.g. ILO 1981; Hammond 1983; Wanberg 1984). The increase in violence among pupils is also evident, as in the example below.

> Police were last night interviewing a 15-year-old boy after a teacher was shot and seriously wounded in front of his class at a Bristol public school. Roderick Findlay, aged 49, was taking a history class with 20 boys at Colston school yesterday morning when a pupil entered brandishing a shotgun.
>
> (The *Guardian*, 6 March 1991)

The previous instance is not a typical example of daily events in British schools but is rather an extreme illustration of classroom violence. However, violence in classrooms in the USA is on the increase to the point that measures have been taken to cope with it. Many schools carry an automatic one-year expulsion for carrying a gun or weapon, and metal detectors are now fitted in the doorways of 16 schools in parts of the USA. This violence is not just aimed at the teachers, but at fellow pupils:

> According to New York City Board of Education, which has 200,000 pupils, there were 1,356 assaults in the 1988–1989 school year. Although this was the first rise in the figures for six years, it included the first killing committed in school, a 17 year old fatally shot in the chest by a fellow student in what was ruled to have been an accident.
>
> (The *Guardian*, 6 March 1991)

The effect of having to witness increasing violence among pupils is just as likely to be stressful for the teacher.

Violence is not the *only* problem facing teachers in schools; they have also to deal with disinterest in education, apathy and the problems that the children may have due to their home backgrounds. Teachers are also finding themselves in the added role of social worker, and are having to observe carefully any evidence of home-related problems experienced by children (e.g. child sexual abuse).

## The type of school as an influence on teacher stress

One question that needs to be addressed in the study of teacher stress is whether or not the type of school has an effect on the nature and levels of stress experienced. There are a number of differing characteristics (i.e. the size of the school, the pupil to teacher ratio, the age of the pupils, the academic pressures) between school types (e.g. primary and secondary schools), that may create problems for teachers. The majority of studies, examining the effects of school type, have focused upon the link between stress and the pupils in these schools, however, the information regarding the type of school and its relationship to the level of stress experienced is very limited. Due to the unequal distribution of the sexes (i.e. predominantly female teachers in primary schools and males in secondary schools), a real comparison without gender bias is difficult (Rudd and Wiseman 1962). However, it has been suggested that stress is a problem at *all* levels of education, though there is an assumption that certain types of school (e.g. inner city, special education) create stress. The majority of studies in this area have considered the effects of teaching in special education (e.g. Pratt 1978), and the problems in dealing with pupils with learning difficulties.

Galloway *et al.* (1982a, b) suggested that teacher stress may be mediated by the school organisation and school climate, despite objectively unfavourable conditions. Pratt (1978) attempted a rather different approach, hypothesising that teacher stress increased in 'poor' schools, as pupil age increased. In this small-scale study of 124 primary teachers, 'poor' schools were identified by the number of school meals given free. Pratt found that the older the class, the greater the stress reported by the teacher, which would suggest that secondary teaching would be the most stressful. The limitations mean that no thorough conclusions may be drawn concerning differences between primary and secondary school teachers and this is largely because studies have failed to utilise standard measurements and large cross-sectional samples.

## Relationships with management

A great deal of overlap may be found between the stress related to relationships with management in schools and the organisational structure and climate of the school itself. A number of features will be discussed in later sections of this chapter (i.e. involvement in decision making and level of participation), but here we shall address issues that are more related to the personal characteristics of the manager (in this case the headteacher), that may create stress for his or her subordinates.

Research has shown that particular individuals in a working environment may cause undue stress to others, because they do not recognise the inter-personal feelings and sensibilities in social interaction (Sutherland and Cooper 1991). Levinson (1978) has devised the label 'abrasive personalities' to describe this character type. These people are usually achievement oriented, intelligent, hard driving, though less efficient with regard to emotional situations. It is suggested that if a leader is of this personality type, then stress may result for the subordinates. For example, if the headteacher of a primary school has the above characteristics, is a perfectionist and is self-centred, then this might create feelings of inadequacy and conflict between staff.

Another relevant feature is that of leadership style, as this is a potential source of stress for employees in whatever type of occupation. The effects of exposure to an authoritarian style of leader has been well documented by Lewin *et al.* (1939). If a headteacher, for example, does not engage in par-ticipation, encourage feedback on his or her own decisions or performance, and does not give recognition for good work, the headteacher–teacher relationship could be at risk. The reactions to this type of leadership style may vary from being passive and repressive (e.g. resulting in elevated levels of blood pressure) or anger and more overt displays of conflict (e.g. aggres-sion). This can create stressful situations for all teachers in that same school. It must be noted, however, that the actual climate or culture of the school may encourage particular forms of management style.

## CAREER DEVELOPMENT

The list of potential stressors that are apparent in the area of career development have been identified as consisting of two major clusters (Marshall 1977). These are:

1 *lack of job security* – i.e. the fear of redundancy, obsolescence, forced early retirement, and the fear of being banned from practice;
2 *status incongruency* – i.e. under- or over-promotion and frustration at having ambitions thwarted and reaching a 'career ceiling'.

An added dimension to this with regard to the teachers' experience is job insecurity and the threat of redeployment, school closure and the subsequent potential job change or loss of job.

## Lack of job security

Some of the common features of working life are the fear of job loss and the threat of redundancy, and these have been found to have links with several serious health problems, including ulcers, colitis and alopecia (Cobb and Kasl 1977), and increased muscular and emotional complaints (Smith *et al.* 1981). With job insecurity follows subsequent deterioration of the morale and motivation of a workforce, which may lead to a negative impact on their job performance, efficiency and commitment.

Teaching has always been believed to be a very secure job, and yet increasingly this is not necessarily the case. The insecurity of teachers' jobs is well documented (e.g. Needle *et al.* 1981; Wanberg 1984). Individuals having to relocate are particularly vulnerable to stress as actual job change is a potential source of high stress (Lazarus 1981). In addition, the rapid pace of change within teaching, both in terms of the nature and requirements of the job, and the technologies and materials with which they have to deal, means that teachers need to consider retraining and a possible career change.

## Status incongruence

This is a feature that is also relevant to the section concerning relationships at work, and refers to the situation where the actual status bestowed on an individual does not match that individual's status expectations and beliefs. This is of particular relevance to teachers at the moment, as they complain they are suffering from a poor public image in terms of prestige, salary and respect for their professional status (e.g. Laughlin 1984; Wanberg 1984).

Under-promotion has also been found to be related to stress in teachers (e.g. Fimian 1983; Wanberg 1984) and thwarted ambitions are a cause of job insecurity. Criteria for promotion are unpredictable and uncertain, and this reinforces an external locus of control in the individual (Kyriacou and Sutcliffe 1979b). Other problems may result from discrimination resulting in restricted job mobility for women (Wanberg 1984). Further related to this is the lack of advancement opportunities in the profession as a whole (Eskridge 1984; Mykletun 1984).

Most people would be able to provide a number of reasons to support their need for career progression. Promotion up the career ladder determines the availability and extent of financial and, therefore, material rewards, but of equal importance is the enhanced status resulting in higher levels of self-esteem and personal challenge.

## Occupational 'Locking-In'

When an individual has minimal opportunity to move from his or her present job this is known as 'Occupational Locking-In'. This may be due to a lack of suitable employment alternatives in the marketplace, or the inability to obtain a different job within the current organisation. For teachers, this may be the result of the feeling that their training does not equip them to move to jobs outside of teaching. Teachers feel they are boxed in as 'educationalists', and are anxious about moving out into the world of work that is far removed from education. Many have moved from school to teacher training college and then straight into the school environment. This 'perceived occupational immobility' may be real or imagined but whatever, it may have an impact on the teacher's feelings of self-worth.

Job dissatisfaction may result from the feeling of being trapped and mental well-being may be reduced (Sutherland and Cooper 1986). Wolpin and Burke (1986) found that those professionals who reported being 'locked-into' their job had lower feelings of self-worth, more negative encounters in their marriages, and less marital satisfaction. They reported more depression, poorer physical health, and less life satisfaction. This suggests, therefore, that teachers may well be professionals who are vulnerable to this source of pressure.

## ORGANISATIONAL STRUCTURE AND CLIMATE

Another feature important in determining the levels of stress that teachers experience is the structure and climate of the school in which they work. On a general level, Cooper and Marshall (1978) refer to the potential threat to autonomy, freedom and identity that this may impose. It is possible, therefore, to suggest that any organisation has a corporate 'personality' that determines the way it treats the members within it. The important element is not just how the organisation treats its workers, but how the individuals *perceive* the actual culture, climate and customs that exist, and how they react to this in terms of their job satisfaction, commitment to the organisation and other behavioural outcomes (e.g. absenteeism).

Structural stressors also include the effects of highly interdependent departments, and a high degree of departmental specialisation and formalisation, with little opportunity for individual advancement. These are problems that often occur for teachers as they may compete with other departments within schools for resources for example. Other stressors include poor communication, an inadequate amount of feedback about performance, inaccurate or ambiguous measurement criteria for performance and unfair control systems (Brief *et al.* 1981). Other features that may be relevant to teachers at present are those concerning participation in decision making, lack of effective consultation and communication, and restrictions on behaviour (e.g. lack of sanctions to deal with unruly pupils).

### Participation in decision making

On a general level, when we talk of participation in this context we are referring to the involvement of subordinates with their superiors in the managerial decision-making process (Tannenbaum and Massarik 1989), where decisions have to be made with regard to organising, directing and controlling responsible subordinates in the process of coordinating the purpose of the company or business. Effective involvement in decision making can result in improved performance and positive psychological and behavioural reactions (Miller and Monge 1986). Teachers have recently been expressing resentment at the lack of involvement in many of the changes that are taking place within education and, consequently, their schools. Traditionally the job of the teacher has been one that involved a great deal of autonomy. In the light of the recent changes taking place within education, we may suggest that this is yet another source of pressure for teachers.

**Performance appraisal**

The process of being evaluated by others can be a very stressful experience for some people, especially if the results of the evaluation have an effect on job prospects and career progression (Baron 1986). At the time of the research, teachers were facing the prospect of teacher appraisal, a new addition to the HRM changes in schools. In addition to this formal appraisal, the very job of a teacher necessitates that they are on show all day, in front of the pupils. Their actual performance is to a large extent evaluated every time a pupil takes an examination, or parents visit for a 'parents evening'.

**Organisational culture**

A pattern of basic assumptions – invented, discovered, or developed by a given group as it learns to cope with its problems of external adaptation and internal integration – that has worked well enough to be considered valuable and, therefore, to be taught to new members as the correct way to perceive, think and feel in relation to those problems.

(Schein 1985)

It may well be that the culture within schools has an effect on the levels of stress that teachers experience. On a general level, organisational culture is generally believed to be concerned with shared values and norms and is a major force for organisational change. More overt and crucial aspects of culture are the norms and behaviours, dominant values, rules and regulations, and overall ethos that make up the organisation. There may be a problem when there is a gap between what an employee expects the job to entail and what the rules say has to be done. To some extent, cultural problems are arising within schools. Many changes are taking place that are transforming a great deal of the ethos (i.e. a move towards an emphasis on financial management and changes in the curriculum). Many teachers complain that teaching is not what it used to be. There is also a greater move towards the pastoral aspects of the job. A further problem is that younger teachers who are new to the profession will have a different expectation of what the job entails compared to the older teachers who will be there to help them settle in. This may create a conflicting culture within some schools.

Additional pressures facing teachers are those consisting of social aspects, that is, legislation which limits responses to social situations (Needle *et al*. 1981), the financial and social deprivation of children (Pratt 1978; Tellenbeck *et al*. 1983), parent–pupil relationships (Wilson 1980), the macro-environment (Pettigrew and Wolf 1981), and public pressures (*Instructor* 1979). This suggests that teachers' problems do not just result from limitations within their own organisation but also the structure and climate of society.

## THE HOME/WORK INTERFACE

So far this chapter has concentrated on the sources of pressure in the teacher's working environment. There are however, potential stressors that exist in the life of the teacher, outside the work arena and affecting behaviour at work, which require consideration when assessing the sources and impact of teacher stress. Potential stressors include stressful life events, pressure resulting from conflict between organisational and family demands, financial difficulties, and conflicts between organisational and personal beliefs. Events occurring in the home may be both a source of stress and a source of support, just like relationships at work, and may also mitigate or exacerbate the effects of stressors experienced in the work environment.

In the case of teachers, the main stresses from the home/work interface are those resulting from dual-career couples and relationships between work and family.

### Dual-career couples

One aspect of home life that may help exacerbate pressure is that of being part of a dual-career couple. One of the major problems facing dual-career families is that of society's attitude towards them (i.e. the 'traditional' family set up is still regarded as the norm). The term 'dual-career family' was first coined by two sociologists, Rhona and Robert Rapoport (1971). They were describing families in which both heads of the household pursue a professional career, while maintaining a family relationship. Some of the stressors of being a member of a dual-career family are outlined by Lewis and Cooper (1989):

• *Conflict* – caused by the traditional expectations concerning the roles of women and men.

- *Overload* – how do couples cope with the demands of work and family?
- *Role cycling dilemmas* – how do they schedule important events (e.g. job relocations) so that overload may not be experienced simultaneously by both partners?
- *Relationship dilemmas* – dual-career couples usually lack role models for equal relationships and so may experience some difficulty in breaking away from the traditional expectations of both themselves and friends and parents.
- *Dilemmas of equality* – though they may attempt to maintain a sense of equality, problems may result when, for example, one partner's job may require relocation, etc.

Though this is a largely unexplored area with regard to teachers, in a profession such as this, which has such a large proportion of women, the stress of being a dual-career couple is bound to be a feature to be considered in the teacher stress phenomenon.

**Relationships between work and family**

The interaction between home and work and the 'juggling' that this often necessitates can create stress. Research has revealed that family-based strains can result from four possible sources:

- *Role pressure or overload* (e.g. due to homemaking);
- *Interpersonal conflicts* (between couples and between parents and children);
- *Role captivity* (where they are bound by one role, but would prefer another);
- *Restructuring of family roles through time* (Pearlin and Turner 1987).

Glowinkowski and Cooper (1985) proposed the idea of 'spillover' – where a relationship exists between home and work that leads to similar experiences and reactions in the two domains. Support for this hypothesis has been found by Bromet *et al.* (1988), who reveal a positive association between occupational stress and marital stress. 'Compensation', on the other hand, is a process in which an individual seeks opposite experiences and satisfactions at work and at home, in order to make up for deficiencies in one of the settings (Gutek *et al.* 1988).

There have been findings in this area related to teachers. In a study by Cooke and Rousseau (1984), results revealed that although the demands of the family conflicted with the demands of work, the family also provided comfort and support to the teacher. This enabled them therefore to overcome some of the more harmful physical effects that are usually associated with stress (i.e. headaches, loss of sleep) better than those teachers who were still single. There is a problem in drawing conclusions from findings such as these, in that there are probably many differences between the lifestyles of unmarried and married teachers.

## ASPECTS OF THE INDIVIDUAL TEACHER AND THE RESPONSE TO STRESS

We have emphasised the point in earlier sections of this book that the situation teachers find themselves in will not necessarily be stressful but may be affected by the interaction between the situation and the individual characteristics of the teacher involved. Evidence shows that in certain environments and under particular levels of pressure, some individuals survive the strain while others do not. Therefore, the experience of stress can be a very personal phenomenon, with stress resulting from an individual teacher perceiving the stressors and threats as far outweighing his or her available resources to meet the demands. Some teachers are therefore more susceptible than others, but we need to discover why this is the case and focus on features of the environment and the teacher's own characteristics that lead to reduced resistance and increased vulnerability. There are many features that predispose a teacher to deal with stress in a particular way (i.e. age, experience, life events, life stages and ability, personality, behavioural disposition, attitudes, values and needs).

On a general level, this 'person-facet' has been described further with regard to personality dispositions, a set of learned responses (Innes 1981) and personal conditioning variables (McMichael 1978). These ideas presume that there exists a stable personality profile (i.e. behavioural dispositions, coping styles and ability to adapt) with styles that affect how a person responds to stress. Schuler (1982) further discusses internal qualities of the individual under the heading of needs and values, abilities and experience, and personality characteristics of the person. These are all important to the individual's perception of the work environment. A summary of these facets of the individual can be seen in Table 3.1, resulting from work by Beehr and Newman (1978).

While we were selecting the individual aspects of teachers to be examined in this study, attention was paid to those which were deemed appropriate to teachers and repeatedly reported by other studies (e.g. gender and age). Also, of major importance to this investigation was the study of Type A behavioural style (e.g. time conscious behaviour, hard driving, etc. – see later in this chapter) which has been a largely neglected area with regard to teachers. Much research has examined biographical variables (e.g. Simpson 1962; Capel 1987) by exploring comparisons between teachers' experience of stress dependent upon their sex, age and teaching experience. Some studies (Cichon and Koff 1978; Kyriacou and Sutcliffe 1978a) report that individual characteristics of teachers, such as age, sex, teaching experience and level of qualification, do not correlate significantly with perceived stress and stressors (Catterton 1979). Kyriacou and Sutcliffe (1979a) report slightly different findings. They found that male heads of departments and female teachers reported greater stress than their colleagues. Moracco *et al.* (1983) found that although there were no significant relationships between similar characteristics and stress, it appeared

*Table 3.1* Facets of the job stress–employee health research domain: the personal facet

---

1.  Psychological condition (personality traits and behavioural characteristics)
    - Type A
    - ego needs
    - need for clarity/ intolerance for ambiguity
    - introversion/extraversion
    - internality/externality
    - approval seeking
    - defensiveness
    - intelligence
    - abilities
    - previous experience with stress
    - impatience
    - intrapersonal conflicts
    - self-esteem
    - motives/goals/aspirations
    - typical anxiety level
    - perceptual style
    - values (human, religious etc.)
    - personal work standards
    - need for perfection
    - satisfaction with job and other major aspects of life

2.  Physical condition
    - physical fitness/health
    - diet and eating habits
    - exercise, work, sleep and relaxation patterns

3.  Life stage characteristics
    - human development stages
    - family stages
    - career stages

4.  Demographics
    - age
    - education (amount and type)
    - sex
    - race
    - socio-economic status
    - occupation, avocation

---

*Source*: Beehr and Newman (1978)

that sex, teaching experience and school environment had some bearing on the stress levels that teachers experienced. In a review of the research literature, Hiebert and Farber (1984) concluded that gender, age and teaching experience were related to teacher stress, whereas Mykletun (1984) found that biographical variables had only a low or moderate influence on stress levels.

Other researchers also report significant interactions. Feitler and Tokar (1982) claim that teachers' stress levels do vary with age, school location and grade level taught, although not with teaching experience. More specifically teachers between the ages of 31 and 44, urban teachers, and those teaching at senior grade levels reported higher levels of stress. The latter finding is supported by Pratt (1978). According to Laughlin (1984) biographical variables play a major role in teachers' perceptions of stress and found that sex, age, type of school (i.e. primary or secondary), positions held, and qualifications were significant in predicting stress among teachers. Young female teachers and secondary teachers reported greater stress with pupil recalcitrance; males and primary teachers found curriculum demands stressful; middle career teachers reported high levels of stress from lack of professional recognition; and older teachers found curriculum changes stressful. There is therefore little consistency in the research findings; however, it seems to be generally acknowledged that certain biographical characteristics of teachers are potential moderators of the impact stress will have, and some of these will be explored in more detail in subsequent sections of this chapter.

### Age, experience and level of ability and its relationship to the experience of stress

An important characteristic that may modify a teacher's response to stress is age, and this is because at each stage in life an individual may experience a particular vulnerability, and/or a particular mechanism of coping (McLean 1979).

Age may affect the impact of stress in two ways:

- the age and biological condition of the person may mediate the response in that he or she is more easily fatigued and finds the work too difficult (e.g. long hours, etc.);
- past experiences affect the way they perceive the stress that they experience (e.g. previous failure to cope).

Age and experience have also been linked to the extent of stress in teaching in that it has often been suggested that the highest levels of stress might be experienced by recent entrants to the profession (usually younger teachers). This may be due to the fact that they have not yet acquired the expertise required to cope with the job. A study by Coates and Thoresen (1976) concluded that younger and less experienced teachers felt greater stress than their colleagues from pressures associated with discipline, poor promotion prospects and management issues.

A recent survey by Edworthy (1988) discovered that a major source of stress for younger teachers was the general low ability of pupils. An earlier Australian study by Laughlin (1984) suggested that the chief concerns of younger teachers are the pupils, whereas for those in their middle years the major source of stress is career aspects, and the actual teaching itself is the problem for older teachers. A look at the literature, in general, highlights the issue that middle-aged teachers may face – a fear of obsolescence linked with their mid-life crisis. Therefore, as Warnat (1980) explains, this may result in middle-aged teachers worrying that their skills are somewhat outdated and what experience they have is of little value to the profession. It is difficult when attempting to compare the experiences of younger and older teachers to eradicate the effect of *actual* experience and so often it is necessary to consider these two together. Researchers may not always make this point clear, but generally speaking this is the case in the majority of the pieces of research in this area.

The implications of the findings so far may imply that teachers learn to cope with the particular stressors they face at one level, they then move onto another concern. The aforementioned study by Laughlin (1984) was not a longitudinal one and therefore the changing concerns of the same teacher throughout his or her career are not presented. Dunham (1984b) has attempted to explain how apparently skilled teachers may become stressed, suggesting that skilled and experienced teachers facing changes in external demands may suffer when they discover that their previously developed coping skills are largely inadequate.

Nias (1985) has pointed out that consolidation and extension of a teaching career does not necessarily depend upon age or experience, but largely relies on luck. In a study of 99 'Post Graduate Certificate in Education' (PGCE) students, she followed their careers by means of extended and extensive interviews over a period of nine years. From periods ranging from three months to two years, the probationers saw teaching as a 'status passage necessarily marked by suffering'. For a number of the group, this continued for as long as four years. Some of these left teaching but a number of others kept on trying. Nias discovered that the factors that influenced their decision to stay or leave the profession were complex, but mainly rested on support or lack of support from colleagues, superiors, family and friends. Nias drew no major conclusions other than that she emphasised the probationers view of themselves as teachers (which they had chosen to be) and successful people (which they hitherto had been academically), and highlighted the probationers' dependence on pupils for recognition and validation of their role as teachers.

An earlier, more general, study by Taylor and Dale (1971) attempted a postal survey of some 3,588 probationers in their first year of service. A third of the sample felt that they were experiencing stress due to the need to adapt to teaching. They were given a list of 132 problems and were then asked to identify the three most relevant to them and their situation. Dealing with mixed ability children was the problem that came top most often for the probationers. The same exercise was also given to the headteachers of the probationers' schools, and they were asked to indicate what *they* believed to be the three major problems facing probationers in their schools. *Most* heads selected the problem of classroom discipline as being the major sources of worry for probationers. There could be various explanations for this. Perhaps headteachers believed that this, though largely unadmitted, was the major problem, or that they felt that probationers *needed* to worry about it. Another option is that perhaps the probationers' fears of teaching mixed ability children were deep rooted somehow in problems of discipline.

Smilansky (1984) raised an interesting point with a small-scale study of teachers in Israel. The study required that teachers were judged by headteachers, pupils and parents. The 'better judged' teachers reported a higher level of job stress than did their colleagues. This raises a number of questions regarding the vulnerability of these particular teachers to stress. It may be that those with conscientious and highly professional standards may be most at risk, but a question that needs to be addressed asks whether or not stress impairs a teacher's effectiveness.

## THE CONTRIBUTION OF BEHAVIOURAL STYLE TO THE STRESS RESPONSE

### Type A behaviour

Type A behavioural style is one of the most widely investigated 'person-based' characteristics that may influence the stress relationship (Ivancevich and Matteson 1984), though there has been less examination of the effect of this on stress in teachers. Particular 'styles' of behaviour have been found to act as modifiers in individual responses to stress, by affecting the relationship between psychosocial stressors and strains (Van Dijkhuizen and Reiche 1980). Friedman and Rosenman (1959) studied the Type A/ Type B concept and suggested that this was a set of attitudes, emotional reactions and behaviour patterns that was linked to the patients in their study exhibiting 'stress diseases' (i.e. coronary heart disease). They found a strong correlation between Type A behaviour and coronary heart disease (Friedman and Rosenman 1974). It is important to understand that Type A is not a '*trait*' but rather a set of overt behaviours – an individual's way of confronting a situation. However, this style is still a habitual coping mechanism produced in the presence of personal and environmental demands.

### *The concept of Type A behaviour*

In the late 1950s, cardiologists Friedman and Rosenman (1959) observed that their coronary heart disease patients shared a characteristic pattern of behaviours and emotional reactions that they named Type A behaviour (TAB), described as an 'action-emotion complex'. This behaviour pattern involves hostility, aggressiveness, competitiveness and a sense of time urgency; patients may also be unrelenting, hard driving and achievement oriented. More obvious characteristics are hurriedness and an explosive speech pattern, quick motor movements, a sense of guilt or unease when not working or when relaxing, and a generally impatient disposition. Type A individuals do not like being prevented from rapidly overcoming obstacles in their way. Perhaps the best way for readers to gain a better understanding of the Type A phenomenon is to complete the Bortner (1969) questionnaire that follows, to obtain their own Type A/B profile and then to read some of the comments that describe how to spot a Type A.

## TYPE A BEHAVIOUR AND HOW TO MEASURE IT

Circle the number (1–11) for each dimension which best fits your behavioural style.

| | | |
|---|---|---|
| Casual about appointments | 1 2 3 4 5 6 7 8 9 10 11 | Never late |
| Not competitive | 1 2 3 4 5 6 7 8 9 10 11 | Very competitive |
| Good listener | 1 2 3 4 5 6 7 8 9 10 11 | Anticipates what others are going to say (nods, attempts to finish for them) |
| Never feels rushed (even under pressure) | 1 2 3 4 5 6 7 8 9 10 11 | Always rushed |
| Can wait patiently | 1 2 3 4 5 6 7 8 9 10 11 | Impatient while waiting |
| Takes things one at a time | 1 2 3 4 5 6 7 8 9 10 11 | Tries to do too many things at once, thinks about what will do next |
| Slow deliberate talker | 1 2 3 4 5 6 7 8 9 10 11 | Emphatic in speech fast and forceful |
| Cares about satisfying him/herself no matter what others may think | 1 2 3 4 5 6 7 8 9 10 11 | Wants good job recognised by others |
| Slow doing things | 1 2 3 4 5 6 7 8 9 10 11 | Fast (eating, walking) |
| Easy going | 1 2 3 4 5 6 7 8 9 10 11 | Hard driving (pushing self and others) |
| Expresses feelings | 1 2 3 4 5 6 7 8 9 10 11 | Hides feelings |
| Many outside interests | 1 2 3 4 5 6 7 8 9 10 11 | Few interests outside work/home |
| Unambitious | 1 2 3 4 5 6 7 8 9 10 11 | Ambitious |
| Casual | 1 2 3 4 5 6 7 8 9 10 11 | Eager to get things done |

Now add up your scores on the 14 sets of statements.

Scoring: Below 70 = Type B; 70–89 = Type B+; 90–110 = Type A; 110 upwards = Type A
*Source:* Bortner (1969)

# HOW TO SPOT THE TYPE A PERSONALITY

Type As:

- Tend to feel or reveal to others an impatience with the rate at which events take place and find it particularly difficult to restrain from hurrying the speech of others. They tend to resort to the device of saying very quickly, over and over again, 'uh huh, uh huh,' or 'yes, yes, yes' to someone who is talking. This can have the effect of urging someone to hurry up. They also tend to finish the sentences of the person who is speaking.

- Possess the habit of explosively accentuating various key words in ordinary speech without need and tend to utter the last few words of sentences far more rapidly than the opening words. This may signify underlying aggression and an impatience even with spending time on their own speech.

- Tend to always move, walk and eat rapidly. In fact they try to do everything rapidly.

- Often attempt to do two or more things at the same time, such as thinking about an unrelated issue when listening to someone else speak. In a similar fashion, they can be identified if, while involved in leisure pastimes or something enjoyable, they continue to ponder business or professional problems e.g. while eating their breakfast they try to dry their hair, or drive their car. This is called 'polyphasic' activity and is one of the most common traits of the Type A.

- Can be recognised by certain tell-tale characteristics and gestures e.g. nervous tics, using clenching fists, and banging hands on tables for emphasis.

- Tend to want to turn all conversation back to themselves and the things that they are interested in. If this strategy does not work, then they pretend to listen but really remain preoccupied with their own thoughts.

- Almost always feel vaguely guilty when they attempt to relax or do nothing for even just a few hours.

- No longer notice the more interesting or lovely things encountered during their day.

- Try to schedule more and more in less and less time. A by-product of this is the fact that they make fewer allowances for anything unpredictable which might disrupt their plans. A core aspect of the Type A personality is having a chronic sense of time urgency.

- Do not show sympathy for their own type, instead, on meeting another Type A, tend to compete and challenge them – this situation tends to arouse all their hostile and competitive feelings.

Type B individuals, on the other hand, are free of these traits, do not suffer from time urgency and impatience, do not harbour 'free floating hostility', play to relax and can 'relax without guilt'.

Based on Watts and Cooper (1992)

*Type A behaviour and occupational stress*

How would we identify the Type A teachers in their work setting? Based on Brief *et al.* (1983), Type A teachers may be identified as those who:

- work long hours constantly under deadlines and conditions of overload;
- take work home on evenings and at weekends; they are unable to relax;
- often cut holidays short to get back to work, or may not even take a holiday;
- constantly compete with themselves and others; also drive themselves to meet high, often unrealistic standards;
- feel frustrated in the work situation;
- are irritable with work efforts and their pupils;
- feel misunderstood by their headteachers.

With the increasing pressures on teachers today from the National Curriculum, LMS, assessment, etc., teachers are perhaps being encouraged to show and develop more and more of these Type A symptoms and behaviour.

**Teacher personality and its effect on the experience of teacher stress**

The study of teachers' personality and its relationship to their experience of stress has been largely neglected in research, in particular with regard to Type A behaviour. Two studies of particular importance are those of Pratt (1976) and Kyriacou and Sutcliffe (1979b). In the first study, Pratt utilised the Eysenck Personality Inventory (EPI) on 124 primary school teachers and reported significant correlations between his measure of reported stress and both neuroticism and extraversion. A problem does occur when interpreting these results with regard to neuroticism, as stress has been found to be positively related to neuroticism scores, in that scores increase when the individual is experiencing stress, suggesting that the scores may be measuring similar aspects of the individual's disposition (Humphrey 1977).

In a study of 130 UK secondary school teachers, Kyriacou and Sutcliffe (1979b) investigated the locus of control effect as revealed by a number of authors (e.g. Chan 1977). This is where individuals experience stress related to the degree to which they perceive themselves as having a lack of control over the potentially threatening situation. This may be due to an inability to deal with the demands or the lack of adequate coping mechanisms being available. They looked at the association between self-reported teacher stress and Rotters Internal-External Locus of Control (I–E) scale (Rotter 1966). A Likert scale (i.e. 1–5 from strongly agree to strongly disagree) was employed in the study and a significant correlation was obtained between self-reported teacher stress and externality. Therefore, teachers exhibiting external control reported higher levels of teacher stress.

A study by Cox *et al.* (1978) investigated the experience and behaviour of 100 UK school teachers and 100 matched semi-professionals using three questionnaires. Information concerning specific complaints (e.g. diabetes), hospitalisation, risk factors associated with CHD, estimated general health, smoking, drinking, sleeping and obesity were gathered using the General Health Questionnaire (GHQ). In addition, the Jenkins Activity Survey (JAS) was used to measure 'Type A' personality (Jenkins *et al.* 1968). The third measure employed was the General Well-Being questionnaire designed by Cox *et al.* (1978). When they compared the responses of the two groups of subjects on the three questionnaires they found only two differences, both on the GHQ. Results revealed that female teachers sleep longer than male teachers and non-teachers, and teachers drink less than non-teachers, but no personality differences were found.

**The effects of gender on the experience of teacher stress**

Two features have for a very long time marked off schoolteachers from other professional or semi-professional groups. The first of these features is that of representing the largest absolute number of women in any such group (other than nurses), the second that of having a preponderance, but not an overwhelming preponderance, of women as compared with men.

(Kelsall 1980)

The fact that there is a preponderance of females in teaching has important implications for the level and nature of stress experienced by teachers if there is a gender effect on the stress response. Here we address the issues of gender effects in (a) occupational stress generally and (b) stress in the teaching profession, as research has shown that gender has an effect on the type, level, and outcomes of stress experienced. In addition, an interaction may exist between gender and moderators of stress (i.e. Type A behaviour and coping styles).

Research has highlighted stressors which are experienced by both sexes, but particular research has uncovered stressors unique to women (e.g. Nelson and Quick 1985). These factors may be encountered by men, but perhaps less often. The stressors specific to women include discrimination (e.g. traditional discrimination, their special career planning needs, lower salary and a comparative lack of advice and support), stereotyping (e.g. of particular personality traits), the marriage/work interface (e.g. childcare, career/family conflicts), and social isolation (to avoid the mother, seductress, pet, fair maiden role entrapment – see Davidson and Cooper 1983).

In terms of managerial level, female managers are found to be particularly affected by stressors resulting from job insecurity (i.e. fear of being laid off), office politics, competition, lack of teamwork and mutual support (Davidson and Cooper 1992).

Studies have indicated that there are gender differences in the experience of stress in teaching, one of these being with regard to job satisfaction. Researchers have reported that women teachers report greater dissatisfaction than their male colleagues with regard to classroom situations and pupil behaviour, whereas male teachers tend to report higher dissatisfaction with administration, participation and need for professional recognition and their career situation (Kyriacou and Sutcliffe 1978b; Laughlin 1984). Also, women tend to report higher levels of satisfaction from the job generally (Maxwell 1974; Laughlin 1984; Patton and Sutherland 1986). However, the greatest level of overall job dissatisfaction was reported by male teachers in large comprehensive schools. Female teachers in primary schools reported the least dissatisfaction (Cox *et al.* 1978).

One of the problems in interpreting male/female differences is that female teachers have a tendency to be primary school teachers, and there has been no direct comparison between females in primary and secondary schools. This sex bias in school type may also explain why females report a greater level of satisfaction overall than males, due to the fact that they have probably been largely drawn from the primary sector, which tends to exhibit greater levels of satisfaction anyway (Rudd and Wiseman 1962; Maxwell 1974; Laughlin 1984; Patton and Sutherland 1986). It is also evident from the literature that teachers who report high levels of satisfaction can also report high levels of stress (Kyriacou 1987) and so it does not follow that the more satisfied women may also be the least stressed.

In terms of mental well-being, studies have revealed that the reported incidence of headaches, tearfulness and exhaustion is higher among female teachers (Kyriacou and Sutcliffe 1978b; Dunham 1984b). A point regarding the emotional expression of female teachers is that they perhaps use this as a coping mechanism, and find open expression easier than their male counterparts. A further confounding variable could be that female teachers are more able to admit to stress. In addition, research has shown that they suffer more than men from 'minor-mood' disorders and from depression, though there is not a preponderance of females among cases treated by psychiatrists (Goldberg and Huxley 1980). Though it is important to look at male and female differences in teaching experience, care must be taken when interpreting manifestations of stress between the sexes and the controls employed to ensure that we are not really measuring school type effects for example.

An age/sex interaction has been uncovered in relation to absence rates and decisions to leave the profession. Young female teachers have higher voluntary absenteeism than their colleagues, in particular their married female colleagues with children (Simpson 1962, 1976). According to a DES survey (1973b), young female teachers tend to report a desire to leave teaching more often than males, although the rationale behind this decision may be positive (i.e. to have a baby) rather than negative (Nias 1985). However, in contrast to these findings, Kyriacou and Sutcliffe (1978b) found that fewer women than men reported an intention to leave the profession, though they too found that having a baby was the most common reason for female teachers having the intention to leave. This issue needs further probing in order to gain a greater insight into the motivation of female teachers, but it may well be the case that stress at work makes women choose to leave the profession rather than purely for maternity leave. Men in these studies gave poor salary, poor promotion prospects and general dissatisfaction as their reasons for leaving.

Turning to the actual sources of stress, a study of 493 Australian teachers by Laughlin (1984) found that women reported more stress concerning pupils and curriculum demands whereas men emphasised participation and professional recognition. A well-documented explanation of the differences in their concerns is that women are greatly under-represented in promoted teaching posts.

While there has been a wealth of research regarding women and management, the investigation of the problems facing women teachers has been largely neglected. The teaching profession warrants detailed study owing to the fact that there are so many women in this occupational group. Therefore, as this is an occupation within which women are employed in large numbers, it provides a good opportunity to compare men and women in terms of (a) achieved professional status and (b) stress outcomes related to the job. The absence of women in managerial positions in teaching suggests that this is a profession where women do not achieve the same status as their male counterparts (DES 1976). Kelsall (1980), citing a DES survey, revealed that:

> Within any given sector of education . . . it is clear that women have a smaller share of the higher-status posts than their numerical strength would lead one to expect. Thus, although . . . women formed a little over 43 per cent of the full-time teaching force in maintained secondary schools in England and Wales, they only had 18 per cent of the headships.

Therefore, although the organisation of teaching may be beneficial for women with regard to maternity leave, there would appear to be barriers to promotion for women in schools. So, the kinds of questions that we shall address later in this book, concerning the effects of gender on teaching experience, will be:

1 How are women teachers represented in positions of management and status measured by the career demographics of managerial level and salary obtained?
2 What are the effects of any differences in women's experiences of teaching as reflected in the stress outcomes of job satisfaction, mental ill health and reported pressure with the job?

These types of issues and questions have been neglected in the study of teachers' experience at work.

## The effect of coping on the experience of teacher stress

The state of well-being an individual teacher experiences is not only influenced by the previously described behavioural/personality dispositions and demographics, but also by the way the teacher copes with the stressful experiences and situations. This ability can be drawn from resources within the teacher or from the surrounding environment. Coping has been included in a number of models of teacher stress (e.g. Kyriacou and Sutcliffe 1978a; Lazarus 1976), and may be defined as the behaviour exhibited by the individual with the intention of bringing about a subsequent reduction in the experience of stress.

In terms of teachers and their methods of coping, there is little empirical evidence, as most of the literature is experiential, anecdotal or suggestive in nature as opposed to experimental (Kyriacou 1980d). Kyriacou studied the issue of coping and produced a descriptive, though not evaluative, account of teachers' coping behaviours (Kyriacou 1980d). There have also been a number of investigations into the methods teachers use to cope with stress in their jobs (Dewe 1985; Dunham 1983; Kyriacou 1980c, d). Kyriacou (1980c) gave teachers a list of 33 coping methods and asked them to rate these coping actions (on a five-point scale from 'always' through to 'never') in response to the request 'Please consider each statement in the list below and indicate how frequently you use such actions to cope with stress at work'. Using the statistical method of factor analysis (see Chapter 6 for a fuller explanation of this method), he found that the responses could be grouped into three categories: 'express feelings and seek support', 'take considered actions' and 'think of other things'. The most frequently used actions in the sample of comprehensive school teachers were 'try to keep things in perspective', 'try to avoid confrontations', and 'try to relax after work'.

Further categorisations of stressors were obtained for New Zealand primary teachers by Dewe (1985). Factor analysis identified the five categories of 'attempts to ride the situation', 'rational task-oriented behaviour', 'a conservative approach to teaching', 'utilising colleague support' and 'putting things into perspective'.

Over the last few years attempts have been made to evaluate the effectiveness of in-service courses for teachers, designed to help them deal more effectively with stress, but these have led to many conflicting results (Docking 1985; Woodhouse et al. 1985). It would appear from the results, however, that the development of more pragmatic skills (i.e. improving time management) outweighs the benefits of psychological stress reduction techniques. This, however, may be due to the fact that the former are more identifiable and tangible. The majority of studies have recommended that this style of coping is essential for teachers (Iwanicki 1983; Sparks 1983).

An important point to note is that, so far, the majority of studies and recommendations for coping have focused on the individual teacher and what he or she can do. Researchers are now emphasising the need to examine the whole school context as an organisation to be managed as Cox *et al.* (1989) argues that:

> studies on stress in schools have generally failed to develop past the established paradigms of considering the teachers' experience in isolation from their organizational context. This is somewhat surprising as, at the same time, many studies report that the problems faced by teachers are organizational (or managerial) in origin.

They believe that the narrow approach of just examining teacher-based reasons for stress has prevented researchers reaching proper solutions, explaining the effects on the organisation, and also:

> have often made very general recommendations, focused on the individual teacher, e.g. relaxation training, access to a counsellor, use of tranquillizers, etc. Sadly, these individually orientated 'band aids' have further detracted from the important role that the organization plays in determining teachers' experiences. Equally, neglecting this organizational perspective, has led to a failure to ask and answer questions about the health and performance of the organization itself òr about organizational solutions to these problems.

Kyriacou (1987) suggests improvements in management practices, organisational and administrative arrangements, staff relationships, working conditions, and curriculum processes that minimise the stress within the school's control.

## Social support as a moderator of teacher stress

A previous section in this chapter on 'relationships at work' revealed how the effects of teacher job stress can be moderated by the degree and nature of support they receive from others within and outside of the teaching environment. The influence of each type of support may be variable, but it can come from a number of sources (i.e. social, organisational and family networks). On a general level, a lack of social support has been found to have serious physiological symptoms (e.g. increased risk of coronary heart disease) (Herd 1988) and higher levels of symptomology (Cobb 1976).

A problem inherent in the study of social support and its effects is that there is no clear agreement as to its definition and how it alleviates stress (Mackay and Cooper 1987). Thoits (1982) provides a possible definition of social support: 'that subset of persons in the individual's total social network upon whom he or she relies for socio-emotional aid, instrumental aid, or both'.

If schools were to provide a 'teacher-counsellor', Phillips and Whitfield

(1980) reported that 50 per cent of teachers in comprehensive schools would make use of this person, as they tended to make use of a 'trusted colleague' with whom to discuss their professional problems.

A comment on the difficulty of implementing sufficient social support is made by Cooper and Marshall (1975), and is relevant to teachers:

> People suffer, in fact, because it is contrary to our cultural norm to admit that one is under stress. Stress is viewed as closely linked to weakness, incompetence and unreliability (none of which are attractive employee characteristics), as well as mental illness. Understandably, the employer is least likely to admit his inability to cope in the actual work situation – it is here that he knows the most damage can be caused.

Kyriacou (1981a) points out the problem of deciding whether social support is a palliative or direct action technique. He proposes that the benefits from social support can be grouped into three categories.

1 Social support enables teachers to receive sound advice from colleagues about new direct action techniques they could use to deal with stress.
2 They can discuss problems and difficulties with colleagues, enabling teachers to get some of their concerns, that have perhaps been excessively developed, back into true perspective – a typical counselling technique (e.g. Ellis 1978).
3 Social interaction with colleagues offers the most important sources of relieving tension that has built up during a period of stress, e.g. staffroom humour (Woods 1979).

Previous sections have discussed the pressures associated with the organisational structure and management of schools. Research suggests that a headteacher should facilitate good support within schools, and as Kyriacou (1981a) says: 'many schools are proud to think of themselves as a caring community for their pupils. It is time to put more effort into providing a mutually caring community for their staff.'

In conclusion, the main sources of stress for a particular teacher will depend on what he or she perceives as a demand that cannot be met, and which will threaten his or her mental and/or physical well-being. There are, therefore, a range of stressors in the teaching environment. The following chapters will highlight our large-scale study into teacher stress to tease out these sources and outcomes.

# Part II
# A study of teacher stress

*Read not to contradict and confute, nor to believe and take for granted, nor to find talk and discourse but to weigh and consider.*
(Francis Bacon, *Essays*, 50, 'Of Studies')

# 4 Who are the teachers?

For every person who wants to teach, there are approximately thirty who don't want to learn – much.

(Sellar and Yeatman, *And Now All This* 1932)

The purpose of this second part of the book is to present the findings of the major nationwide study of stress among the UK teaching profession carried out by the authors. This chapter will explain how the study was carried out and will provide a profile of the teachers in the sample. Chapter 5 will present the data regarding the teachers' reactions to the stress in teaching and Chapter 6 will examine the major sources of pressure in teaching and their effects.

A certain amount of statistical 'jargon' (will be used in these chapters) and for ease of interpretation, those who have little or no statistical knowledge can refer to the glossary of terms provided in Appendix 1.

## GETTING THE DATA

To enable us to meet the aims of our study (as outlined in the Preface to this book), we needed to gather a large amount of data from a wide range of teachers in terms of teaching grade, school type and location. In addition, we needed to gather information about perceived sources of stress and how teachers attempt to cope with that stress. We also wanted to gain information about the way they react to these stressors.

### Gaining access to UK teachers

One of the key problems for any researcher is gaining access to people when the information to be obtained is of a highly sensitive nature – especially when the researchers, as in this case, are working outside of the system under scrutiny. Due to the perceived prevalence of stress among teachers, we were very fortunate to obtain access with very few barriers as teachers were keen to share their experiences with us. In order to pick up where previous research had left off, we planned to study a nationwide sample, and subsequently gained permission and support from the NASUWT, the second largest teaching union in the UK. A random sample of NASUWT members was obtained with the full cooperation and support of the union.

## Interviewing teachers

Having gained union support, the researchers made contact with union representatives within a number of schools in the North West as this was a convenient location for the researcher involved. It was decided that a sufficient number of interviews with teachers should be conducted (i.e. 40). In advance of the interviews, a phone call was made to the appropriate contact at each school to enable them to prepare and explain the purpose of the study to the school teachers. The phone call outlined the purpose of our study and indicated briefly the proposed content and aims of the interviews, emphasising the degree of confidentiality.

We decided to carry out the interviews for the following reasons:

- to obtain detailed qualitative data about the job of teaching and the teaching environment within which teachers work;
- to determine which aspects of a teacher's job might be stressful, and the behavioural outcomes that result from stress in teaching;
- to obtain up-to-date information to help design the Teacher Stress Questionnaire.

A total of 40 interviews were conducted in seven schools, a mix of primary and secondary in inner city, rural and suburban locations. The majority of these were recorded in full, with the consent of the interviewee teacher on audio tape, to be transcribed for further analysis. At one school, due to time constraints, a group interview was conducted with three teachers taking part. In the primary schools it was often necessary to conduct interviews in the classroom, and these interviews often took longer as they had to stop and start, due to disturbances. But this helped the researchers gain an insight into the actual environment in which teachers work, as they had to spend the whole day at the school, across the lunch times and breaks, etc.

Initially the researchers had a structured interview schedule, where questions were drawn up formally prior to the interview. It soon became apparent, however, that teachers were very keen to talk openly about their experience, and so a less formal semi-structured interview was employed. All information was written up after the interview, whether from notes or from the audio tape.

Teachers were selected for interview mainly by the process of voluntary contribution and availability. In some schools (i.e. in the primary sector), it was possible to interview all teachers during the school day. However, in the secondary schools, as one day only had been allocated for each school, representatives usually asked for interested and willing volunteers prior to the chosen day. Time slots were not allocated due to the impracticability of this for teachers, and so it was a case of fitting them in when it was convenient, to a loose schedule. Each interview lasted between 30 and 60 minutes; with some lasting longer. At the beginning of each interview the researcher provided the interviewees with a brief outline to the project, and they were then asked to provide information about their background, family situation, education, employment history and their current job within teaching. They were also asked about the things that they found positive and negative in the job of teaching, what had been their original reasons for entering the profession and how they saw the job of teaching now. They were also asked to detail the effects on their home life, any teacher training they had experienced, their future plans, and other employment experience and opportunities.

## Gathering the data: the Teacher Stress Questionnaire

Having carried out the interviews within the schools, we designed a questionnaire that would obtain the data which would meet the aims and objectives of the study. The questionnaire was based on the view of stress that we have adopted (i.e. the interactive model of stress outlined in Chapters 1 to 3), and by comments and issues raised and examined with the teachers during the interviews. The questionnaire can be found in Appendix 2 and consists of six sections designed in such a way as to operationalise the main stressors and strain factors.

The questionnaire comprised the following (though not in this order): (1) demographic questions, asking for information regarding the teacher's personal and job demographics concerning biographical items (e.g. sex and age), professional and career (e.g. years in teaching, teaching grade), school (e.g. number of pupils) and job details (e.g. number of hours worked); (2) a measure of behavioural style, which was a Type A Behaviour questionnaire; (3) a Coping Style Inventory; (4) a Sources of Job Pressure measure designed from the rich interview data. The remaining two sections were measures of 'strain' and comprised (5) mental health and (6) job satisfaction. Additional strain measures were also included for ease in the demographic section, to obtain information with regard to teachers' health-related behavioural responses to stress (e.g. smoking, drinking and intention to leave the profession), as these have been found to be potentially important indicators of stress (Cooper *et al.* 1988b).

The following sections provide more detail with regard to the measures used in the study.

### Mental health

Psychological well-being and mental health were measured by the Crown–Crisp Experiential Index (formerly the Middlesex Hospital

Questionnaire) (Crown and Crisp 1979). This inventory comprises of six subscales, but for the purpose of this study only three were used:

**1 Free-floating anxiety** This cannot be seen to be related to any specific cause but is the experience of dread, tension or indefinable terror without cause and panic. The questions investigate the possible existence of feelings of worry, unease, tension and restlessness, i.e.:

- Do you often feel upset for no obvious reason?
- Have you ever felt as though you might faint?
- Do you feel uneasy and restless?
- Do you sometimes feel really panicky?
- Would you say you are a worrying person?
- Do you often feel 'strung up' inside?
- Have you ever had the feeling you were 'going to pieces'?
- Do you have bad dreams which upset you when you wake up?

**2 Somatic concomitants of anxiety** This is the type that manifests itself in the form of headaches, aches and pains, and breathlessness. The questions in this section refer to appetite loss, digestion upset, tiredness, exhaustion and sleep disturbance, i.e.:

- Are you troubled by dizziness or shortness of breath?
- Do you often feel sick or have indigestion?
- Do you sometimes feel tingling or prickling sensations in your body, arms or legs?
- Has your appetite got less recently?
- Do you feel unduly tired and exhausted?
- Can you get off to sleep alright at the moment?
- Do you often suffer from excessive sweating or fluttering of the heart?
- Has your sexual interest altered?

**3 Depression** This is best described as a mood of sadness, difficulty in thinking clearly and a slowing down of actions and activity. This means that the implications for an organisation (e.g. a school) might be that performance and effectiveness may be decreased. The items included in this section are:

- Can you think as quickly as you used to?
- Do you often feel that life is too much effort?
- Do you regret much of your past behaviour?
- Do you wake unusually early in the morning?
- Do you experience long periods of sadness?
- Do you have to make a special effort to face up to a crisis or difficulty?
- Do you find yourself needing to cry?
- Have you lost your ability to feel sympathy for other people?

Some questions have only two options, and therefore score 0 or 1; others have three options and score 0, 1 or 2. Altogether, this gives a total potential score of 36 and so a total overall mental health score can also be obtained. It has been noted that this global total may have greater applicability and be a better indicator of pathological symptomology than the three subscales, which are taken as discrete and individual entities. This measure was used because the researchers had a large amount of comparative data for this scale, and also the scale has been found to be highly reliable and valid (Crown and Crisp 1979).

*Job satisfaction*

Warr *et al.*'s (1979) Job Satisfaction Scale was used (slightly modified) in order to measure job satisfaction. This scale consists of 15 items/questions, measured on a 7-point 'Likert' type rating scale for each item, assessing the degree of job satisfaction from being 'extremely dissatisfied' at one end of the scale to 'extremely satisfied' at the other. Results can be obtained for total job satisfaction with a range of 15 to 105, but the scale can be further subdivided into five smaller scales measuring satisfaction with the following aspects of the job:

**1 Intrinsic job satisfaction** This asks questions concerning satisfaction with the job itself, i.e.:

- The freedom to choose your own method of working.
- The recognition you get for good work.
- The amount of responsibility you are given.
- Your opportunity to use your abilities.
- Your chance of promotion.
- The amount of variety in your job.
- The attention paid to suggestions you make.

**2 Extrinsic job satisfaction** This aims to discover how satisfied teachers are with the other aspects of the job, i.e.:

- The physical working conditions.
- Your fellow teachers.
- Your immediate boss.
- Your rate of pay.
- Your hours of work.
- Industrial relations between management and staff in your school.
- Your job security.
- The way your school is managed.

**3 Job itself intrinsic satisfaction** This group of questions deals with actual features inherent in the job, i.e.:

- The freedom to choose your own method of working.
- The amount of responsibility you are given.
- Your opportunity to use your abilities.
- The amount of variety in your job.

**4 Working conditions satisfaction** This deals with the features in the actual working environment and is a subset of extrinsic satisfaction, covering specifically the actual working conditions, i.e.:

- The physical working conditions.
- Your fellow workers.
- Your immediate boss.
- Your hours of work.
- Your job security.

**5 Employee relations satisfaction** This is a group of questions which deal with a cluster of intrinsic and extrinsic features of the job. They aim to measure satisfaction with the level of individual recognition received and the style of management experienced, i.e.:

- Your chance of promotion.
- The way you school is managed.
- The attention paid to suggestions you make.
- The recognition you get for good work.
- Your rate of pay.
- Industrial relations between the management and teachers in your school.

*Sources of teacher stress*

The interviews we conducted with teachers were content analysed and a 'Sources of Job Pressure' inventory of 98 items was designed, which assessed sources of teacher stress (on 6-point Likert-type scales). It is clear from the literature that pressure is not always negative in its effect, and, therefore, it is important to investigate those sources of pressure that lead to stress-related outcomes (e.g. mental ill health). Chapter 6 will present the results of factor analysis, performed upon the 98 item inventory. The items themselves can be seen at the end of Chapter 5.

*Type A behaviour*

Type A behaviour pattern has long been believed to be a strong predictor of cardiovascular disease and other stress-related illnesses. A Type A individual may be characterised as one who is extremely competitive, aggressive, an achievement striver, hasty, impatient, restless, hyper-alert, emphatic in speech, tense facially and considers that he or she is permanently under the pressure of time and responsibility. This study employed Bortner's (1969) 'Type A' behavioural style inventory, consisting of a 14-item bipolar adjectival scale measured on an 11-point Likert-type continual rating scale (see page 66, Chapter 3). This yields a single score ranging from 14 to 154, i.e. low (or Type B) to high Type A behaviour.

*Coping*

Individuals will adopt various coping strategies to deal with the stress they experience. Teachers' strategies for coping were measured by using the coping scale from the Occupational Stress Indicator (OSI) (Cooper *et al.* 1988a). The scale consists of 28 items rated on a 6-point Likert scale ranging from 'never used by me' to 'very extensively used by me'. The scale is not to be used as a total coping score, but rather as six subscales, namely:

**1 Social support** This subscale measures the degree to which individuals rely on others as a means of coping with stress. It can take various forms and may not necessarily be in the form of talking. The subscale recognises that the mere existence of supportive relationships will itself be significant. Items are:

- Seek support and advice from my superior.
- Talk to understanding friends.
- Have stable relationships.
- Seek as much social support as possible.

**2 Task strategies** This subscale measures the way the individual copes with stress by reorganisation of work. These range from organisational, in the micro sense of tasks, but may also entail reliance upon organisational processes in the wider sense. The overall underlying theme is coping with work organisation. Items are:

- Reorganise my work.
- Plan ahead.
- Use distractions (to take my mind off things).
- Set priorities and deal with problems accordingly.
- Resort to rules and regulations.
- Delegation.
- Try to avoid the situation.

**3 Logic** As expected, individuals can cope with stress by adopting an unemotional and rational approach to the situation. This may involve the suppression of any feelings that might be expressed but will also involve actively trying to be objective. Items are:

- Try to deal with the situation objectively in an unemotional way.

- Suppress emotions and try not to let the stress show.
- Try to 'stand aside' and think through the situation.

**4 Home and work relationships**  It has already been stated that the overall relationship between work and home life is an extensive one. This subscale recognises the dual role that this relationship can possess and examines its role in coping strategies. Again, this may take many forms from the existence of certain qualities in home life to what the individuals do when they are there. Items are:

- Resort to hobbies and pastimes.
- Having a home that is a 'refuge'.
- Deliberately separate home and work.
- Expand interests and activities outside work.

**5 Time**  One of the major commodities that people have to negotiate with is time. 'Time management' is itself sold as a valuable skill to be learned. This subscale recognises this and its importance as a coping strategy. Items are:

- Deal with problems immediately as they occur.
- 'Buy time' and stall the issue.
- Effective time management.
- Force one's behaviour and lifestyle to slow down.

**6 Involvement**  This is a coping type that appears quite diverse in content, but the underlying theme that runs throughout it involves the process of the individuals being submerged in or committed to the situation. In other words, coping by forcing themselves to come to terms with 'reality'. Items are:

- Try to recognise my own limitations.
- Look for ways to make the work more interesting.
- 'Stay busy'.
- Not 'bottling things up' and being able to release energy.
- Use selective attention (concentrating on specific problems).
- Accept the situation and learn how to live with it.

*Social Support*

Following the scale on stress-coping strategies, and in order to gather some information on main providers of social support, teachers were asked to indicate who they turned to when they experienced stress. The list of potential sources of social support were both home and work related and consisted of the following:

- fellow teachers;

- spouse or partner;
- relative;
- friend outside of work;
- headteacher;
- other.

## Distribution of the questionnaires

The previously described six sections were compiled in a 16-page booklet (see Appendix 2), together with instructions on how to complete the questionnaire and a covering letter explaining the purpose of the study with clear instructions for completion and emphasising confidentiality and anonymity. In addition, a letter was included in the package from the union involved, stressing their support for the project.

Questionnaires were printed and graphically designed by the union involved, and they were sent to a sample of 5,000 teachers nationwide who were employed within schools and colleges in the UK. These were drawn randomly from the NASUWT membership list by selecting every twentieth member (membership in alphabetical order). The teachers were members of one of the largest teaching unions in the UK, and were from a variety of teaching backgrounds in terms of teaching grade, school type, sector, area and region. A response rate of 36 per cent (*n*=1,790) was obtained before our agreed cut-off date, with further questionnaires received but not included due to incompletion or the fact that teachers had left the profession or questionnaires were returned because of the wrong address. This is an expected and acceptable sample size for a postal survey (Sutherland and Cooper 1991), and, as subsequent sections will show, the distribution of 'teacher-type' in the sample was representative of the union membership. The data obtained from the 1,790 usable questionnaires was then analysed by computer using SPSS (Statistical Package for the Social Sciences). This package means that data can be analysed speedily and effectively by the use of a file which contains all of the data plus a command file where statistical commands are placed dependent upon the analysis required.

## BIOGRAPHICAL DATA OF THE TEACHERS

The results of this section will be presented in terms of personal, professional, job, career and school demographics. Within each section, the results will address each question in turn as they appeared on the questionnaire.

### Sex

Teaching has long been viewed as a female profession. Although there is indeed a preponderance of women in the primary teaching sector, this does not apply to the secondary sector. (The majority of NASUWT members are in the secondary sector.) Therefore, as Table 4.1 shows, almost three-fifths of the teachers are male (59 per cent, $n=1,052$) with 41 per cent female ($n=730$).

Enquiries made to the NASUWT revealed that, as with all other subgroup distributions (i.e. sector, school type, etc.), this was a similar distribution to the actual union membership as a whole. Therefore, we may conclude that the sample of teachers examined in this study is truly representative of the union membership from which it was randomly selected. Further analysis of the differences between male and female teachers can be seen in Chapters 5 and 6.

## Age

As shown in Table 4.2, the teachers range from 22 to 65 years of age, with an average age of 40.2 years. Therefore, this was a middle-aged population with the majority (22.9 per cent) of teachers aged between 35 and 39 and 22.4 per cent between 40 and 44. There would appear to be a normal distribution with regards the other age bands, with 2.6 per cent aged between 22 and 24, 7.8 per cent between 25 and 29, 14.4 per cent between 30 and 34, 15.9 per cent between 45 and 49, 8.6 per cent between 50 and 54, 4.1 per cent between 55 and 59 and the remaining 1.3 per cent of teachers aged 60+. As age is considered to be a determining factor in the experience of stress in teachers, further analysis will investigate the influence of age on stress outcomes in Chapter 6.

### Marital status

Table 4.3 reveals that almost three-quarters (74.7 per cent) of the teachers report that they are married, with a further 4.2 per cent cohabiting, 15 per cent single, 3.8 per cent divorced, 1.5 per cent separated and the final 0.7 per cent widowed. This means that the majority of teachers have some form of social support in the home, although it must be remembered that relationships at home may themselves be a source of stress.

### Partners' working pattern

Each teacher was asked to give information regarding his or her partner's working pattern. A total of 73.3 per cent of their partners work full-time, 22.6 per cent part-time and the remaining 4.1 per cent work occasionally (see Table 4.4). Recent research has highlighted the problem facing dual-career families, and so it must be recognised that teachers will be experiencing these home-life pressures in addition to their work-related ones (Cooper and Lewis 1993). The much suggested claim that 'teachers marry teachers' was not entirely substantiated by the finding that less than half (46.1 per cent) of the sample have teaching partners.

*Table 4.1* Sex of teachers

|        | n     | %    |
|--------|-------|------|
| Male   | 1,052 | 59.0 |
| Female | 730   | 41.0 |

*Table 4.2* Age distribution of teachers

| Age range (years) | n | % |
|-------------------|-----|------|
| 22–24 | 46 | 2.6 |
| 25–29 | 140 | 7.8 |
| 30–34 | 256 | 14.4 |
| 35–39 | 407 | 22.9 |
| 40–44 | 398 | 22.4 |
| 45–49 | 283 | 15.9 |
| 50–54 | 153 | 8.6 |
| 55–59 | 73 | 4.1 |
| 60+ | 24 | 1.3 |

Mean = 40.22 (range = 22–65)

*Table 4.3* Marital status of teachers

|           | n     | %    |
|-----------|-------|------|
| Married   | 1,328 | 74.7 |
| Single    | 267   | 15.0 |
| Cohabiting| 75    | 4.2  |
| Divorced  | 68    | 3.8  |
| Separated | 27    | 1.5  |
| Widowed   | 13    | 0.7  |

*Table 4.4* Working pattern of teachers' partners

|                  | n     | %    |
|------------------|-------|------|
| Not working      | 183   | 13.1 |
| Working partner  | 1,213 | 86.9 |
| Full-time        | 895   | 73.3 |
| Part-time        | 276   | 22.6 |
| Occasionally     | 50    | 4.1  |
| Teaching partner | 667   | 46.1 |

## Number of children

Two out of every three teachers have at least one child (see Table 4.5). A large majority of teachers have children living at home (i.e. 16 per cent pre-school, 30 per cent have children in primary school and 22.5 per cent at secondary). We can see therefore that the majority of teachers have domestic commitments beyond their teaching role. Also, as the questionnaire did not ask for details of other dependents (i.e. elderly relatives, etc.), this figure is perhaps an underestimation of the real extent of their domestic responsibilities.

## WHAT TYPES OF SCHOOLS DO THEY TEACH IN?

### Region in which they teach

The majority of teachers in our sample are from the North West, North East and the Midlands (see Table 4.6). This is not surprising as it reflects, very accurately, the distribution of these areas within the actual union membership itself. As the numbers in different areas, though reflecting union membership, are not entirely representative of these areas as a whole (i.e. only a small number of Scottish teachers choose to join the NASUWT in preference to their own regional union), it was decided that it was probably not appropriate to examine regional differences in symptoms of stress.

### Type of school in which they teach

In terms of the type of school in which the teachers work (see Table 4.7), 1.4 per cent ($n$=25) are nursery teachers, 22.2 per cent ($n$=390) primary, 4.6 per cent ($n$=80) middle school teachers, 5.4 per cent ($n$=95) special, 63.8 per

*Table 4.5* Number and age of children

|  | $n$ | % |
| --- | --- | --- |
| None | 586 | 32.7 |
| One | 281 | 15.7 |
| Two | 660 | 36.9 |
| Three | 200 | 11.2 |
| Four or more | 63 | 2.9 |
| Mean (for those with children) = 2.06 (range = 0–10) | | |
| Pre-school | 286 | 16.0 |
| Primary school | 537 | 30.0 |
| Secondary school | 403 | 22.5 |
| Tertiary college | 150 | 8.4 |
| Other, e.g. university, married, etc. | 349 | 19.5 |

*Table 4.6* Region in which they teach

|  | n | % |
|---|---|---|
| Scotland | 45 | 2.5 |
| Northern Ireland | 146 | 8.2 |
| Wales | 109 | 6.1 |
| North West | 347 | 19.4 |
| North East | 276 | 15.4 |
| Midlands | 357 | 19.9 |
| South West | 146 | 8.2 |
| South East | 150 | 8.4 |
| East Anglia | 85 | 4.1 |
| Greater London | 129 | 7.2 |

*Table 4.7* Type of school in which they teach

|  | n | % |
|---|---|---|
| Nursery unit/school | 25 | 1.4 |
| Primary | 390 | 22.2 |
| Middle | 80 | 4.6 |
| Special | 95 | 5.4 |
| Secondary | 1,120 | 63.8 |
| Sixth-form college | 22 | 1.3 |
| Tertiary college | 2 | 0.1 |
| FE college | 21 | 1.2 |

cent ($n$=1,120) secondary, 1.3 per cent ($n$=22) sixth-form college teachers, 0.1 per cent ($n$=2) teach in tertiary colleges and 1.2 per cent ($n$=21) are employed in FE colleges (see Table 4.7). For the purpose of this study, the major emphasis examined will be between primary and secondary, as these constitute the majority of the sample. Later chapters will examine the effects of working in primary and secondary schools, and for the purposes of analysis the nursery and primary teachers will be combined, as will the middle and secondary, constituting 90 per cent of the sample.

**Area in which they teach**

Thirty-eight per cent of the teachers are teaching in towns ($n$=672), 29 per cent ($n$=512) are in the suburbs, 16.8 per cent ($n$=296) are inner-city teachers and the remaining 16.1 per cent (n=284) are teaching in rural areas (see Table 4.8).

*Table 4.8* Area in which the schools are based

|  | n | % |
| --- | --- | --- |
| Town | 672 | 38.1 |
| Suburban | 512 | 29.0 |
| Inner-city | 296 | 16.8 |
| Rural | 284 | 16.1 |

### Sector in which the schools are based

Teachers were asked to indicate which sector they taught in and the results can be seen in Table 4.9. The vast majority of teachers (i.e. 83.4 per cent, $n=1,480$) were teaching in the state sector with 13.5 per cent ($n=239$) working in voluntary-aided schools. Three per cent of the respondents ($n=54$) were teaching in independent schools.

### Size of the school (i.e. number of teaching staff and number of pupils)

The average number of staff in the schools was 43.66 (see Table 4.10), but there is a great variety in numbers and size of schools in terms of staffing levels and pupil numbers where the mean number is 706.89. The number of auxiliary helpers in schools, however, does not reflect the need for support, as the average number of added helpers in the classrooms was only 2.44, despite the size of the school in question.

### JOB AND CAREER DEMOGRAPHICS

### Level of education

Data concerning the level of qualifications obtained by the teachers (Table 4.11) reveals that 51 per cent ($n=909$) had a Certificate of Education, 20 per cent ($n=355$) had a BEd, 26 per cent ($n=470$) had a PGCE and 2 per cent ($n=38$) had obtained an MEd. A small number (1 per cent, $n=15$) had obtained a PhD. In terms of the number of qualifications obtained by the teachers, on average teachers have 1.3 each, with 26.7 per cent of the sample having two or more qualifications.

### Current job title

Of the sample, 33 (1.8 per cent) were headteachers, 5 per cent ($n=89$) deputy heads, 28.7 per cent ($n=513$) heads of department, 13.8 per cent ($n=247$) promoted teachers and 37.4 per cent ($n=669$) main-scale teachers (see Table 4.12).

*Table 4.9* Sector in which the schools are based

|  | n | % |
|---|---|---|
| State | 1,480 | 83.4 |
| Voluntary-aided | 239 | 13.5 |
| Independent | 54 | 3.0 |

*Table 4.10* Number of teaching staff and pupils in school

|  | n | % |
|---|---|---|
| *Teaching staff* | | |
| 1–10 | 276 | 15.9 |
| 11–20 | 260 | 15.0 |
| 21–30 | 112 | 6.4 |
| 31–40 | 177 | 10.3 |
| 41–50 | 244 | 14.0 |
| 51+ | 666 | 38.4 |

Mean = 43.46 (range = 1–450)

|  | n | % |
|---|---|---|
| *Pupils* | | |
| 7–200 | 217 | 14.2 |
| 201–400 | 327 | 19.0 |
| 401–600 | 227 | 13.1 |
| 601–800 | 279 | 16.2 |
| 801–1,000 | 309 | 18.0 |
| 1,001+ | 431 | 19.5 |

Mean = 706.79 (Range = 7–10,000)

|  | n | % |
|---|---|---|
| *Auxiliary helpers* | | |
| None | 552 | 31.9 |
| 1–5 | 990 | 57.3 |
| 6–10 | 158 | 9.2 |
| 11–15 | 20 | 1.1 |
| 16–98 | 8 | 0.5 |

Mean = 2.44 (Range 1–98)

## Length of time in teaching career and current position

On average, teachers were in the profession for 15.6 years (see Table 4.13). Over half of the sample had been teaching for 10 or more years, demonstrating that this is a very experienced workforce. Teachers had been in their current position for an average of 7.2 years.

## Incentive allowance held

Table 4.14 shows that 60 per cent (*n*=1,060) of the teachers had obtained an incentive allowance for their post. The most frequently acquired levels are '2' (42 per cent) and '4' (19 per cent).

*Table 4.11* Level of education

|  | n | % |
|---|---|---|
| *Type of qualification* | | |
| Certificate of Education | 909 | 51.0 |
| MEd | 38 | 2.0 |
| BEd | 355 | 20.0 |
| PGCE | 470 | 26.0 |
| PhD | 15 | 1.0 |
| Other | 511 | 28.6 |
| *Total number of qualifications* | | |
| One | 1,311 | 73.3 |
| Two | 440 | 24.6 |
| Three | 33 | 1.8 |
| Four | 2 | 0.1 |
| Mean = 1.3 | | |

*Table 4.12* Current job title

| Title | n | % |
|---|---|---|
| Headteacher | 33 | 1.8 |
| Deputy head | 89 | 5.0 |
| Head of department | 513 | 28.7 |
| Promoted teacher | 247 | 13.8 |
| Main-scale teacher | 669 | 37.4 |
| Other | 239 | 13.4 |

**Style of contract**

Table 4.15 reveals that 95 per cent (*n*=1,090) are employed to teach full time, 3.3 per cent (*n*=59) part time and 1.9 per cent (*n*=33) teaching on supply.

**Workload and responsibilities**

Almost half of the teachers were responsible for an average of 8.78 members of staff in the schools in which they teach. The type of school and the variety in sizes of schools has to be taken into account and is reflected in the range of number of staff for whom teachers are responsible, as shown in Table 4.16 (e.g. teachers in small primary schools, where the only real opportunity for staff responsibility lies with the headteacher).

**Workload in school**

Table 4.17 shows data concerned with teachers' workload in school. On average, there are 27.5 hours in the pupil week, and, of these, 21.85 are spent with pupils. In addition, teachers spend almost 6 hours on other

*Table 4.13* Length of time in teaching

|  | n | % |
| --- | --- | --- |
| *Years in teaching career* |  |  |
| 1 or less | 53 | 3.0 |
| 2–5 | 133 | 7.4 |
| 6–10 | 282 | 15.8 |
| 11–20 | 875 | 49.0 |
| 21+ | 444 | 24.8 |
| Mean = 15.62 (range = 1–40 years) |  |  |
| *Years in current position* |  |  |
| 1 or less | 323 | 20.2 |
| 2–5 | 547 | 31.2 |
| 6–10 | 406 | 23.3 |
| 11–20 | 424 | 24.2 |
| 21+ | 49 | 1.1 |
| Mean = 7.22 (range = 0–34 years) |  |  |

*Table 4.14* Incentive allowance held

|  | n | % |
| --- | --- | --- |
| *Allowance held?* |  |  |
| Yes | 1,060 | 60.0 |
| No | 708 | 40.0 |
| *Level of allowance* |  |  |
| 1 | 170 | 16.1 |
| 2 | 442 | 41.9 |
| 3 | 84 | 8.0 |
| 4 | 205 | 19.4 |
| 5 | 43 | 4.1 |
| Headteacher | 31 | 2.9 |
| Deputy head | 77 | 7.3 |

*Table 4.15* Style of contract

|  | n | % |
| --- | --- | --- |
| Full time | 1,690 | 94.8 |
| Part time | 59 | 3.3 |
| Supply | 33 | 1.9 |

*Table 4.16*  Responsibility for staff

|  | n | % |
|---|---|---|
| *Responsibility?* | | |
| Yes | 825 | 46.5 |
| No | 948 | 53.5 |
| *How many?* | | |
| 1–5 | 466 | 58.0 |
| 6–10 | 201 | 25.1 |
| 11–30 | 103 | 12.8 |
| 30+ | 33 | 4.1 |
| Mean = 7.67 (range = 1–82) | | |

*Table 4.17*  Workload in school

|  | n | % |
|---|---|---|
| *Hours in the pupil week* | | |
| 5–10 | 6 | 0.3 |
| 11–15 | 4 | 0.3 |
| 16–20 | 1 | 0.8 |
| 21–25 | 596 | 34.4 |
| 26–30 | 844 | 48.6 |
| 31–35 | 219 | 12.6 |
| 36+ | 52 | 15.4 |
| Mean = 27.5 (range = 5–100)* | | |
| *Actual teaching hours spent with pupils* | | |
| 0–5 | 20 | 1.1 |
| 6–10 | 39 | 2.3 |
| 11–15 | 106 | 6.1 |
| 16–20 | 483 | 27.7 |
| 21–25 | 776 | 44.5 |
| 26–30 | 261 | 15.0 |
| 31–35 | 40 | 2.3 |
| 36+ | 17 | 0.9 |
| Mean = 21.85 (range = 0–55) | | |
| *Average number of hours on other directed time activities* | | |
| 0 | 143 | 8.2 |
| 1–5 | 1,054 | 60.8 |
| 6–10 | 338 | 19.4 |
| 11+ | 201 | 11.6 |
| Mean = 5.99 (Range = 0–100)* | | |
| *Hours cover for absent colleagues in last week* | | |
| None | 686 | 38.9 |
| 1–5 | 1,019 | 57.9 |
| 6+ | 57 | 3.2 |
| Mean = 1.35 (range = 0–120)* | | |

Table 14.7 cont.

|  | n | % |
|---|---|---|
| *Number of times accepted absent colleague's pupils last term* | | |
| None | 1,023 | 58.8 |
| 1–5 | 421 | 24.2 |
| 6–10 | 179 | 10.3 |
| 11–20 | 116 | 6.7 |
| Mean = 2.88 (range = 0–100)* | | |
| *Number of teachers involved in extra-curricular activities* | | |
| Yes | 960 | 54.2 |
| No | 810 | 45.8 |
| *Average number of hours per week* | | |
| 0 | 9 | 1.0 |
| 1–5 | 824 | 88.9 |
| 6–10 | 71 | 7.6 |
| 11–15 | 15 | 1.6 |
| 16–20 | 7 | 0.8 |
| 21+ | 1 | 0.1 |
| Mean = 2.92 (range = 0–40) | | |
| N.B. * extreme scores actually provided by teachers. | | |

directed time activities. Another feature of the working day in schools is the problem of having to cover for absent colleagues. The sample were covering for an absent colleague at least 1.35 times a week, which may have disrupted their particular system of working or prevented them from using vital time that they originally had available. Throughout the previous term, they reported having to accept the class of an absent colleague three times on average, though there is a great deal of variation in this, and 54.2 per cent of teachers also got involved in extra-curricular activities, for an average of 2.92 hours per week.

## Workload out of school

Table 4.18 shows that teachers are spending an average of 2.87 hours a week marking; 3.96 hours preparing for lessons and a further 1.73 assessing pupils at home. This adds up to 8.53 hours on average that teachers' school work infringed upon their home life, which may or may not be a problem, depending upon family and social commitments.

## TEACHER'S BEHAVIOURAL STYLE

### Coronary prone behaviour

Type A coronary-prone behaviour is made up of a cluster of traits, and is characterised by extremes of competitiveness, impatience,

*Table 4.18* Average hours spent working at home each week

|  | n | % |
| --- | --- | --- |
| *Marking* | | |
| None | 443 | 25.0 |
| 1–5 | 1,088 | 61.4 |
| 6–10 | 214 | 12.1 |
| 11–15 | 20 | 1.1 |
| 16–20 | 7 | 0.4 |
| Mean = 2.87 (range = 0–20) | | |
| *Preparation* | | |
| None | 154 | 8.7 |
| 1–5 | 1,249 | 70.4 |
| 6–10 | 324 | 18.3 |
| 11–15 | 38 | 2.1 |
| 16–24 | 8 | 0.5 |
| Mean = 3.96 (range = 0–24) | | |
| *Assessment* | | |
| None | 462 | 26.2 |
| 1–5 | 1,245 | 70.8 |
| 6–10 | 53 | 2.9 |
| 11–20 | 2 | 0.2 |
| Mean = 1.73 (range = 0–20) | | |
| *Total hours* | | |
| 0 | 103 | 5.9 |
| 1–5 | 450 | 25.5 |
| 6–10 | 677 | 38.5 |
| 11–15 | 344 | 19.6 |
| 16–20 | 147 | 8.3 |
| 21+ | 38 | 2.2 |
| Mean = 8.53 (range = 0–50) | | |

aggressiveness, and feelings of being continuously under pressure from time and from the challenge of responsibility.

(Hingley and Cooper 1986)

Measurements of Type A behaviour were taken by administering the Bortner scale of 14 items to the teachers. The overall mean score for the sample was 101.70 (range = 44–148). Teachers fall predominantly into the Type A classification, with 61.3 per cent of the sample exhibiting Type A behaviour (taking scores 98–154 as indicative of Type A). It is possible to further divide Type A into Types A and B, giving four categories: $A_1$ (112–154), $A_2$ (98–111), $B_3$ (70–97) and $B_4$ (14–69). Rosenman *et al.* (1964) report a normal distribution of Type A scores within the general population, i.e. $A_1$ = 10 per cent, $A_2$ = 40 per cent, $B_3$ = 40 per cent, $B_4$ = 10 per cent. In an adapted version of the Bortner scale, Davidson and Cooper (1980a) studied 135 UK female executives and reported that 61.5 per cent of the sample were Type A and that:

Table 4.19 Percentage of teachers who are Type A or Type B with subgroup percentages

| Category | Range | Total | | Males | | Females | | Primary | | Secondary | | Senior | | Middle | | Main scale | |
|---|---|---|---|---|---|---|---|---|---|---|---|---|---|---|---|---|---|
| | | n | % | n | % | n | % | n | % | n | % | n | % | n | % | n | % |
| $A_1$ | 112–154 | 490 | 28.8 | 252 | 25.0 | 237 | 34.4 | 120 | 30.2 | 324 | 28.4 | 33 | 28.7 | 233 | 32.2 | 224 | 26.0 |
| $A_2$ | 98–111 | 554 | 32.5 | 333 | 33.2 | 219 | 31.9 | 124 | 31.1 | 375 | 32.9 | 37 | 34.8 | 231 | 31.9 | 283 | 32.7 |
| $B_3$ | 79–97 | 613 | 36.0 | 392 | 38.9 | 218 | 31.7 | 147 | 36.9 | 410 | 36.0 | 41 | 35.6 | 243 | 33.6 | 329 | 38.2 |
| $B_4$ | 14–69 | 45 | 2.6 | 29 | 2.9 | 14 | 2.0 | 7 | 1.8 | 31 | 2.7 | 1 | 0.9 | 17 | 2.3 | 27 | 3.1 |
| | Mean | 101.70 | | 100.24 | | 103.98 | | 102.15 | | 101.73 | | 102.24 | | 103.01 | | 100.53 | |
| | S.D. | 16.49 | | 16.48 | | 16.17 | | 16.13 | | 16.65 | | 15.52 | | 16.52 | | 16.52 | |
| | Range | 44–148 | | 44–146 | | 53–148 | | 56–144 | | 44–148 | | 60–145 | | 47–148 | | 44–143 | |

Total number of teachers Type A 1,044 (61.3%)
Total number of teachers Type B 658 (38.7%)

*THREE-WAY SPLIT**

| Category | Range | Total | | Males | | Females | | Primary | | Secondary | | Senior | | Middle | | Main scale | |
|---|---|---|---|---|---|---|---|---|---|---|---|---|---|---|---|---|---|
| $A_1$ | 111–154 | 527 | 31.0 | 270 | 26.8 | 256 | 37.2 | 128 | 32.2 | 350 | 30.7 | 36 | 31.3 | 252 | 34.8 | 239 | 27.7 |
| $A_2$ | 93–110 | 694 | 40.7 | 419 | 41.7 | 249 | 39.7 | 160 | 40.2 | 470 | 41.2 | 48 | 41.7 | 279 | 38.5 | 367 | 42.5 |
| $A_3$ | 14–92 | 481 | 28.3 | 317 | 31.5 | 159 | 23.1 | 110 | 27.6 | 320 | 28.1 | 31 | 27.0 | 189 | 26.7 | 257 | 29.8 |

*$A_1$ = 1 standard deviation below the mean; $A_2$ = the mean distribution; $A_3$ = 1 standard deviation above the mean.

the sample contained over twice the proportion of the most extreme Type A1 individuals, who are most at risk in terms of stress-related illness.

Davidson and Cooper (1983) also studied almost 700 women managers and found that they had a statistically significant higher mean score of 81 as compared to their male colleagues, who had a score of 79. Though it is not possible to make direct comparisons between these studies and the current study due to the use of an adapted version of the Type A scale, we can see that, using a thumbnail guide, teachers are indicating higher coronary-prone behaviour than expected. In addition, when we examine the teachers' scores in relation to the norms provided by the designers of the scale, we can see that almost three times the expected proportion of extreme Type $A_1$'s are present in this sample (see Table 4.19). We found that this proportion was consistent across the grade levels and types of school, though female teachers revealed the highest proportion of Type $A_1$. This reinforces the findings of the previously mentioned researchers who revealed higher levels of Type A in women as compared to their male colleagues. Further analysis was carried out in order to examine the effects of Type A on the stress outcomes experienced by teachers (e.g. mental ill health), and this will be presented in Chapters 5 and 6.

Subsequent discussion will address the sources of this stress, in more detail but the following chapter will present findings with regard to how the teachers are responding to their working environments.

# 5   How teachers respond to the job of teaching

'Exactly what do you mean by "guts"?' 'I mean', Ernest Hemingway said, 'grace under pressure!'

(Ernest Hemingway: an interview with Dorothy Parker 1929)

The previous chapter provided a profile of the teachers in our sample, in particular the personal, professional and job-related demographics of their experience. In Chapter 2 we outlined the previous findings with regard to teachers and their responses to stress. In this chapter we shall examine the way in which this particular sample of UK teachers respond to the job of teaching; the level of job satisfaction they experience; the presence of emotional and psychological strain as a response to the job; and how this manifests itself in the form of health behaviours such as alcohol consumption, smoking, self-reported absence and intention to leave the teaching profession. Chapter 3 presented evidence from previous research into the sources of teacher stress. In this chapter we shall examine the sources of stress that UK teachers report and assess the methods they use in order to cope with these. In order to get a more detailed picture, we shall explore particular subgroups of teachers within the sample (e.g. male versus female teachers, primary versus secondary teachers, and those at varying levels of grade). Where statistically significant differences are found between groups, these will be reported. In addition, to help obtain a clearer picture as to the extent of the problem of teacher stress, normative data will be used where available.

## HOW SATISFIED ARE UK TEACHERS?

It is important to see job dissatisfaction as something which may be a direct response to stress. In order to measure job satisfaction in this study, the 15-item inventory outlined in the previous chapter was used. The inventory chosen comprised questions which are scored from 1 to 7, meaning that for any individual teacher the job satisfaction score could range from 15 to 105, with a mean score for a normative population of graduates of 74.6. We found that the mean score for the teachers in this sample was 59.6, which is significantly below the normative level. Overall, therefore, it appears that teachers are very dissatisfied with their job. When comparisons are made with other occupational groups, these findings are even more persuasive. Table 5.1 shows that the teachers are significantly less job satisfied than other professional groups such as tax officers (Cooper and Roden 1985), a general population of graduates (Warr *et al.* 1979) and a sample of nurses (Cooper and Mitchell 1990). A clearer picture emerges when each individual item is examined in Table 5.2. Each of the 15 items in the scale measured one aspect of job satisfaction and the table shows the mean scores obtained for each of these and the percentage of teachers scoring high on satisfaction. Teachers are revealing the highest levels of dissatisfaction with 'extrinsic' aspects of the job (i.e. their 'rate of pay', 'chances for promotion' and working conditions). Teachers do find some aspects of their job favourable, particularly those that deal with freedom to choose their own way of working, variety and, especially, their fellow teachers.

When interviewing the teachers prior to the distribution of the questionnaire, it was found that many felt that supportive staff within the school was a great factor in reducing or coping with stress. Many teachers talked of the need to return to the staffrooms prior to leaving school, so as to share a problem and gain moral support. These relationships, and the sense of humour shared with other staff, are important ways of dealing with the stress of teaching, as the job of a classroom teacher is a fairly isolated one. Judging by the findings, it can be seen that the satisfaction arising from teaching is more to do with the *intrinsic* aspects of the job, and the dissatisfying aspects are those *extrinsic* to the job. The whole thing is summarised eloquently by one female secondary teacher who lamented:

> I don't find the work particularly satisfying at the moment . . . there just seems a great deal of effort with very little that actually comes out of it, whereas in the 'old days' there was a great deal of satisfaction in the work itself.

### Differences between subgroups in the sample

A gender difference was observed in that female teachers were found to be reporting a significantly higher level of job satisfaction than males in the sample (see Table 5.3). This was with regard to all aspects of satisfaction, except those concerned with 'working conditions', where male and female teachers were reporting comparable levels.

Those teachers with Type A behavioural style reported lower levels of job satisfaction than those who reported a Type B profile (see Table 5.4). This is true of all subscales of satisfaction, *except* that concerning 'employee relations'.

With regard to school type, primary teachers were reporting higher levels of job satisfaction than their secondary colleagues (see Table 5.5) and on all aspects except 'job itself/intrinsic satisfaction'. However, this

*Table 5.1* Teacher job satisfaction as compared to other occupational groups

| Group | n | Mean | SD | t | p⩽ |
|---|---|---|---|---|---|
| Teachers | 1,790 | 59.6 | 15.1 | | |
| Tax officers | 185 | 62.0 | 15.8 | 2.1 | 0.05 |
| General population norms | 340 | 74.6 | 11.3 | 19.2 | 0.001 |
| Nurses | 104 | 72.8 | 11.6 | 9.9 | 0.001 |

*Table 5.2* Job satisfaction: in order of most satisfaction

| Job satisfaction item* | Mean | % scoring 6 or 7 |
|---|---|---|
| Your fellow teachers | 4.90 | 40.9 |
| The amount of variety in your job | 4.83 | 42.3 |
| The freedom to choose your own method of working | 4.80 | 42.4 |
| Your job security | 4.67 | 44.2 |
| The amount of responsibility you are given | 4.60 | 40.5 |
| Your immediate boss | 4.25 | 35.1 |
| The attention paid to suggestions you make | 3.96 | 21.5 |
| Your opportunity to use your abilities | 3.92 | 25.0 |
| Your hours of work | 3.85 | 22.0 |
| The physical working conditions | 3.81 | 19.7 |
| Industrial relations between management and teachers in your school | 3.49 | 17.1 |
| The recognition you get for good work | 3.43 | 14.4 |
| The way your school is managed | 3.21 | 11.5 |
| Your chance of promotion | 2.95 | 13.5 |
| Your rate of pay | 2.90 | 10.1 |

*Note*: * Each item scored 1–7; the higher the score, the higher the satisfaction. Items with a mean score of below '4' indicates a level of dissatisfaction with this particular aspect of the teachers' job.

*Table 5.3* Job satisfaction: comparison of male and female teachers

| Sex | n | Mean score | Significant difference |
|---|---|---|---|
| Male | 1,052 | 58.83 | |
| Female | 730 | 60.51 | ($p ⩽ 0.021$) |

*Table 5.4* Job satisfaction: comparison of Type A and Type B individuals

| Type | n | Mean score | Significant difference |
|---|---|---|---|
| Type A | 1,044 | 58.95 | |
| Type B | 658 | 61.02 | ($p ⩽ 0.005$) |

difference may be gender based as male teachers in *both* sectors report comparable levels of 'intrinsic job satisfaction' and 'working conditions' satisfaction, and female teachers in both sectors are similar with regard to working conditions.

In terms of differences between the various teaching grades, major differences occur (see Table 5.6). Senior managers are significantly *more* satisfied on all aspects of satisfaction except 'working conditions', where all three groups report similar levels. On most aspects, main-scale teachers are reporting the *least* satisfaction, except with regard to 'extrinsic job satisfaction' and 'working conditions', where teachers in middle management report the lowest levels.

## Habit-forming behaviours

The harmful effects of a psychological dependency upon cigarettes, alcohol and drugs as a means of coping are well documented and have been described in Chapter 2. Smoking and drinking in abnormally high levels costs the nation vast amounts of money each year in days lost from work due to illness and death. High levels of these behaviours are more evident in highly stressful occupations, and so it was decided to investigate these further in teachers.

### Smoking

Teachers were asked if they smoked or not. If 'yes', then they were asked to state the level of smoking (i.e. number of cigarettes, cigars and pipefuls smoked per day) and changes in smoking behaviour in the last three months prior to the survey. Recent figures suggest that the percentage of professional people who now smoke is in fact only 17 per cent. Teachers are not much higher, as 18.6 per cent smoke an average of 12 cigarettes per day, with 33.3 per cent smoking 20 or more cigarettes per day (see Table 5.7). Thirty-seven per cent of 'smoking' teachers declared that they had smoked more than usual in the last three months, and on average they believed that 45.5 per cent of their smoking was for stress release. Although not an excessive number of teachers smoke, it was still quoted as a concern in the initial interviews, and it was observed that a small number can still cause smoke-filled staffrooms, and it would appear from the figures that the smokers are in fact rather heavy smokers.

### Alcohol consumption

In addition to questions concerning smoking behaviour, a number of questions were asked with regard to the level of drinking, as much research has discussed the link between excessive drinking as a form of stress release.

Throughout the preliminary interview stage, the researchers were made

*Table 5.5* Job satisfaction: comparison of primary and secondary teachers

| School type | n | Mean score | Significant difference |
|---|---|---|---|
| Primary | 415 | 62.57 | |
| Secondary | 1,200 | 58.37 | $(p \leqslant 0.000)$ |

*Table 5.6* Job satisfaction: comparison of teachers at various grades

| Grade | n | Mean score | Significant difference |
|---|---|---|---|
| Main scale | 908 | 58.73 | |
| Middle | 760 | 59.63 | |
| Senior | 122 | 65.18 | $(p \leqslant 0.0001)$ |

*Table 5.7* Smoking behaviour of teachers

| | n | % |
|---|---|---|
| *Cigarette smoking* | | |
| Smokers | 332 | 18.6 |
| Non-smokers | 1,454 | 81.4 |
| *Number of cigarettes smoked by teacher per day* | | |
| Cigarettes: 0 | 82 | 25.2 |
| 1–50 | 38 | 11.6 |
| 6–10 | 50 | 15.3 |
| 11–15 | 40 | 12.3 |
| 16–20 | 75 | 23.0 |
| 21–30 | 30 | 9.2 |
| 31+ | 11 | 3.4 |

Mean = 12.33 (range = 0–100)

| | n | % |
|---|---|---|
| *Changes in teachers' smoking in the last three months* | | |
| More than usual | 122 | 36.4 |
| Same as usual | 189 | 56.4 |
| Less than usual | 24 | 7.2 |
| *Proportion of smoking for stress release* | | |
| 0 | 70 | 21.3 |
| 1–10 | 21 | 6.4 |
| 11–20 | 19 | 5.8 |
| 21–30 | 21 | 6.4 |
| 31–40 | 10 | 3.1 |
| 41–50 | 69 | 21.0 |
| 51–60 | 12 | 3.7 |
| 61–70 | 17 | 5.2 |
| 71+ | 89 | 27.1 |

Mean = 45.51 (range = 0–98)

aware of the increased dependency of teachers upon alcohol as a way of coping with stress. One male secondary teacher was very concerned with his own observations and remarked:

> I find that far more of the teachers that I know drink more now, not only in a social way, but when they get home from school . . . several of the staff here, the first thing they do when they get home at night is pour themselves a drink.

It is difficult to obtain reliable reports of the level of alcohol consumption as it is affected by 'social desirability', but, it was decided that five questions would be included: whether the teacher drank alcohol; the number of units consumed per week; whether the teacher had felt a need to cut down on drinking; and changes in alcohol consumption in the last three months. In addition they were asked to say how much of their drinking was for stress release (see Table 5.8). Of the overall sample, 88.1 per cent drink, consuming an average of 11.40 units per week. Twenty-one per cent of teachers are consuming the equivalent of, or above, the recommended safe limit of 21 units per week. Twenty-nine per cent feel the need to cut down on their drinking, and 17 per cent consumed more than usual in the three months prior to the survey. On average, they consider at least 23.9 per cent of their drinking to be a form of stress release. Almost 20 per cent of male teachers are drinking more than the 'safe' limit with 14 per cent of female teachers drinking above the level recommended for women.

## Use of drugs

Eighteen per cent of the sample of teachers are taking some form of prescribed drug (see Table 5.9). Of these, 28 per cent are taking anti-depressants, 12.7 per cent regularly and 15.3 per cent occasionally, and 25 per cent are taking sleeping pills, 6.8 per cent regularly and a further 18.6 per cent occasionally. On average, teachers are drinking 3.7 cups of coffee or 3.15 cups of tea per day.

## Withdrawal behaviours

A key feature of this study was to examine the withdrawal behaviours of teachers (i.e. intention to leave the profession and self-reported absence) (see Chapter 2). The findings provided some very interesting points regarding these two stress manifestations.

## Intention to leave the profession

The introductory chapters outlined the importance to the profession of an assessment of teachers' intention to leave. This topic has not been studied in great detail in the field, and yet is of major importance due to the

*Table 5.8* Alcohol consumption of teachers

|  | n | % |
| --- | --- | --- |
| Drinkers | 1,571 | 88.1 |
| Non-drinkers | 212 | 11.9 |
| *Units of alcohol consumed per week\** | | |
| Males | 13.80 | |
| Females | 7.56 | |
| Overall mean = 11.40 (range = 0–100) | | |
| *Felt need to cut down* | | |
| Yes | 473 | 28.7 |
| No | 1,176 | 71.3 |
| *Changes in drinking habits over previous three months* | | |
| More than usual | 264 | 16.9 |
| Same as usual | 1,158 | 74.1 |
| Less than usual | 140 | 9.0 |
| *Proportion of drinking for stress release* | | |
| 0 | 698 | 44.8 |
| 1–10 | 167 | 10.7 |
| 11–20 | 89 | 5.7 |
| 21–30 | 106 | 6.8 |
| 31–40 | 33 | 2.2 |
| 41–50 | 246 | 15.7 |
| 51–60 | 33 | 2.2 |
| 61–70 | 23 | 1.4 |
| 71+ | 163 | 10.5 |
| Mean = 23.88 (range = 0–98) | | |

\* Recommended weekly intake for males is up to 21 units – 186 male teachers, i.e. 19.6 per cent are drinking above this 'safe' limit. Recommended weekly intake for females is up to 14 units – 86 teachers, i.e. 14 per cent of female teachers are drinking above this recommended 'safe' limit.

amount of teachers leaving the profession, and the dwindling numbers choosing teaching as a career.

Teachers were asked a number of related questions; whether they had actively considered leaving the teaching profession within the last five years, and their actual turnover intentions. Of the teachers in the sample, 66.4 per cent have actively considered leaving during this period (see Table 5.10). Twenty eight per cent said that they were actively seeking alternative employment, with 13.3 per cent currently seeking premature retirement.

Comments from teachers further enhance the picture of a profession attempting to escape, as one female primary teacher explained:

> If I got a chance of getting out, I would do . . . but the risk of getting out is too great . . . I don't know anybody over 50 who wouldn't get out if they were given the opportunity.

*Table 5.9*  Drug-taking behaviour of teachers

|  | *n* | % |
|---|---|---|
| *Currently on prescribed drugs* | | |
| Yes | 322 | 18.4 |
| No | 1,430 | 81.6 |
| *If yes, which of the following* | | |
| Anti-depressants: Regularly | 34 | 12.6 |
| Occasionally | 41 | 15.2 |
| Never | 194 | 72.1 |
| Sleeping pills: Regularly | 20 | 7.2 |
| Occasionally | 52 | 18.5 |
| Never | 209 | 74.4 |
| (*Cups per day*) | *Mean* | *Range* |
| Coffee | 3.67 | 0–25 |
| Tea | 3.15 | 0–20 |

*Table 5.10*  Intention to leave the profession

|  | *n* | % |
|---|---|---|
| Number who have actively considered leaving the profession in the last five years | 1,181 | 66.4 |
| Number currently seeking alternative employment | 456 | 27.6 |
| Number currently seeking premature retirement | 181 | 13.3 |

The results of the survey were quite startling as (a) a very large percentage of teachers intended to leave and (b) a large percentage of these 'escapees' were very young. Of the 66 per cent of the sample intending to leave the profession, quite a considerable number are actually putting these intentions into practice, and seeking alternative employment or premature retirement. Previous research has suggested that males and females differ in their reasons for wanting to leave (e.g. women say that they want to leave to start a family). The kinds of reasons teachers gave in the current study, revealed that men and women provided very similar rationales for leaving, both wanting more from the actual job itself, in the form of improved status, chances for promotion and better pay. From the open-ended comments teachers made, the following *restraining* factors (see Chapter 2) may need to be measured in future research:

- the financial risk of leaving teaching;
- the fear of having no other training (i.e. perceived occupational immobility);
- apathy and the problems of being 'stuck in a rut'.

Many other studies have discussed how the more positive features of the job may restrain the intention to leave (i.e. status acquired), but this study highlighted the more negative aspects (i.e. the risk factors). It may be that teachers do not like to take risks; for example, one female head of department in a secondary school lamented:

> Once you have been a teacher, you can't do anything else, your qualifications are no good for anything else. To start a new career now – I would have to start at the bottom of something and I could not afford to live without my salary, and yet there is no way I could transfer to another job without more training. But then – the thought of being in this job for the next 30 years, I just couldn't stand the thought of it – what I'm actually doing now.

A comparison between potential 'leavers' and 'non-leavers' revealed many differences. Leavers are significantly less satisfied, have poorer mental health, consume more alcohol, take more time off work, and report higher levels of pressure from *all* aspects of the job except 'job insecurity'. They also display higher levels of Type A behavioural style and make greater use of 'home/work relationship' coping strategies. This shows that the intention to leave is not purely an arbitrary decision, and that these two groups of teachers are very different in their actual experience and perception of the job. The effect of 'intention to leave' is examined in more detail in Chapter 6.

### Self-reported sickness and absence from work

Absence rates are often used as a general indicator of occupational stress. It was not possible to obtain absence records for the group of teachers over the previous 12 months, as this was a totally random selection and completely anonymous, and so the study relied upon teachers' self-reported rates of absence. The results for the overall sample suggest that absence rates are low in comparison to national figures, with the individual teacher losing on average 7 working days per year (see Table 5.11). Eighty- two per cent ($n=1,467$) of teachers have had 10 or less days off in the last year, with 8.1 per cent ($n=144$) taking 20 or more days off work. It must also be remembered that these average figures need to be considered in relation to the fact that teachers have approximately 13 weeks away from school per year through school holidays, and so the figures may be substantially affected if we consider a *real* rather than an *academic* year.

### Illness in the last 12 months: what kinds of illnesses are they experiencing?

Twenty-three per cent ($n=413$) of the sample reported having a significant illness in the last year, and Table 5.12 shows the type of illnesses experienced. It must be considered that the questionnaire did ask for 'significant illness', therefore this may have resulted in many illnesses 'slipping through the net' if teachers did not consider them of sufficient importance to merit attention. This suggests that the question was open to individual perception as to how the word 'significant' should be interpreted and, therefore, the figures should be regarded as conservative estimates.

As can be seen from Table 5.12, the major illnesses experienced are those which are now viewed as highly stress-related – persistent viral problems, chest, throat and bowel problems and those associated with anxiety and depression. Teachers also suffer from problems connected with their backs and necks.

The levels of absence reported by the teachers are not particularly high. However, it is important to note that many teachers reported the added problems of absence from school creating problems for other staff when they have to find cover for lessons. The work and responsibility is still there when they return to school (e.g. pressures of reaching examination standard in a given time) and so they may be more reluctant to stay off work. Often within schools, there is no one else who can adequately cover for the teacher. In addition, as many of the teachers are women with families, they tend to save their days for an occasion when one of their children may be ill, as one female primary teacher in inner city London explained:

> Most stressful of all, I find, is my 'double jeopardy' situation of being a lone parent and needing to be at home when my daughter is sick, as well as when I am. . . . I now try to keep my 'sick' time for my daughter, and have often worked when ill myself, though the work I do is far from up to my usual standard.

The study should have asked teachers to estimate the number of occasions they go into work feeling ill as they could not afford to be off school. The study discovered that a great deal of guilt results, and this may determine teacher absence. We must not presume that teachers will take time off when they need to or want to, as this may not be the case. The previous teacher added:

> My present school is somewhat better than previous ones (where there was horrific pressure to 'make her (sick daughter) go to school and let them handle it!' But even in this relatively humanitarian school, pressures such as non-availability of supply staff and the cover ruling mean that there is still considerable implicit criticism, pressure and use of guilt to manipulate ('Oh dear, and you *have* had so much time off sick this term already').

**Differences between the subgroups in the sample**

An examination of the subgroups in the sample revealed no significant differences between groups, in terms of absenteeism rates, but those teachers with intentions to leave the profession had significantly more days off in the last 12 months. This suggests a link between these two types of

*Table 5.11* Self-reported absence and illness

|  | Mean | Range |
|---|---|---|
| Number of days absent in last year | 7.04 | 0–365 |
| Approximate number due to stress-related causes | 3.78 | 0–300 |

|  | n | % |
|---|---|---|
| *Number with a significant illness in last year* | | |
| Yes | 413 | 23.4 |
| No | 1,353 | 76.7 |

*Table 5.12* Major significant illnesses in the last 12 months

| Illness | n | %* |
|---|---|---|
| Persistent virus (e.g. flu, myalgic encephalomyelitis (ME)) | 71 | 17.19 |
| Back problems (e.g. degeneration of the spine) | 49 | 11.86 |
| Anxiety and depression | 43 | 10.41 |
| Bowels and stomach (e.g. irritable bowel syndrome) | 41 | 9.93 |
| Chest and lung problems (e.g infections and pains) | 35 | 8.47 |
| Throat and voice | 27 | 6.54 |
| High blood pressure and hypertension | 26 | 6.30 |
| Severe headaches and migraines | 23 | 5.57 |
| Asthma | 20 | 4.84 |
| Problems with eyes and ears | 20 | 4.84 |
| Skin allergies (e.g. shingles, excema) | 14 | 3.39 |
| Cancer-related illness | 13 | 3.15 |
| Ulcers | 12 | 2.91 |
| Heart problems | 12 | 2.91 |
| Exhaustion and tiredness | 5 | 1.21 |
| Sinusitis | 5 | 1.21 |

* Represents those who reported experiencing an illness.

withdrawal behaviours and that absence need not be related to actual illness, but a desire to be away from the job, as one male head of department in an inner-city secondary school explained:

> I don't find anything satisfying about teaching at the moment. It's just a hard drag into work. You get up some days when you think 'I'd hate to go into work today', you wake up with that feeling, and it's a day that you particularly don't like. Well, the whole of this year has been like that for me.

## Mental health

The Crown–Crisp Experiential Index (CCEI) (1979) was used to measure mental ill health in this study. However, only three of its subscales were used, which makes comparisons between teachers' overall scores and those of other occupational groups in terms of overall mental ill health not possible. A great deal of information can nevertheless be gleaned from observing the three subscale CCEI scores, particularly if they are seen in the light of Crisp's (1977) recommendation that no more than 5–10 per cent of the general population should score as high or higher than psychoneurotic outpatients. Table 5.13 gives the psychoneurotic mean scores for each of the three subscales for both males and females and also provides the percentages of teachers who score as high or higher than this 'case-ness' sample.

This is followed by Table 5.14 which presents the mean scores and standard deviations for each of the three subscales, for male and female teachers, as compared to other occupational groups. The table shows that teachers are suffering from higher levels of mental ill health on most aspects when compared to these other 'highly stressed' groups of workers. The only case where the teachers' scores are *not* higher than other groups is with regard to female teachers and levels of free-floating anxiety. Female teachers are suffering from comparable levels to female tax officers (Cooper and Roden 1985) and female dentists (Cooper *et al.* 1987). However, it must be noted that these are two other highly stressed groups and all of the mean scores are high.

Further evidence for these findings can be found in quotes from the teachers that have been cited in the press:

> One (teacher) told researchers she attempted suicide after suffering 'morbid preoccupations with the implications of the National Curriculum', others said that they burst into tears in the classroom after lessons and suffered from panic, shaking and heart flutters.
>
> (Brace 1990)

*Free-floating anxiety*

In comparison with normative data and that of other comparable occupational groups, both male and female teachers report significantly greater levels of free-floating anxiety. A further disturbing finding is that in some cases up to 24 per cent of the sample are suffering from levels at or above the levels achieved by psychoneurotic outpatients. Free-floating anxiety may be defined as indescribable terror and tension without a cause. As the profession is undergoing mass change, lessening control and poor status, this is not really a very surprising outcome. However, care must be taken when interpreting these findings, because the question arises as to whether this is due to the situation *now* or if teachers are naturally more anxious. The situation in which teachers are finding themselves may be inducing anxiety, as the work now requires many changes, increased demands with little knowledge of the situation, and better expectations – but few added resources to do the job.

*Table 5.13* Percentage of teachers scoring as high as, or higher than, psychoneurotic outpatients

| Subscale measure | Psychoneurotic outpatients* (Mean) | Teachers (%) |
| --- | --- | --- |
| *Males (n=133)* | | |
| Free-floating anxiety | 9.7 | 20.7 |
| Somatic anxiety | 8.0 | 20.1 |
| Depression | 7.7 | 25.0 |
| *Females (n=173)* | | |
| Free-floating anxiety | 11.0 | 23.8 |
| Somatic anxiety | 8.9 | 19.6 |
| Depression | 7.6 | 26.2 |

*Note*: * Crisp 1977.

*Somatic anxiety*

Both male and female teachers report higher levels of somatic anxiety than the norm or other highly stressed occupational groups. This suggests that, as well as the psychological effects, teachers are unable to dissipate and cope with the physical effect of stress. Up to 21 per cent of teachers are suffering from levels at or above the psychoneurotic level.

*Depression*

As with somatic anxiety, both males and females were reporting higher levels of depression than the norm or other highly stressed occupational groups and up to 26 per cent are suffering from levels at or above the psychoneurotic level – a very disturbing find.

**Differences between the subgroups in the sample**

Differences in the mental ill health of male and female teachers has already been discussed. However, there were a few other subgroup differences worth noting. With regard to school type, and after allowing for the effect of female preponderance in the primary sector, it was safe to say that both male and female primary teachers were reporting higher levels of mental ill health on all of the scales. With regard to teaching grades, no significant differences were found, although senior teachers were consistently reporting poorer levels on all measures of mental well-being. Of most importance is that whatever the differences between the groups, all teachers compare poorly to other occupational groups, though perhaps teachers are more vocal in their feelings due to current pressures. It may also be the case that this is a particularly stressful time for teachers, and one that is being reflected in the high levels of mental ill health obtained. A study by Chakravorty (1989)

*Table 5.14*  Mental ill health of teachers compared to other occupational groups

| Group | n | Mean | SD | t | p (= or <) |
|---|---|---|---|---|---|
| *Free-floating anxiety* | | | | | |
| Females: Teachers | 730 | 7.1 | 4.0 | | |
|     Population | 415 | 5.4 | 3.5 | 7.42 | 0.001 |
|     Tax officers | 131 | 6.9 | 3.9 | 0.56 | N.S. |
|     GPs | 335 | 4.5 | 3.3 | 10.98 | 0.001 |
|     Dentists | 85 | 6.5 | 3.5 | 1.42 | N.S. |
| Males:   Teachers | 1,052 | 5.7 | 4.0 | | |
|     Population | 340 | 2.8 | 2.8 | 14.26 | 0.001 |
|     Tax officers | 185 | 5.0 | 3.6 | 2.44 | 0.05 |
|     GPs | 1,439 | 3.7 | 3.0 | 14.30 | 0.001 |
|     Dentists | 399 | 5.1 | 3.6 | 2.86 | 0.05 |
| *Somatic concomitants of anxiety* | | | | | |
| Females: Teachers | 730 | 5.3 | 3.3 | | |
|     Population | 415 | 5.7 | 3.3 | 2.02 | 0.05 |
|     Tax officers | 128 | 4.2 | 3.0 | 3.64 | 0.05 |
|     GPs | 335 | 2.7 | 2.2 | 15.37 | 0.001 |
|     Dentists | 85 | 3.7 | 2.7 | 4.65 | 0.001 |
| Males:   Teachers | 1,052 | 4.7 | 3.2 | | |
|     Population | 340 | 4.3 | 3.0 | 2.27 | 0.05 |
|     Tax officers | 185 | 3.8 | 3.3 | 3.73 | 0.01 |
|     GPs | 1,439 | 2.4 | 2.3 | 21.70 | 0.001 |
|     Dentists | 399 | 3.4 | 2.7 | 7.73 | 0.001 |
| *Depression* | | | | | |
| Females: Teachers | 730 | 5.6 | 3.3 | | |
|     Population | 415 | 4.4 | 2.5 | 6.85 | 0.001 |
|     Tax officers | 130 | 4.9 | 3.0 | 2.26 | 0.05 |
|     GPs | 335 | 3.4 | 2.4 | 11.95 | 0.001 |
|     Dentists | 85 | 3.7 | 2.8 | 5.37 | 0.001 |
| Males:   Teachers | 1,052 | 5.1 | 3.5 | | |
|     Population | 340 | 3.2 | 2.3 | 10.20 | 0.001 |
|     Tax officers | 184 | 4.0 | 3.0 | 4.10 | 0.001 |
|     GPs | 1,439 | 2.9 | 2.7 | 17.30 | 0.001 |
|     Dentists | 399 | 3.9 | 3.0 | 6.10 | 0.001 |

revealed that major changes facing teachers have often subsequently resulted in poor mental well-being (see Figure 5.1). Peak incidents of mental illness followed two periods of administrative reorganisation in 1979 and 1983.

This is further reinforced when the results from the current study are compared with those obtained by Kyriacou and Pratt (1985). Using the same measure of mental ill health, they found that levels of mental ill health in teachers were comparable with those of the population norms (i.e. Crown and Crisp 1979). Table 5.15 shows that, in contrast, the teachers in this

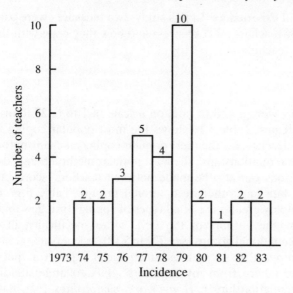

*Figure 5.1* Incidence of mental illness among school teachers
*Source:* Chakravorty (1989)

*Table 5.15* Comparison of our results with those of Kyriacou and Pratt (1985)

|  | UK | North of England* |
|---|---|---|
| *Free-floating anxiety* | | |
| Males | 5.7 | 4.0 |
| Females | 7.1 | 6.3 |
| *Somatic anxiety* | | |
| Males | 4.7 | 3.7 |
| Females | 5.3 | 4.5 |
| *Depression* | | |
| Males | 5.1 | 3.0 |
| Females | 5.6 | 4.4 |

*Note*: * Kyriacou and Pratt (1985): males = 37; females = 90.

study exhibit far more severe levels than the sample of Kyriacou and Pratt (1985) taken from the North of England, as well as the norms, reflecting the enormous changes that have taken place since the 1985 study.

## Coping strategies used by the teachers

As the literature suggests, the ability to cope with the demands arising in one's environment is a crucial factor in determining the levels of stress that an individual experiences. In this study, two measures were used to obtain data on how teachers react to stress and how they cope with the pressures involved in teaching.

## Coping

Respondents were asked to rate, on a scale of 1 to 6, 28 items, describing coping strategies. Table 5.16 shows the most popular coping strategies in order of preference, i.e. the most popular coping mechanism for teachers is 'having stable relationships'; the least popular method being 'delegation'.

Comparisons can also be made between teachers' scores and those of normative data and other occupational groups. Table 5.17 reveals that teachers employ greater use of all types of coping strategies than the norms provided by the authors of the OSI. More specifically, in comparison to other occupational groups (see Table 5.18), teachers use greater amounts of '*social support*' (e.g. 'seek as much social support as possible'; 'seek support and advice from my superiors'; 'talk to understanding friends'; 'have stable relationships'); '*Home/work relationships*' (e.g. 'having a home that is a "refuge"'; 'resort to hobbies and pastimes'; 'deliberately separate "home" and "work"'; 'expand interests and activities outside work') and '*Involvement*' (e.g. 'try to recognise my own limitations'; 'look for ways to make the work more interesting'; 'stay busy'; 'not bottling things up and being able to release energy'; 'use selective attention (concentrating on specific problems)'; 'accept the situation and learn to live with it'), but comparable levels of '*Task strategies*' (e.g. 'reorganise my work'; 'plan ahead'; 'use distractions (to take your mind off things)'; 'set priorities and deal with problems accordingly'; 'resort to rules and regulations'; 'delegation'; 'try to avoid the situation'); '*Logic*' (e.g. 'try to deal with the situation objectively in an unemotional way'; 'suppress emotions and try not to let the stress show'; 'try to stand aside and think through the situation') and '*Time*' (e.g. 'deal with problems immediately as they occur'; 'buy time and stall the issue'; 'effective time management'; 'force one's behaviour and lifestyle to slow down').

## Mobilised social support

Much research has stressed the importance of social support networks in enabling individuals to cope with the stress they experience, therefore it was considered important to include such a measure in this study of teachers. Table 5.19 reveals the most popular sources of support as far as the teachers in our study are concerned.

As can be seen from the table, the most popular source of support for teachers experiencing undue pressure is their spouse or partner followed by a 'work source' (i.e. a work colleague). Headteachers are less likely to be sought as producers of support in the event of stress.

*Table 5.16* The most popular coping strategies used by teachers

| Coping style item | Mean | SD | % scoring 5 or 6* | n |
|---|---|---|---|---|
| Have stable relationships | 4.86 | 1.14 | 90.0 | 1,782 |
| Deal with problems immediately as they occur | 4.79 | 1.01 | 92.4 | 1,784 |
| Having a home that is a refuge | 4.54 | 1.38 | 79.1 | 1,779 |
| Plan ahead | 4.52 | 1.07 | 87.4 | 1,783 |
| Set priorities and deal with problems accordingly | 4.45 | 1.02 | 86.6 | 1,782 |
| Look for ways to make the work more interesting | 4.43 | 1.14 | 85.0 | 1,782 |
| Suppress emotions and try not to let stress show | 4.26 | 1.29 | 75.6 | 1,782 |
| Try to recognise my own limitations | 4.24 | 1.06 | 82.8 | 1,781 |
| Try to deal with the situation objectively and in an unemotional way | 4.21 | 1.07 | 80.8 | 1,784 |
| Reorganise my work | 4.18 | 1.04 | 80.7 | 1,780 |
| Try to 'stand aside' and think through the situation | 4.12 | 1.01 | 79.1 | 1,782 |
| Use selective attention, concentrating on specific problems | 4.10 | 1.12 | 75.2 | 1,772 |
| Deliberately separate 'home' and 'work' | 4.06 | 1.56 | 61.8 | 1,178 |
| Talk to understanding friends | 3.99 | 1.46 | 68.5 | 1,782 |
| Effective time management | 3.98 | 1.12 | 72.1 | 1,772 |
| Resort to hobbies and pastimes | 3.96 | 1.49 | 65.5 | 1,781 |
| 'Stay busy' | 3.94 | 1.34 | 66.3 | 1,780 |
| Expand interests and activities outside work | 3.87 | 1.42 | 62.3 | 1,783 |
| Accept the situation and learn to live with it | 3.83 | 1.19 | 69.1 | 1,784 |
| Use distractions (to take my mind off things) | 3.76 | 1.30 | 60.6 | 1,785 |
| Not 'bottling things up' and being able to release energy | 3.75 | 1.34 | 58.0 | 1,783 |
| Seek support and advice from my superiors | 3.37 | 1.30 | 54.0 | 1,783 |
| Seek as much social support as possible | 3.26 | 1.28 | 44.8 | 1,780 |
| Resort to rules and regulations | 3.18 | 1.16 | 42.7 | 1,786 |
| Force one's behaviour and lifestyle to slow down | 3.12 | 1.17 | 38.3 | 1,779 |
| Try to avoid the situation | 3.00 | 1.26 | 33.8 | 1,782 |
| 'Buy time' and stall the issue | 2.86 | 1.23 | 30.0 | 1,781 |
| Delegation | 2.85 | 1.21 | 32.1 | 1,773 |

*Note*: * The overall percentage of teachers scoring 5 or 6 is used to indicate the strength of preference – that is, the strategy was 'extensively' or 'very extensively' used by them.

## Sources of stress in the job

Transcriptions of the 40 interviews carried out in the first phase of the study were content analysed and, based on our knowledge of the sources of occupational stress generally and a thorough literature review of the findings on teacher stress, an inventory of 'Sources of job pressure' was

*Table 5.17* Comparison of teachers' stress-coping strategies with OSI normative data

|  | n | Mean | SD | t | p (= or ≤) |
|---|---|---|---|---|---|
| *Social support* |  |  |  |  |  |
| Teachers | 1,765 | 15.48 | 3.36 | 6.71 | 0.001 |
| OSI | 156 | 13.54 | 3.56 |  |  |
| *Task strategies* |  |  |  |  |  |
| Teachers | 1,749 | 25.90 | 3.79 | 19.26 | 0.001 |
| OSI | 156 | 20.51 | 2.90 |  |  |
| *Logic* |  |  |  |  |  |
| Teachers | 1,776 | 12.59 | 2.38 | 3.32 | 0.001 |
| OSI | 156 | 11.75 | 1.77 |  |  |
| *Home and work relationships* |  |  |  |  |  |
| Teachers | 1,763 | 16.43 | 4.04 | 4.57 | 0.001 |
| OSI | 156 | 14.98 | 3.57 |  |  |
| *Time* |  |  |  |  |  |
| Teachers | 1,761 | 14.74 | 2.21 | 2.81 | 0.005 |
| OSI | 156 | 14.23 | 2.14 |  |  |
| *Involvement* |  |  |  |  |  |
| Teachers | 1,748 | 24.30 | 3.60 | 21.62 | 0.001 |
| OSI | 156 | 18.32 | 3.02 |  |  |

*Source*: Cooper *et al.* (1988a)

*Table 5.18* Comparison of teachers' stress-coping strategies with other occupational groups

| Strategy | Occupational group | | | | | |
|---|---|---|---|---|---|---|
|  | Teachers (n=1,748 to 1,776) | | Management consultants* (n=105) | | Middle managers* (n=48) | |
|  | Mean | SD | Mean | SD | Mean | SD |
| Social support | 15.48 | 3.36 | 14.21 | 2.61 | 13.77 | 2.28 |
| Task strategies | 25.90 | 3.79 | 25.78 | 2.89 | 24.94 | 3.11 |
| Logic | 12.59 | 2.38 | 12.80 | 1.78 | 12.60 | 1.62 |
| Home/work relationships | 16.43 | 4.04 | 13.46 | 3.84 | 14.48 | 2.81 |
| Time | 14.74 | 2.21 | 14.35 | 1.74 | 13.50 | 1.57 |
| Involvement | 24.30 | 3.60 | 22.38 | 2.85 | 22.33 | 2.36 |

*Source*: Cooper *et al.* (1988a)

*Table 5.19* Frequency of respondents' choice of social support

| Source of support | n | % |
|---|---|---|
| Spouse/partner | 1,264 | 70.7 |
| Work colleague | 1,403 | 58.3 |
| Friend (outside of work) | 688 | 38.5 |
| Relative | 346 | 19.3 |
| Headteacher | 223 | 12.5 |

designed and included in the questionnaire. From this we could discover which pressures were seen as detrimental and lead to stress outcomes. A total of 98 items were included in the scale, and many of these covered areas identified in the model in Chapters 1 and 3.

Table 5.20 reveals how teachers responded to this questionnaire. The table shows all 98 items along with the mean score obtained and the percentage of teachers who reported high levels of pressure (i.e. a score of 5 or 6). A score of 1 indicates low pressure and 6 indicates that the item provided the teacher with a very definite level of pressure. The items are presented in descending order. The results show that the item causing the most pressure for teachers is 'lack of support from the government', which has a mean score of 5.39, and 85 per cent of the teachers rated this as 5 or 6. As well as this item, teachers are experiencing a very high level of pressure from 'the lack of information as to how the changes are to be implemented' (with a mean score of 5.30); 'the constant changes taking place within the profession' (mean score 5.30); and 'society's diminishing respect for my profession' (mean score of 5.19).

*Table 5.20* Sources of pressure in the teacher's job

| Item | Mean | SD | % 5 or 6 | n |
|---|---|---|---|---|
| Lack of support from the government | 5.39 | 1.11 | 85.1 | 1,782 |
| The lack of information as to how the changes are to be implemented | 5.30 | 1.05 | 84.0 | 1,783 |
| The constant changes taking place within the profession | 5.30 | 1.05 | 83.6 | 1,785 |
| Society's diminishing respect for my profession | 5.19 | 1.13 | 80.8 | 1,782 |
| The move towards a 'National Curriculum' | 4.89 | 1.26 | 71.3 | 1,781 |
| A salary that is out of proportion to workload | 4.88 | 1.29 | 68.3 | 1,781 |
| Having to produce 'assessments' of pupils | 4.79 | 1.20 | 67.8 | 1,773 |

*Table 5.20*  cont.

| Item | Mean | SD | % 5 or 6 | n |
|------|------|------|------|------|
| Dealing with basic behavioural problems | 4.78 | 1.36 | 69.2 | 1,775 |
| Lack of non-contact time | 4.77 | 1.34 | 66.8 | 1,763 |
| Being a good teacher does not necessarily mean promotion | 4.76 | 1.37 | 65.3 | 1,765 |
| Having to be a 'Jack of all trades, master of none' | 4.74 | 1.42 | 65.9 | 1,778 |
| The lack of value placed on actual teaching itself | 4.74 | 1.41 | 66.4 | 1,776 |
| Knowing that my absence will create problems for other staff | 4.72 | 1.45 | 68.3 | 1,768 |
| Administrative tasks | 4.68 | 1.28 | 64.0 | 1,779 |
| Overall lack of resources | 4.66 | 1.32 | 65.2 | 1,778 |
| Dealing with children who demand immediate attention | 4.65 | 1.36 | 62.8 | 1,778 |
| Teaching those who do not value education | 4.61 | 1.45 | 63.5 | 1,773 |
| Lack of time to resolve problems with individual pupils | 4.56 | 1.35 | 60.7 | 1,774 |
| Inability to plan ahead due to constant changes | 4.54 | 1.43 | 60.1 | 1,776 |
| Teaching those who take things for granted | 4.54 | 1.36 | 58.4 | 1,777 |
| The advent of local management of schools | 4.46 | 1.41 | 55.6 | 1,767 |
| Taking work home interferes with family life | 4.41 | 1.61 | 58.6 | 1,772 |
| Teachers can have little influence over school decisions as a whole | 4.40 | 1.32 | 51.6 | 1,773 |
| Lack of parental 'back-up' on matters of discipline | 4.36 | 1.53 | 54.5 | 1,775 |
| Witnessing increasing aggression between pupils | 4.29 | 1.56 | 52.6 | 1,777 |
| The likely introduction of 'teacher appraisal' | 4.26 | 1.51 | 50.4 | 1,782 |
| No recourse to sanctions in the school | 4.25 | 1.57 | 50.8 | 1,757 |
| The hours spent marking at home | 4.24 | 1.57 | 52.3 | 1,765 |
| Maintaining discipline | 4.23 | 1.53 | 51.2 | 1,776 |
| Having to work through breaks and lunchtimes | 4.23 | 1.59 | 53.3 | 1,774 |
| Having to manage the school on a tight budget | 4.22 | 1.64 | 52.9 | 1,752 |
| Lack of support from the local authority | 4.20 | 1.51 | 47.5 | 1,763 |
| Lack of chances for promotion | 4.19 | 1.65 | 51.7 | 1,773 |
| The 'unpredictability' of 'cover' periods | 4.19 | 1.60 | 51.4 | 1,732 |

*Table 5.20* cont.

| Item | Mean | SD | % 5 or 6 | n |
|---|---|---|---|---|
| When pupils try to 'test' you all the time | 4.13 | 1.54 | 47.4 | 1,778 |
| When 'cover' for absent colleagues leads to 'large' classes | 4.12 | 1.73 | 52.3 | 1,699 |
| The integration of pupils with special educational needs | 4.12 | 1.68 | 50.7 | 1,762 |
| When my performance is assessed by others | 4.03 | 1.59 | 45.7 | 1,771 |
| Increasing involvement with 'pastoral' issues | 4.01 | 1.55 | 44.7 | 1,770 |
| The 'hierarchical' nature of the structure of my school | 4.00 | 1.61 | 43.5 | 1,764 |
| Verbal aggression from pupils | 4.00 | 1.71 | 45.1 | 1,771 |
| The number of interruptions in class | 3.97 | 1.53 | 41.8 | 1,766 |
| Lack of consensus among staff on matters of discipline | 3.95 | 1.58 | 43.3 | 1,775 |
| Lack of auxiliary support | 3.89 | 1.60 | 40.5 | 1,772 |
| Lack of clerical assistance | 3.89 | 1.66 | 42.9 | 1,765 |
| The constant 'answering back' from pupils | 3.88 | 1.68 | 41.9 | 1,772 |
| Lack of participation in decision making in the school | 3.86 | 1.47 | 36.4 | 1,766 |
| Poor staff communications | 3.86 | 1.48 | 36.4 | 1,779 |
| Having to 'cover' in unfamiliar areas of the curriculum | 3.84 | 1.60 | 40.1 | 1,740 |
| Having to attend parents' evenings | 3.83 | 1.41 | 34.9 | 1,767 |
| The need for constant decision making in the classroom | 3.82 | 1.52 | 38.8 | 1,771 |
| Feeling that apart from teaching I have no other employable skills | 3.80 | 1.85 | 45.3 | 1,776 |
| The number of daily confrontations in the class | 3.79 | 1.64 | 39.3 | 1,768 |
| Conflict between the needs of my department/class and the views of senior management | 3.78 | 1.55 | 37.3 | 1,764 |
| Building and maintaining relationships with pupils | 3.77 | 1.58 | 39.7 | 1,777 |
| Poor working conditions | 3.76 | 1.62 | 36.6 | 1,777 |
| Having to teach in overcrowded classrooms | 3.71 | 1.70 | 39.4 | 1,761 |
| The size of the classes that I teach | 3.67 | 1.68 | 35.9 | 1,768 |
| Relationships with pupils' parents | 3.67 | 1.40 | 29.2 | 1,771 |
| The amount of noise in the school | 3.65 | 1.57 | 33.7 | 1,773 |
| High demands from parents for good results | 3.65 | 1.50 | 31.2 | 1,765 |
| Lack of support from the headteacher | 3.59 | 1.75 | 36.5 | 1,759 |
| Awareness of pupils' social and financial deprivation | 3.55 | 1.54 | 29.4 | 1,778 |

*Table 5.20*  cont.

| Item | Mean | SD | % 5 or 6 | n |
|---|---|---|---|---|
| Conflict between my department and others for resources | 3.53 | 1.47 | 27.1 | 1,746 |
| The inadequate implementation of change in my school | 3.49 | 1.52 | 28.8 | 1,772 |
| Not enough opportunity to make my own decisions | 3.47 | 1.39 | 23.4 | 1,780 |
| Parental attitudes towards my adherence to union policies, e.g. strikes | 3.45 | 1.74 | 32.3 | 1,766 |
| Lack of job security within the profession | 3.44 | 1.70 | 30.8 | 1,778 |
| The unfamiliarity of the demands that I face | 3.37 | 1.54 | 26.3 | 1,775 |
| Intra-staff rivalry, i.e. within the school | 3.33 | 1.59 | 25.9 | 1,770 |
| Feeling that my training is not appropriate | 3.30 | 1.69 | 28.2 | 1,777 |
| Continually having to form new relationships | 3.30 | 1.51 | 23.4 | 1,781 |
| Lack of support from the school governors | 3.29 | 1.50 | 23.1 | 1,751 |
| The lack of clarity concerning my role within the school | 3.28 | 1.56 | 25.2 | 1,774 |
| The number of supervisory activities I have to perform at school | 3.28 | 1.53 | 24.1 | 1,741 |
| Poor staff–student ratios | 3.26 | 1.69 | 28.2 | 1,767 |
| Academic pressure within the school | 3.25 | 1.51 | 22.6 | 1,773 |
| Vandalism of the school premises | 3.22 | 1.62 | 24.4 | 1,770 |
| Unrealistically high expectations of others concerning my role | 3.21 | 1.53 | 22.6 | 1,761 |
| Too little responsibility within the school | 3.18 | 1.53 | 21.2 | 1,766 |
| Poorly defined schemes of work | 3.17 | 1.60 | 24.5 | 1,766 |
| Uncertainty about the degree of area of my responsibility | 3.13 | 1.54 | 21.5 | 1,768 |
| Reacting too personally to pupils' criticism | 3.10 | 1.49 | 19.5 | 1,775 |
| Physical aggression from pupils | 3.05 | 1.83 | 25.7 | 1,773 |
| Increasing pressures from school governors | 3.00 | 1.49 | 18.0 | 1,756 |
| The threat of redeployment | 2.95 | 1.79 | 24.9 | 1,764 |
| Truancy | 2.94 | 1.63 | 20.1 | 1,764 |
| Teaching to exam standard | 2.91 | 1.72 | 24.0 | 1,731 |
| Over-emotional involvement with the pupils | 2.82 | 1.51 | 27.0 | 1,769 |
| Lack of 'social support' from fellow teachers in my school | 2.81 | 1.46 | 14.2 | 1,765 |
| The neighbourhood in which my school is based | 2.69 | 1.69 | 19.2 | 1,770 |
| Lack of support from my union | 2.62 | 1.51 | 13.8 | 1,770 |

*Table 5.20*  cont.

| Item | Mean | SD | % 5 or 6 | n |
|------|------|------|------|------|
| My staff do not understand the pressures I am under as a manager | 2.58 | 1.56 | 14.2 | 1,601 |
| My school is too 'traditional' and slow to move with the times | 2.56 | 1.42 | 11.8 | 1,765 |
| The use of school bells | 2.44 | 1.56 | 13.6 | 1,745 |
| Duration of the summer holidays | 2.15 | 1.45 | 9.8 | 1,768 |
| Racial tensions within the school | 2.00 | 1.36 | 6.8 | 1,750 |
| Promotion has led to too few class contacts with pupils | 1.97 | 1.30 | 6.8 | 1,717 |

The perceived pressure from lack of governmental support was high-lighted by many of the teachers during the interviews and can be seen more clearly by many of the quotes given in the following chapter.

When the main sources of pressure are examined, it can be seen that there are a number of links between them. The most outstanding sources are connected to change, its pace and implementation. They are also concerned with the implication of this change (i.e. diminishing respect for teachers, inadequate salary and the amount of paperwork that these changes have introduced).

The following chapter will examine in more detail the underlying themes of groups of stressors which teachers are reporting. As the scale designed for the teachers was unique to the study it was not possible to compare the findings with other groups. However, just by examining the types of responses and the high levels of pressure reported, we can see that there are high levels of negative pressure in this particular group of teachers.

# 6 Sources of pressure in the job of teaching

Felix qui potuit rerum cognoscere causas – Lucky is he who has been able to understand the causes of things.

(Virgil)

The previous two chapters in this part of the book have discussed the way teachers react to their working environment, the causes of stress in terms of their personality, and the major sources of stress that they report. This chapter aims to explore the sources of teacher stress in more detail and will (1) determine the major sources of stress for teachers; (2) discover which cause the most damage; and (3) discover what proportion of experienced stress can be attributed to the personality of the individual teacher. In Chapter 3 it was suggested that the Type A behavioural style may lead to individuals being more prone to stress. In Chapter 4 we noted that, as a group, teachers display high levels of Type A behaviour which may make them particularly prone to stress. The interesting questions raised for this chapter are: 'To what extent does this behavioural style contribute to the level of stress revealed by teachers?' and 'To what extent does this style, along with coping mechanisms and other individual characteristics, moderate the effect that the environmental stressors have on such outcomes as mental health and job satisfaction?' From the ensuing discussion we can be more confident in the relevance of the recommendations we make in the final chapter of this book. In addition, the previous chapter revealed that our UK teachers report the greatest pressure from 'lack of support from the government' and the 'pace and implementation of change'. How does this type of pressure manifest itself? Do teachers drink more, attempt to leave and become more job dissatisfied? Or, indeed, are these stressors more contemporary in their nature and, subsequently, do they have less impact than the more intrinsic features of the job (e.g. pupil behaviour)? Are any of these sources of pressure actually reducing the possibility of stress outcomes (i.e. eustress – see Chapter 1), or do they have less obvious effects on outcomes? Are there any other effects for which we have not measured?

Therefore, in this chapter we are trying to delve deeper and get closer to the real causes of stress for our sample of teachers. In order to do this, advanced statistical analyses are used in the form of *factor analysis* and *multiple regression analysis*. Multiple regression is used to determine the relationships between the stress outcomes in which we are interested (i.e. mental ill health, job dissatisfaction, intention to leave, sickness absence, habit-forming behaviours) and the potential sources and causes of these outcomes (i.e. Type A behaviour, coping methods, pressures in the job).

Many of the potential causes of stress for teachers (e.g. biographical data of age, length of time in career, etc.) are represented for each teacher by single total scores. This is not the case for all of the variables in the study. Sources of job pressure and stress-coping mechanisms are more effectively examined when broken down into factors or categories. It was also decided for the purpose of this study to break down the Type A scale into separate factors. As we are attempting to provide effective recommendations for stress management, it is more beneficial if we go as far as possible to identify maladaptive behaviours. Therefore, before carrying out regression analysis, we reduced the large range of variables in each of the three scales (sources of job pressure, coping, and Type A) to a manageable number. This was done by using factor analysis, which allows us to reduce a large number of item variables into a few factors, consisting of elements which are strongly related to each other. For example, the 'Sources of Pressure You Face in Your Job' score consists of 98 items, and was not designed to be a scale with a singular score. An overall 'stress' score could be obtained, but would not be as informative, as the major aim of this study was to identify the sources of pressure that lead to stress outcomes and suggest recommendations for action. Factor analysis breaks down the 98 items by identifying underlying themes or dimensions. When applied it may give us a 'feel' for the major stressors experienced by teachers, the methods used to cope with those stressors and the varying behavioural styles that teachers employ. We shall present the factors we found, and then the results of the more detailed multiple regression analysis. (A glossary of terms can be found in Appendix 1.)

## FACTOR ANALYSIS OF SOURCES OF PRESSURE IN THE TEACHER'S JOB

From the factor analysis, 10 separate 'teacher stress' factors were identified. We have given these 10 factors subjective names for convenient reference. Table 6.1 shows the items which constitute each factor and these are from Section 5 of the questionnaire, entitled 'Sources of Pressure You Face in Your Job' (see Appendix 2). Each of these factors is now discussed with an interpretation of each.

### Pupil/teacher interaction

This factor of 10 items is rather a wide category, in that it covers pupils' actual behaviour and the resulting pressure from dealing with that

*Table 6.1* Factor analysis of the sources of pressure in the job

---

*Factor 1: Pupil/teacher interaction*
Verbal aggression from pupils
Number of daily confrontations in the class
Answering back from pupils
Maintaining discipline
Pupils trying to test you all the time
Dealing with basic behavioural problems
Teaching those who do not value education
Witnessing increasing aggression between pupils
Lack of parental back-up on matters of discipline
Physical aggression from pupils

*Factor 2: Management/structure of the school*
The hierarchical nature of my school
Lack of participation in decision making in my school
Conflict between the needs of my department and the views of
    senior management
Lack of support from the headteacher
Poor staff communications
Teachers can have little influence over school decisions as a whole
Too little responsibility within the school
Intra-staff rivalry, i.e. within the school
Not enough opportunity to make my own decisions

*Factor 3: Class sizes/overcrowding*
Having to teach in overcrowded classrooms
Poor staff–student ratios
The size of the classes that I teach

*Factor 4: Changes taking place within education*
Constant changes taking place within the profession
The move towards a 'National Curriculum'
The lack of information as to how the changes are to be implemented

*Factor 5: Appraisal of teachers*
High demands from parents for good results
When my performance is assessed by others
Having to attend parents' evenings
Academic pressure within the school
The likely introduction of 'Teacher Appraisal'

*Factor 6: Concerns of management*
My staff do not understand the pressures I am under as a manager
Unrealistically high expectations of others concerning my role
The number of supervisory activities I have to perform at school

*Factor 7: Lack of status/promotion*
Being a good teacher does not necessarily mean promotion
Lack of chances for promotion
Society's diminishing respect for my profession
A salary that is out of proportion to workload
Lack of support from the government
The lack of value placed on actual teaching

*Table 6.1* cont.

---

*Factor 8: 'Cover' and staff shortages*
Having to cover in unfamiliar areas of the curriculum
The unpredictability of cover periods
When cover for absent colleagues leads to classes that are too large
Inability to plan ahead due to constant changes

*Factor 9: Job insecurity*
The threat of redeployment
Lack of job security within the profession

*Factor 10: Ambiguity of the teacher's role*
Uncertainty about the degree or area of my responsibility
Poorly defined schemes of work
Unfamiliarity of the demands that I face
Feeling that my training is not adequate
The lack of clarity concerning the teacher's role within the school
The inadequate implementation of change in the school

---

behaviour. The discovery of this as the major factor is not surprising when we examine previous findings with regard to teacher stress and the traditional view of what is stressful in teaching. As was outlined in Chapter 3, one of the key features in a teacher's job is the constant responsibility for others. In addition, the teachers in this sample were largely drawn from the secondary sector and so were dealing with large classes, often with very little auxiliary support in the classroom.

These teachers are experiencing problems from all aspects of pupil behaviour (i.e. verbal and physical aggression) and, in addition, have to deal with the lack of parental back-up (e.g. with respect to discipline problems). This is why the word 'interaction' is used rather than just 'pupil misbehaviour' as it includes features that affect how the teachers are equipped to deal with the problems. The difficulty of physical aggression from pupils is increasingly evident in schools. One female supply teacher, describing her last school, explained:

> The children were so unbelievably aggressive, it was just a battle, I couldn't believe that children of 8 and 9 years old would just square at you continually and just refuse to do anything, not only to me but to teachers that had been teaching in the school for 10 to 15 years.

In addition, they have to witness increasing aggression *between* the pupils themselves, as she went on to say: ' . . . play time and the children did not know how to play, it was just a battle.'

A further problem lies with the need to deal with those who do not appreciate the value of education. One female secondary teacher explained:

If you are first of all trying to convince people there is a reason they should be there, and then you confront the discipline problem, and then you are trying to get over what it is you are trying to get over (i.e. the actual subject). It's a very difficult situation.

As a further example, a male head of department in a secondary school explained:

Few of the pupils in my school appear to value education and many are positively antagonistic towards what we have to offer. I often feel like a door-to-door salesman, trying to sell a product which people do not want to buy. Few pupils enter the room EXPECTING to have to work and work done at home shows little evidence of real interest or effort in many cases. Presentations on TV with their slick, 'expense-no-object' production, cannot be matched in the classroom with limited resources and over-filled time. Little appears to interest or excite anymore. 'Boring' is a word used about so many things, not just school work.

A female main-scale teacher explained that the problem of dealing with discipline even intrudes into her private life:

It has not been unusual for my dreams, on holidays, to feature some of my present or previous classes – often involving crazy situations where I feel I have virtually no control! I don't need to be a professional psychologist to recognise anxiety relating to class management and discipline when I see it.

A female promoted teacher in a secondary school further explained that parents do not even agree as to what they expect from the teacher, which exacerbates the problem:

A great degree of pressure at the moment is coming from parents, who are led to believe that all they have to do is demand what they want for their children/child and we will provide immediate success. The difference in expectations is incredible – from one set of parents who want the child to have complete freedom to do exactly as he/she wants, regardless of the safety or well-being of others – to others who expect under fives to be academic robots who should be capable of producing 'visible excellence' throughout the day and provided with at least 1 hour's homework each evening. Trying to accommodate these extremes or wishes/demands with my own expectations is becoming impossible.

An additional fear comes from the threat of violence. Two female promoted teachers recalled their experiences for us:

I found the experience of being attacked by a pupil extremely disturbing. Even though I know I was in no way to blame, I still experience deep feelings of failure because of this, and this incident is a large factor in my leaving teaching.

'... a kid tells you to 'f\*\*\* off' or something and you can take it very personally, especially when you first start here.

Over the course of the school day a teacher may be faced by a large number of such confrontations, as one male teacher in an inner-city secondary school remarked on the sources of stress: 'You are in so many confrontation situations a lot of the time.'

Several aspects of pupil attitude and behaviour have been identified as causing teacher stress. Teachers have to deal with *disinterest* in education, aggression and many other aspects which may have a particular effect on their job satisfaction.

## Management/structure of the school

This second factor, consisting of nine items, reflects concern with the organisational structure of the school and the way in which the school is managed.

Many of the problems and resulting pressures mentioned in this factor could be alleviated with improved management as they involve the pressures from staff relationships. As one female secondary teacher recalled of her last school:

A lot of pressure was due to the attitudes of the staff. A lot of elitist attitudes from people or less elitist attitudes, it's hard to define, but there was a lot of conflict, staff conflict.

Many of the problems result from the lack of opportunity to take part in decisions and from not being consulted, as one male main-scale teacher in a sixth-form college explained:

In this particular institution one of the stress factors is the style of leadership. Very dynamic, very directive, very objective and non-consultative generally.... That has caused stress in the staffroom as teachers feel that they are not consulted.... If you go to discuss something, you don't discuss it, you get told *how* to do it.

Teachers complain that headteachers do not always seem to recognise the problems that members of their staff face, as one male teacher in a primary school explained:

My present headteacher is dynamic and has very strong leadership qualities but is a very poor personnel manager, showing lack of interest in staff as individuals – only interested in the work they produce. At the 'chalk-face' in education, appreciation of your efforts by an immediate superior makes all the difference to any pressure under which one is working.

**Class sizes/overcrowding**

This factor comprises three items, and deals with the issue of overcrowding in school and the resulting class sizes. The problem resulting from having too many pupils in school and in too few classrooms is far too great for some teachers. One teacher described how she had problems at her last nursery school, but that now there was less stress as:

> Now the staff/pupil ratio is 1–15 and at some times even better with voluntary helpers, mums, etc.

Class reduction was mentioned frequently as a remedy for reducing stress. A female teacher explained:

> For me the key solution to the problem of teacher stress is *smaller classes*. It is frustrating having 30 plus first years/second years/third years who all need attention, some needing constant help – and having to pitch a lesson somewhere that will just about do for everyone, and yet very little opportunity to give positive help – tending to suppress the requests for help/symptoms of attention seeking.

The evidence in the study suggests that teachers have on average only 2.4 auxiliary supporters in their classrooms. This is very low when we consider the average class sizes and that a large proportion of the teachers are in secondary schools. In fact, 32 per cent of the sample had no auxiliary helpers present in the school. This suggests that class sizes can lead to subsequent problems with teaching a wide range of abilities in one class, and also some feelings of guilt at having to neglect those children with the greater needs.

**Changes taking place within education**

The many changes taking place within education have taken their toll; teachers are reporting 'change' as being a major cause of pressure. One male head of department explained that in his secondary school this had been particularly a result of the way major reorganisations within schools had been carried out:

> The greatest stress in my career has been experienced when schools are reorganising. Having been through the mill on THREE occasions where one has to reapply for one's own position, or has to enter a competitive situation with colleagues – over a lengthy consultation period, this can depress and wear one down. In many cases I have witnessed depression and anger from resentful colleagues.

He further explained that this was to do with the *way* change is implemented:

> Changes in education seem to be unending and each 'flavour of the

month' must be given priority – until the next band-waggon rolls along, with many staff seeking promotion, only too eager to jump aboard. Change is needed but the way it is introduced leaves much to be desired.

One secondary headteacher explained that change had left him feeling that he did not really understand the purpose and requirements of the changes:

> As a head, I expend a great deal of energy in understanding each particular change, but rarely feel confident that I understand the overall picture.

They argue that change is usually not accompanied by sufficient resources, and one primary teacher said that she did not have the energy to deal with the increasing demands:

> Confusion and lack of cooperation with resources regarding implementation of the new curriculum, not just monetary but time allocation – non-existent in order to prepare fully, while having a full teaching commitment. No energy left at the end of a normal day's workload to tackle new initiatives. This gives rise to lack of confidence in one's ability to cope – not a healthy situation for teaching.

One of the demanding functions within teaching, and one that is becoming more apparent, is the considerable amount of time teachers have to spend on the 'social' aspects of the job, as one male secondary head of department explained:

> This 'social thing', it's going to have to be increased due to the way that society's going, but if they're going to increase this load on us then they're going to have to give us more time to do the social work and less time teaching.

Therefore, this can be a source of pressure as it means less time on other teaching activities, and has more to do with the changes in the role of the 'educator' within education.

## Appraisal of teachers

These items dealt with the issue of teachers being appraised and evaluated by a number of significant others (i.e. parents, the government and education advisers). As can be seen in the following quote from a female primary teacher, teachers are more fearful of appraisal because they believe that people do not think they are doing a good job in any case:

> I have the inner feeling that, by implication, we are not doing a good job ... that is why we need a National Curriculum, when the government will wave its wand and we will all, as if by magic, become wonderful teachers. I am working damned hard – achieving good results, yet feeling a pressure and resentment that someone has decided I'm going

to do better, by taking on an unknown quantity of extra work . . . frightening!

A male primary head of department explained the pressures from parents' expectations:

> I am reaching the stage where it is becoming physically harder to maintain my standards and I also feel that many parents now expect and almost demand many of the extra-curricular items.

In addition, the teachers are fearful of the possible threat of the implementation of Teacher Appraisal, as one secondary female head of department explained:

> And, of course, appraisal of staff looms ahead, it shouldn't be daunting, in theory a good idea, I suppose, but it will frighten a lot of teachers and encourage resentment between colleagues particularly the assessed and assessors.

This suggests that appraisal can have positive or negative effects, depending on the *culture* of the school.

## Concerns of management

This factor is mainly concerned with the problems of being in a supervisory role, and so is not as relevant for all teachers within the sample. One of the problems facing 'supervisors', particularly headteachers, is the feeling that others do not fully understand the pressures they are under, and this can lead to a sense of isolation, as one secondary female head lamented:

> The head hasn't got anybody to go to. Alright, you've got your deputies around to talk about general things to. But there are certain things that the head can't talk to anybody about and that is the problem.

It would appear, therefore, that there is a lack of communication between the needs and roles of teachers and managers within schools that may be instrumental in bringing about stress, as the previous headteacher went on to say:

> I feel with the new system that's coming in with our Local Financial Management, you don't want a headteacher in this job, you want somebody who is a hard faced administrator who has no thought for children or staff.

A problem discussed by many was the problem of motivating *other* teachers in a time of mass change, as one male deputy headteacher in a secondary school remarked:

> My stress at the moment is motivating staff, good staff. They are well qualified, usually well motivated, but they just don't want to know. They

just want to teach their lessons and then go home. These are the people who used to give up their weekends, their evenings and yet they just say 'Well, if that's what they want, to just treat us like hired labour, then that's what we'll do.'

Another pressure facing heads that may lead to added stress is an increased accountability to outside bodies (e.g. the governors) yet, at the same time, many feel that there is a lack of information and understanding between the roles and level of responsibility that each must have, as one male secondary headteacher explained:

> I am constantly dealing with parts of a jig-saw with the full knowledge that crucial parts will be missing. A head also has the governing body to consider. The government seems to perceive governing bodies as playing a primary role in the management of schools in broad terms. The majority of governors, I feel sure, perceive their role as secondary, and rely greatly on the head to explain all of the changes.

## Lack of status/promotion

This factor was described both as a source of stress and also as a reason for wanting to leave the profession. Included here were concerns about low pay, lack of status, diminished public opinion, and the lack of opportunities for advancement in the profession. One female secondary head of department recalled:

> I remember hearing someone speak years ago, saying it'll be the worse day for the teaching profession once they establish hierarchies. Looking back, I think that's exactly what it has been, what they should've done was to pay teachers, full stop, a good salary, and give the secretarial bit (which after all is what heads of department are doing) one particular allowance to anyone who is prepared to do it, because otherwise there is no incentive. I certainly didn't advise any of my children to go into teaching and thank God neither of them has. The things that you have to go through to progress in education. . . . It's soul destroying.

In addition, the lack of value and worth was a main issue for one male teacher in a nursery school who complained:

> What is unique to the teaching profession is the value placed upon it, in all kinds of ways, but particularly financially. Surely one of the reasons why a job is well paid is because it is some recognition of the high level of stress that is part of it. The teaching profession lacks this recognition and the lack of financial reward can be a cause of persistent resentment and dissatisfaction. It is easier to cope with stress if one is handsomely paid for doing so.

This has not been helped by the number of changes that have taken place, as a female secondary teacher added:

> The amalgamation of scales 1 and 2 to form the 'main professional scale' has caused a great deal of discontent in the profession. Being at the top of scale 2 at the time of changeover meant that teachers like me no longer had any financial advantages for the additional work they were doing and yet were still expected to do it.

They do not believe that they receive much in the way of recognition, as the above teacher added:

> It's one of those jobs where you get very little praise at all, and there is no reason why people should praise you but you are isolated all the time. . . . It's not what I went into. It's a lack of challenge.

The 'bad press' also causes distress, as one female primary deputy head reported:

> Teachers invariably get a bad press. Comments in the media are seldom complimentary and serve to undermine a teacher's confidence as well as his/her standing in the community and among pupils. They are constantly being undervalued, this being of course reflected in their salary level.

The positive image teachers once possessed has now diminished:

> People used to be quite pleased when you said that you were a teacher, but now they're not at all impressed. In general terms, I think that a lot of people tend to think that standards have gone down . . . the various teachers' actions have not helped. I just don't think that they think anything goes on in schools, anything of any value.

Another problem that would appear within this factor, one related to status, is the lack of promotion opportunities. This may help to create a barrier between heads and teachers as many believe in the unfairness of promotion. Teachers do not believe that there are enough opportunities and often resent those in promoted positions, as one male secondary head of department explained:

> You can see people that are apparently not as able, but have got on, and the lack of promotion in teaching at the moment is unbelievable. . . . You get a bit staid, you're stuck in a rut, because things don't happen that you expect to have done . . . you go for something and you get knocked on the head, it puts you off and so you think 'stuff it, I won't do any more of that'.

This seems to be leading to a degree of bitterness within the teaching profession. A general impression gained by the researchers was that many teachers believe that bad teachers are 'promoted *out* of the classroom', but that could just be a lack of knowledge and communication with regard to the headteacher's role. One other female secondary head of department said:

> The way the profession is structured is so basically unfair. I just feel that the whole hierarchy in schools ... is so ludicrous, about being in the right place at the right time with the right vacancy coming up. ... I think it's totally corrupt.

They believe that many of these problems arise from the fact that education itself is not given sufficient credibility, and a secondary male promoted teacher complained:

> 'Outsiders' do not take education seriously, do not generally see it as important except as a young 'training scheme' for work. The value of having expanding horizons of being interested/curious in people/places/ideas/the past for their own sake is being neglected in importance all the time, even though it was never very high in the national psyche. 'If it isn't useful why bother?' is the pervasive attitude now.

However, one of the major problems for many is that they do not think there are enough opportunities for different types of promotion (i.e. not everyone wants to be promoted out of the classroom and yet still want to secure some professional advancement). This was clearly explained in the comments made by a female secondary headteacher:

> I think the structure that they have made for the teachers is bad, because they've got ten years on increments and that's it, unless they happen to get a scale of some kind. Whereas previously if you looked at the salary structure from '0' to 'Scale one', up to senior teacher, there were 25 steps and I think it would've been better to have kept a straight scale and let people go up each year, because experience counts for something, and not everybody wants to come out of the classroom, and if you are promoted, you are promoted out of the classroom and that's the sad part.

### 'Cover' and staff shortages

This factor of four items deals with the issue of 'cover' and staff shortages. This aspect of the teacher's job is causing pressure for all teaching grades. One of the most frequently cited problems in the initial study interviews was the problem of being expected to teach in areas of the curriculum despite having little working knowledge of the subject. As one female secondary supply teacher explained:

> I was teaching maths. I haven't even got an 'O' level in Maths. I was having to work out all the analysis and everything the night before and how to do it, and these kids knew, and they weren't nice kids. You

couldn't say to them – 'Look kids, this is not my area, so just do the best you can.'

This is a problem that obviously has serious implications for personal self-esteem, discipline and control over the class.

It would appear that the problem not only lies with having to teach in unfamiliar areas, but also being in a position where the teacher does not in fact teach his or her own subject at all. As one female secondary supply teacher said:

> I was covering in every subject. . . . I was an English teacher, that's what I do here, but in that school, and for the whole year I was on supply, I never taught one English lesson. I was teaching science, etc. And so I had to be one step ahead all of the time . . . the kids . . . they were trying to outwit you all of the time.

A further element resulting in stress is the problem of department heads having to cope with absent staff and other managerial issues, as one male head of department in a large inner-city secondary school explained:

> I come in the morning and the first stressful thing I've got to do is to cover all the absent staff, and that's a very unpopular thing. Obviously because I'm using up teachers' free time to allocate to absent teachers' work. So it throws everybody's plans. It's about the *most* unpopular job anyone on the management team can do.

Overall, this situation is worsened by the fact that the number of teachers in some schools is in decline (due to many leaving the profession and financial constraints), and many other potential teachers are deciding not to enter teaching as a career. One female main-scale primary teacher remarked:

> I get frustrated because there are not enough of us to give the attention to the children, to give them what they really need. We need more people, one person in a classroom nowadays is definitely not enough.

This problem is not helped by the fact that there is a delay before supply teachers can be brought into school. One female secondary teacher remarked that a solution to stress would be by 'Removing the 3 day waiting period before a supply can be brought in. I lose 3 out of 5 non-contact lessons per week, sometimes all.'

## Job insecurity

Teaching has always been viewed as a rather stable and secure profession, and yet this is not exactly the case at present. Even though certain education authorities are 'crying out' to employ teachers to cover shortages, there is still a threat to job security in terms of redeployment and job loss, in part due to the closure and amalgamation of many schools. One teacher commented factually of his experience at a sixth-form college:

' ... 24 staff have been redeployed this year from the sixth-form college which has put a great deal of stress on our staff for more than a year. Next year approximately 6 staff go, and the same the year after.'

Changes involving school closure have been another source of job insecurity, as one female secondary teacher remarked:

> An additional pressure has been the fact that my school is to close next year, to be replaced by a CTC. Campaigning against this decision has taken much time and energy – all to no avail. Whether it is the result of stress or not, I find myself becoming increasingly irritated especially at home and less able to relax and forget the demands of work.

## Ambiguity of the teacher's role

This factor consisted of six items. All of the other factors together can be seen to lead to situations where the teacher's role has become increasingly ambiguous. Many of the features previously described could also be seen to be describing ambiguity (i.e. changes in the profession, poor management) but at the time of the research there had been a number of specific events that had led to an increasing feeling of ambiguity in the teaching role, e.g. the introduction of the 'National Curriculum', as one teacher explained:

> National Curriculum training, and in particular regarding assessment of teachers and children, is placing great stress upon staff at my school. We have no clear picture as yet of what is expected in formal assessment and are proceeding, as usual, in teaching ourselves.

The teachers discussed at great length the problems of being in an ambiguous position, and, as can be seen in the quotes provided in the other factors, this ambiguity was present across all levels and school types.

## FACTOR ANALYSIS OF THE 'TYPE A' BORTNER SCALE

Chapter 3 explained in some depth the meaning of the concept and measure of Type A behaviour and provided a questionnaire (Bortner 1969) for self-analysis. This same questionnaire was used in the study of UK teachers, and Chapter 4 shows that teachers were displaying high levels of this particular behavioural disposition. In order to obtain a clearer picture of the potential problems associated with Type A and stress, further analysis was performed on the scale.

A factor analysis of the Bortner scale resulted in four meaningful factors utilising 12 of the original 15 questions from the original scale. These factors and their content can be seen in Table 6.2. The most extreme style of Type A behaviour is used as a label for each item and in some cases these are slightly shortened for convenience. Statistical analysis revealed

*Table 6.2* Factor analysis of the Bortner scale

---

*Factor 1: Time conscious behaviour**
Tries to do too many things at once
Always rushed
Impatient while waiting
Emphatic in speech, fast and forceful
Hard driving

*Factor 2: Ambitious/competitive behaviour**
Ambitious
Very competitive

*Factor 3: Efficient behaviour*
Never late
Eager to get things done
Fast (eating and walking)

*Factor 4: Emotionally suppressive behaviour*
Hides feelings
Few interests outside of work/home

---

*Note*: *Statistically reliable factors.

that only two of these subscales were statistically reliable (i.e. the subscales of 'Time conscious behaviour' and 'Ambitious/competitive behaviour'). This means that for this particular sample the other scales created by factor analysis were not statistically sound. Therefore, only these two will be used in the subsequent regression analyses and described in more detail in the following sections.

## Factor interpretation of the Type A (Bortner) scale factors

For the two reliable factors, the following sections will offer some form of interpretation of their meaning and relevance to teachers.

### Time conscious behaviour

This factor is concerned with the way teachers deal with actual events (i.e. whether or not they can take things one at a time; are they rushed when doing things; and can they wait patiently?). This also reveals something about the actual behavioural style of some teachers in terms of the way they talk (i.e. do they speak fast and do they find it difficult to be 'easy-going' about things?). This may be important to teachers in the teaching environment as those high on this factor may be prevented, by the structure of the school, from getting things done and so may suffer from stress in the form of frustration or anxiety or job dissatisfaction, and this may ultimately affect their intention to leave.

*Ambitious/competitive behaviour*

This factor measures whether or not the individuals are ambitious and competitive. This is particularly important when observing teachers in the school environment, as they may be high on this factor but may not be achieving the high status and promotion that this type of behavioural style requires. This may then lead to a number of manifestations of stress (e.g. frustration). Alternatively, a teacher low on this style of behaviour might survive more effectively if the school fails to provide career opportunities.

## FACTOR ANALYSIS OF THE OSI COPING SCALE

As explained in Chapter 4, the coping scale used in this study was the Occupational Stress Indicator (OSI) coping scale (Cooper *et al.*, 1988b). A factor analysis was performed on this scale to see if there was a 'better fit' in terms of the way these questions were categorised into particular themes for this sample of teachers.

The factor analysis reduced the number of variables in the OSI coping scale to eight meaningful, manageable and reliable factors (see Table 6.3). Only two of these were found to achieve sufficient statistical reliability, and therefore will be used in later more intricate statistical analyses (i.e. regression analyses) and these two factors will be interpreted ·in more detail.

### Factor interpretation of the coping scales

*Prioritise/objective coping*

One of the major problems facing teachers at the moment is the extent of change taking place within the profession. It would appear that the items in this factor are used as a way of dealing with school change, overload, Local Management of Schools (LMS), etc. Four of the items are about attempting to achieve efficient time management and making the most of the time available to complete all of these tasks, i.e. 'set priorities and deal with problems accordingly', 'use selective attention', 'effective time management' and 'plan ahead'. In addition, the objective nature of this type of coping strategy is emphasised in that it highlights the need to 'try to deal with the situation objectively in an unemotional way'.

*Hobbies and pastimes*

This factor reflects the need for teachers to take part in extra-work activities as a means of coping with the stressors related to their job. This seems to indicate that a popular coping strategy for the teachers is to have outside interests and make a conscious effort to separate home and work by using distractions in the form of hobbies and pastimes. Details from the

*Table 6.3*  Factor analysis of the OSI coping scale

---

*Factor 1: Prioritise/objective coping*
Set priorities and deal with problems accordingly
Use selective attention (concentrating on specific problems)
Try to 'stand aside' and think through the situation
Effective time management
Plan ahead
Try to deal with the situation objectively in an unemotional way

*Factor 2: Hobbies and pastimes*
Expand interests and activities outside work
Resort to hobbies and pastimes
Use distractions (to take your mind off things)
Deliberately separate 'home and work'

*Factor 3: Mobilised social support*
Talk to understanding friends
Seek as much social support as possible
Not 'bottling things up' and being able to release energy
Seek support and advice from superiors

*Factor 4: Time measures*
'Buy time' and stall the issue
Deal with problems immediately as they occur

*Factor 5: Innovation*
Reorganise my work
Look for ways to make the work more interesting

*Factor 6: Suppression of stress*
Having a home that is a refuge
Suppress emotions and try not to let the stress show
'Stay busy'

*Factor 7: Non-confrontive of the situation*
Try to recognise my own limitations
Try to avoid the situation
Accept the situation and learn to live with it

*Factor 8: Non-involvement and delegation*
Resort to rules and regulations
Delegation
Force one's behaviour and lifestyle to slow down

---

questionnaires, and observation of teachers at work in the school environment, revealed that it is very rare for teachers to find time to relax during the course of the school day. Most of their official break times are taken up with some form of work or supervision, reinforcing the need and importance of hobbies and 'out of work' distractions.

## COMPARING GROUPS OF TEACHERS WITHIN THE SAMPLE

As the items in the 'Sources of pressure' inventory were unique to teachers and designed specifically for this sample, normative and comparative data were not available. Therefore, we could only make internal comparisons by carrying out '*t*-tests' on the data, examining the significant differences between mean scores (e.g. for male teachers compared with female teachers). Of greater interest, however, was the examination of the variations in the experiences within the group. The causes of stress for various subgroups indicated that they varied in the levels of stress they experienced. However, enough similarities occurred to suggest that the teaching profession is a relatively homogeneous group with regard to *particular* stressors of the job, which suggests that implementation of stress management programmes, for the population as a whole, is a realistic possibility.

### Differences between male and female teachers

Female teachers are reporting greater pressures from 'management/ structure of the school', 'large classes and overcrowding', 'appraisal of teachers' and 'job insecurity' as compared to the male colleagues who report greater pressure from 'managerial concerns' (see Figure 6.1). These findings are related to promotional opportunities and status within teaching, as women do not achieve the same levels of status and are thus facing fewer of the associated pressures. In addition, they report higher pressure from 'appraisal', which may be a factor that increases the limitations and barriers to status acquisition and promotion.

### Differences between primary and secondary school teachers

When comparing the two main school types, a number of differences were discovered (see Figure 6.2). Analysis revealed that both male and female primary teachers experience higher pressure than their secondary school counterparts from 'class sizes/overcrowding' and 'appraisal of teachers'. Secondary teachers experience greater pressures from relationship-orientated factors – 'pupil behaviour' and 'management/structure of the school'. In addition, they tend to be more pressurised by features that are contemporary issues in teaching at present (i.e. the shortages in staffing levels and the need for cover).

### Differences between various teaching grades

The type and level of pressure experienced is related to the level of seniority acquired by the teacher, as senior managers suffer more than others from pressures associated with 'ambiguity of role', 'managerial concerns', 'changes taking place within the profession' and problems associated with 'class sizes/overcrowding' (see Figure 6.3). As may be expected, those dealing 'hands on' with pupils (i.e. the main-scale teachers) report greater pressure than other groups from the factor of 'pupil/teacher interaction', and suffer more from 'appraisal of teachers', management/structure of the school and job insecurity. Middle managers report higher levels of pressure from 'lack of status and promotion opportunities'.

### Differences between Type A and Type B individuals

Of particular interest to this study is the effect of behavioural style on reported pressure, as this is a group with a high proportion of Type A individuals in its midst (see Figure 6.4). Type A individuals report significantly more pressure than Type Bs from 9 of the 10 factors, and these especially tend to be concerning features of the job that may prevent them from exerting control over their working environment (i.e. pressures from 'management/structure of the school', 'lack of status and promotion' and 'ambiguity of role'). Type As are also more affected by the pressures resulting from 'managerial concerns'. These findings suggest that although Type As are those individuals who may seek a more stressful working environment, they are aware of these pressures and suffer more in the teaching environment.

### PREDICTING VULNERABILITY TO STRESS

In order to profile the teachers who are most vulnerable to pressure and to explore the more damaging sources of teacher stress, regression analyses were performed on the data. Regression analysis incorporates variables into the 'stress–strain' equation in respect of their level of significance (i.e. the greater the amount of strain predicted, the more powerful the stressor). In addition to examining the total sample of teachers, a number of subgroups were examined in further detail. This was because a number of differences in perceived pressure and stress responses had been discovered during the previous analysis in this chapter. The subgroups were as follows:

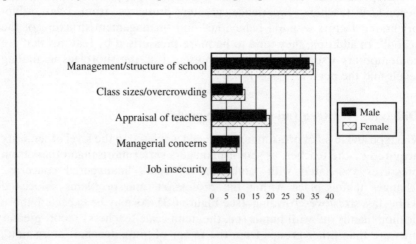

*Figure 6.1* Sources of job pressure: male and female differences

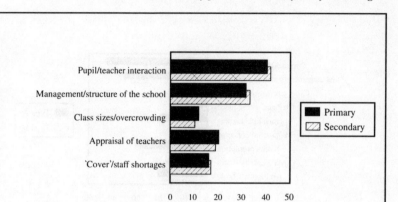

*Figure 6.2* Sources of job pressure: school type differences

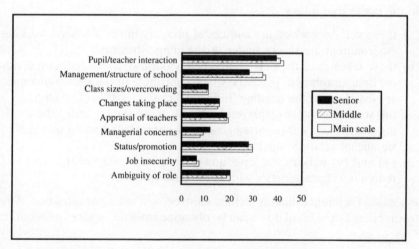

*Figure 6.3* Sources of job pressure: teaching grade differences

- male and female;
- primary versus secondary;
- teaching grade.

The variables used in the regression analyses were the 10 job pressure factors, two 'Type A' subfactors, two coping scale factors, and some teacher demographics (e.g. age, length of time in teaching career, length of time in current job, cover for absent colleague in previous week, and accepting class of absent colleague).

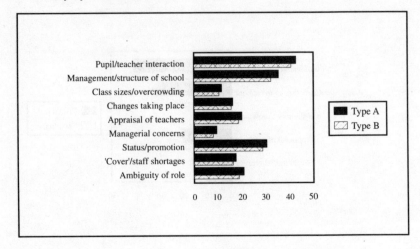

*Figure 6.4*  Sources of job pressure: Type A and Type B differences

**Understanding the regression tables**

In the tables that follow:

(a) those variables which are sources of pressure in the teachers' working environment are shown under the heading 'Stressors';

(b) those features of the personality, behavioural styles and other individual demographics of teachers, which contribute to the stress outcomes, are listed under the heading 'Individual characteristics of teachers';

(c) the stress outcomes displayed by teachers are shown under the heading 'Outcome' (self-reported absence is not included owing to a lack of significant relationships);

(d) (+) and (–) indicate the direction of the relationship of stressors and individual characteristics with stress outcomes.

For ease of reference, figures include all stress outcomes per subgroup. Any further details and breakdown can be obtained from the authors on request.

**Who are the vulnerable teachers?**

Table 6.4 shows the sources of stress outcomes in teachers.

*Mental ill health*

Seven stressors predict 31 per cent of the total mental health explained. Teachers at risk of poor levels of mental health are those displaying a high level of 'time conscious behaviour' and low levels of 'ambitious/competitive behaviour'. In addition, teachers who employ less 'prioritise/objective coping' styles are more prone to mental ill health, especially if they have

*Table 6.4* Who are the vulnerable teachers?

| Stressors | Individual characteristics of teachers | Outcome |
|---|---|---|
| Ambiguity of role (+) | Time conscious behaviour (+) | Mental ill health |
| Lack of status/ promotion (+) | Ambitious/competitive behaviour (–) | Job dissatisfaction |
| Appraisal of teachers (+) | Prioritise/objective coping (–) | Alcohol consumption |
| Number of times covered for absent colleagues in last week (+) | Length of time in teaching career (+) | Free-floating anxiety |
| Number of times accepted the class of an absent colleague (+) | Hobbies and pastimes (+) | Somatic anxiety |
| Management/structure of the school (+) | Age (+) | Depression |
| | Intrinsic job satisfaction (–)* | Intention to leave |
| | Mental ill health (+)* | |

*Notes: Italic* entries predict two or more stress outcomes.
  * Dependent variables linked to intention to leave.

been in the profession longer. Though the individual characteristics appear to make the teacher most vulnerable to mental ill health, there are also damaging stressors in the job itself. Teachers at risk are those suffering from higher levels of pressure from 'ambiguity of role', a 'lack of status/ promotion', and 'appraisal of teachers'. Overall, the mental ill health of teachers is linked to a combination of work pressures, coping mechanisms, behaviour and tenure factors.

## Free-floating anxiety

The causes of free-floating anxiety are very similar to those for mental ill health in teachers (i.e. teachers with high levels of 'time conscious behaviour', 'ambitious/competitive behaviour' and low levels of 'prioritise/ objective coping' experience poorer mental health). Twenty-seven per cent of the mental ill health experienced was explained by these factors, along with pressure from 'ambiguity of role' and 'appraisal of teachers'.

## Somatic anxiety

In attempting to explain somatic anxiety, only 18 per cent of the variance could be explained by individual differences and job stressors. This suggests that responsibility may lie with other factors that this study did not examine. However, the six causes of somatic anxiety are very similar to those predicting overall mental ill health, other than 'ambitious/competitive behaviour', which was excluded and replaced by age (i.e. the older the teachers, the more somatic symptoms they report). In addition, somatic symptoms are more likely to be displayed by those teachers who are more exposed to excessive 'cover for absent colleagues'. Pressure from 'appraisal of teachers' is also more likely to result in greater levels of somatic symptoms.

## Depression

In attempting to explain what causes depression in teachers we had more success, with 26 per cent of the amount of depression explained. Though similar again to the sources of mental ill health, there are some differences. Teachers vulnerable to depression are older, displaying 'time conscious' and 'ambitious/competitive' behaviour, and experiencing pressure from 'lack of status/promotion' and 'ambiguity of role'.

## Job dissatisfaction

Only two of the measured variables are predictors of job dissatisfaction in teachers, and these account for 40 per cent of the variation in job dissatisfaction levels. One source of job pressure, the 'management/structure of the school', is overwhelmingly the most important, followed by 'lack of status/promotion'. It is interesting, as this suggests that only *job* pressure factors are predictors, not demographic or personality variables. These two predictor variables are both related to the professional involvement, decision making, and status of the teacher within teaching. It is important to note that 'lack of status/promotion' is particularly a problem, as it can lead to *both* mental ill health and dissatisfaction.

## Alcohol consumption

Very little of the variance in teachers' alcohol consumption is accounted for by variables measured in our study. Regression analysis revealed that two variables were predictors, accounting for only 2 per cent of the variance. These were increased 'number of times accepting the class of an absent colleague', and the 'length of time' in teaching. It would seem that further investigation is necessary, but the fact that this measurable behavioural manifestation is more likely to be linked to more objective and quantifiable aspects of the teacher's job and working environment is an interesting finding.

## Intention to leave the profession

As it was believed that 'intention to leave' the profession was in fact an attitudinal measure of teacher turnover intentions, we aimed to predict its occurrence. Although 'intention to leave' is itself a dependent variable (i.e. a result of stress), past research has suggested a link between this withdrawal behaviour and other stress outcomes, and so it was believed relevant to include 'mental ill health' and 'job satisfaction' as predictors in the regression analysis. Only three variables predicted 'intention to leave', which accounted for 15 per cent of the variance. Teachers more likely to want to leave the profession are those suffering from higher levels of 'mental ill health', low 'intrinsic job satisfaction', and those who use 'hobbies and pastimes' as a way of coping with stress (i.e. employing interests outside of work).

## Who are the vulnerable female teachers?

### Mental ill health

Seven variables predict mental ill health in women, accounting for 33 per cent of the variance (see Table 6.5). Although similar variables as for the overall sample are involved, pressure from 'appraisal of teachers' is far more a concern for female teachers, than 'ambiguity of role'. Women teachers at risk of mental ill health are also those who are suffering pressure from 'managerial concerns'. Like the total sample, individual characteristics play an important role in the resulting mental ill health, that is, high levels of 'time conscious behaviour' and, interestingly, low levels of 'ambitious/competitive behaviour', although this latter behavioural aspect has less impact on women's mental ill health than that of men in this sample.

*Table 6.5* Who are the vulnerable female teachers?

| Stressors | Individual characteristics of teachers | Outcome |
|---|---|---|
| Appraisal of teachers (+) | Time conscious behaviour (+) | Mental ill health |
| Lack of status/ promotion (+) | Prioritise/objective coping (−) | Job dissatisfaction |
| Managerial concerns (+) | *Length of time in teaching career* (+) | Alcohol consumption |
| Management/structure of the school (+) | *Ambitious/competi ive behaviour* (−) | Intention to leave |
| Ambiguity of role (+) | *Hobbies and pastimes* (+) | |
| Job insecurity (−) | Depression (+)* | |
| Cover/staff shortages (+) | Overall Type A (+)* | |
| | Mental ill health (+)* | |
| | Extrinsic job satisfaction (−) | |

Notes: *Italic* entries predict two or more stress outcomes.
    * Dependent variables linked to intention to leave.

*Job dissatisfaction*

For women teachers there are a range of job stressors and personality factors. In addition to pressure from 'management structure of the school', and 'lack of status/promotion', two additional factors (though less powerful) contributed to job dissatisfaction, 'appraisal of teachers' and low levels of 'ambitious/competitive behaviour'. This is interesting, as low levels of this particular disposition also lead to high levels of mental ill health.

*Alcohol consumption*

Interestingly, differences were found with regard to alcohol consumption in male and female teachers, especially as more variance in female consumption was explained than for male teachers and the total sample. For women teachers, alcohol consumption is predicted by a combination of four variables accounting for 7 per cent of the variance. High levels of alcohol consumption is related to higher levels of coping (using 'hobbies and pastimes'), high levels of depression, low pressure from 'ambiguity of role' and high levels of overall Type A behaviour. The variance contribution was too small to enable us to draw any firm conclusions.

*Intention to leave*

Interestingly, gender differences were found with regard to 'intention to leave'. There are seven variables that predict intention to leave in female teachers, which accounts for 21 per cent of the variance. A female teacher is more likely to leave if she has high mental ill health, low extrinsic satisfaction (e.g. with pay) and has been in teaching for many years; she resorts to hobbies and pastimes as ways of coping, has lower 'job insecurity' pressures, has high pressure from 'lack of status/promotion' and is experiencing problems with 'cover and staff shortages'. This suggests that although the major predictors of mental ill health apply to both men and women, there are very different reasons for leaving, with more of these reasons being connected to the job itself, as far as women teachers are concerned. In addition, contrary to past findings, female teachers are more likely to consider leaving with *increased* tenure.

**Who are the vulnerable male teachers?**

*Mental ill health*

Six variables predict mental ill health in men, accounting for 33 per cent of the variance (see Table 6.6). The pressures related to mental ill health in male teachers almost mirrors that of the overall sample, with the exception of the omission of 'appraisal of teachers'. For men, lower levels of 'ambitious/competitive behaviour' has a strange influence. In addition, the behavioural style of 'time conscious behaviour', along with high levels of pressure from 'ambiguity of role', accounts for a greater contribution to mental ill health.

## Job dissatisfaction

The two predictors of satisfaction in male teachers were identical as for the overall sample and accounted for similar variances (i.e. 40 per cent).

## Alcohol consumption

Regression of alcohol consumption produced very poor predictors for males, as with the total sample. Only one health-related aspect of male teachers' lifestyles was linked to alcohol consumption and for only 1 per cent of the variance (i.e. the number of times they accepted the class of an absent colleague) related to workload and disruption of working day, suggesting that there are other variables, not measured by this study, that account for this behavioural manifestation (i.e. home stressors, social pressures, social desirability, etc.).

## Intention to leave

For male teachers, the findings with regard to predictors of 'intention to leave' almost mirrored that of the total group, with the two major predictors being high overall mental ill health and low intrinsic job satisfaction, accounting for 15 per cent of the variance.

*Table 6.6* Who are the vulnerable male teachers?

| Stressors | Individual characteristics of teachers | Outcome |
| --- | --- | --- |
| Ambiguity of role (+) | Time conscious behaviour (+) | Mental ill health |
| *Lack of status/ promotion* (+) | Ambitious/competitive behaviour (−) | Job dissatisfaction |
| Management/structure of the school (+) | Prioritise/objective coping (−) | Alcohol consumption |
| Number of times accepted the class of an absent colleague (+) | Length of time in teaching career (+) | Intention to leave |
| | Mental ill health (+)* | |
| | Intrinsic job satisfaction (−)* | |

*Notes*: *Italic* entries predict two or more stress outcomes.
    * Dependent variables linked to intention to leave.

**Who are the vulnerable primary teachers?**

As the majority of predictor variables of mental ill health are the same for both primary and secondary teachers and the total sample, only interesting and significant differences will be described.

*Mental ill health*

For primary teachers, a total of eight variables predict 32 per cent of mental ill health measured (see Table 6.7). The two factors of 'prioritise/ objective coping' and 'lack of status/promotion' were not of major significance for primary teachers. Additional variables related to increased pressure from 'appraisal of teachers' and use of 'hobbies and pastimes', 'length of time in teaching career', 'class sizes/overcrowding' and 'management/ structure of the school' were important for those teaching in primary schools. As with secondary teachers, the major predictors of poor mental health are high levels of 'time conscious behaviour' and pressure from 'ambiguity of role'.

*Job dissatisfaction*

Having discovered a difference in the levels of job satisfaction reported by primary and secondary school teachers, it was important to examine any

*Table 6.7* Who are the vulnerable primary teachers?

| Stressors | Individual characteristics of teachers | Outcome |
|---|---|---|
| Ambiguity of role (+) | Time conscious behaviour (+) | Mental ill health |
| Appraisal of teachers (+) | *Ambitious/competitive* | Job dissatisfaction |
| *Job insecurity* (−) | *behaviour* (−) | Alcohol consumption |
| Class sizes/ | *Hobbies and pastimes* (−/+) | Intention to leave |
| overcrowding (+) | Length of time in teaching | |
| *Management/structure of* | career (+) | |
| *the school* (+) | Teaching grade (heads = 1; | |
| Lack of status/ | main scale = 5) (−) | |
| promotion (+) | Mental ill health (+)* | |
| Teaching hours per | Extrinsic job satisfaction (−)* | |
| week (+) | | |
| *Number of times accepted* | | |
| *the class of an absent* | | |
| *colleague* (+) | | |
| Age of the pupils that you | | |
| teach (+) | | |

*Notes*: Italic entries predict two or more stress outcomes.
  \* = Dependent variables linked to intention to leave.

difference in stress factors for teachers in each type of school. Primary teachers' job satisfaction was predicted by four variables accounting for 47 per cent of the variance. The major cause was high pressure from 'management/structure of the school', with low levels of 'ambitious/competitive behaviour', high 'actual teaching hours per week' and high 'amount of class cover for absent colleagues'.

*Alcohol consumption*

Primary school teachers' alcohol consumption was predicted by four variables which accounted for 13 per cent of the variance. Primary teachers consuming high amounts of alcohol are those in higher teaching grades, who accept more classes for absent colleagues, teach older pupils, and are experiencing lower pressure from 'job insecurity'.

*Intention to leave*

As with the total sample and most other subgroups, overall mental ill health was the major predictor of 'intention to leave' for primary teachers. Other variables predictive of this stress outcome were similar to those for female teachers, which is not surprising as primary teachers are predominantly female. Primary teachers intending to leave are those who not only have a higher level of mental ill health, but have lower satisfaction with extrinsic aspects of the job (e.g. pay), make greater use of 'hobbies and pastimes' as a way of coping, have less pressure from 'job insecurity' and feel greater pressure from a 'lack of status/promotion'.

**Who are the vulnerable secondary teachers?**

*Mental ill health*

A total of six variables predict mental ill health (see Table 6.8) in secondary school teachers accounting for 30 per cent of the variance. As with all other subgroups and the total sample, 'time conscious behaviour' and 'ambiguity of role' are the major predictors. The additional four are the same as for the total sample, and those teachers with low levels of 'ambitious/competitive behaviour', low use of 'prioritise/objective coping', and high levels of pressure from 'lack of status/promotion' are older.

*Job dissatisfaction*

As with primary teachers and the total sample, the major predictor of low job satisfaction in secondary teachers is high pressure from 'management/ structure of the school'. However, that is where the similarity with primary teachers ends, with job-dissatisfied secondary teachers experiencing more pressure from 'lack of status/promotion' and 'appraisal of teachers', and having been in their current position for longer. Appraisal is interesting, because although excessive amounts of this kind of pressure are related to low job satisfaction when examined on its own, when considered with the other predictor variables it is actually a source of satisfaction.

## Alcohol consumption

Secondary teachers who are consuming higher levels of alcohol are those who use greater amounts of 'hobbies and pastimes' and less 'prioritise/ objective coping' strategies as methods of coping, are experiencing low pressure from pupil teacher interaction, are more likely to accept the class of an absent colleague, and have been in the teaching profession for a longer period.

## Intention to leave

There are two main predictors of intention to leave in secondary school teachers accounting for 15 per cent of the variable. These mirror those for male teachers – high levels of mental ill health and low levels of intrinsic job satisfaction.

## Who are the vulnerable senior teachers?

### Mental ill health

Three variables predict mental ill health in senior teachers (i.e. head-teachers and deputy headteachers), accounting for 32 per cent of the variance (see Table 6.9). Those experiencing poorer mental health are those who exhibit more 'time conscious behaviour', are experiencing high pressure from 'appraisal of teachers' and use lower amounts of 'ambitious/ competitive behaviour'.

### Job dissatisfaction

As with all other teacher types, the major source of job dissatisfaction in senior teachers is 'management/structure of the school' – the only really significant predictor for this group, accounting for 40 per cent of the variance. A separate regression analysis for heads and deputies revealed that there were no significant predictors for headteachers, though interpretation is difficult due to the sample size. However, it is interesting to note that deputies, when examined alone, had two relevant predictors, i.e. 'management/structure of the school' (43 per cent) and 'lack of status/ promotion', a further 5 per cent.

*Table 6.8*  Who are the vulnerable secondary teachers?

| Stressors | Individual characteristics of teachers | Outcome |
|---|---|---|
| Ambiguity of role (+) | Time conscious behaviour (+) | Mental ill health |
| Lack of status/ promotion (+) | Ambitious/competitive behaviour (–) | Job dissatisfaction |
| Management/structure of the school (+) | Prioritise/objective coping (–) | Alcohol consumption |
| Appraisal of teachers (+/–) | Age (+) | Intention to leave |
| Pupil/teacher interaction (–) | Length of time in current position (+) | |
| Number of times accepted class of an absent colleague (+) | Hobbies and pastimes (+) | |
| | Length of time in teaching career (+) | |
| | Mental ill health (+)* | |
| | Intrinsic job satisfaction (–)* | |

*Notes*: *Italic* entries predict two or more stress outcomes.
　* Dependent variables linked to intention to leave.

*Table 6.9*  Who are the vulnerable senior teachers?[†]

| Stressors | Individual characteristics of teachers | Outcome |
|---|---|---|
| Appraisal of teachers (+) | Time conscious behaviour (+) | Mental ill health |
| Management/structure of school (+) | Ambitious/competitive behaviour (–) | Job dissatisfaction |
| Lack of status/ promotion (+) | Mental ill health (+)* | Alcohol consumption |
| Number of times accepting class of an absent colleague (+) | | Intention to leave |

*Notes*: [†] Headteachers and deputy headteachers.
　* Dependent variables linked to intention to leave.

## Alcohol consumption

Only one variable predicted alcohol consumption in senior teachers (7 per cent) – the greater number of times they have accepted the class of an absent colleague.

## Intention to leave

Some interesting differences emerged with regard to differences in predictors of 'intention to leave' across the three teaching grades. The only common predictor, as with all other subgroups, was overall mental ill health, which was the only predictor of 'intention to leave' in senior teachers, accounting for 27 per cent of the variance.

## Who are the vulnerable middle managers?

### Mental ill health

The teachers who are middle managers at risk of poor mental ill health (see Table 6.10) are those who exhibit high levels of 'time conscious behaviour', have high pressure from 'ambiguity of role', 'appraisal of teachers', and 'lack of status/promotion', and make little use of 'prioritise/objective coping' methods.

### Job dissatisfaction

Those teaching in middle managerial positions are more likely to report job dissatisfaction if they are experiencing high pressure from 'management/ structure of the school', 'appraisal of teachers' and 'lack of status/promotion'. They are also more likely to have been many years in their current position. These variables account for 42 per cent of the variance.

### Alcohol consumption

Higher levels of alcohol consumption in middle managers was only significantly accounted for (1 per cent) by the longer time spent in teaching.

*Table 6.10* Who are the vulnerable middle managers?

| Stressors | Individual characteristics of teachers | Outcome |
|---|---|---|
| Ambiguity of role (+) | Time conscious behaviour (+) | Mental ill health |
| *Appraisal of teachers* (+) | Ambitious/competitive | Job dissatisfaction |
| *Lack of status/ promotion* (+) | behaviour (−) | Alcohol consumption |
| | Prioritise/objective coping (−) | Intention to leave |
| Management/structure of the school (+) | Length of time in current position (+) | |
| Number of hours spent working at home (+) | Length of time in teaching career (+) | |
| | Hobbies and pastimes (+) | |
| | Intrinsic job satisfaction (−)* | |
| | Mental ill health (+)* | |

*Notes*: Italic entries predict two or more stress outcomes.
  * Dependent variables linked to intention to leave.

*Intention to leave*

Those in middle management positions provide a rather different pattern compared to other teaching grades. Intrinsic job dissatisfaction is the major predictor, accounting for 9 per cent of the total variance. Mental ill health follows in importance as a cause of 'intention to leave', plus the greater use of 'hobbies and pastimes' as a way of coping. Also, the teachers who are at greater risk of leaving in this grade are those who spend more hours marking at home.

## Who are the vulnerable main-scale teachers?

*Mental ill health*

Those main-scale teachers at risk of poorer mental ill health (see Table 6.11) are experiencing similar stressors to their colleagues in middle management – that is, high 'time conscious' and low 'ambitious/competitive' behaviour, high pressure from 'ambiguity of role' and 'lack of status/promotion'. They make less use of 'prioritising/objective coping' methods, and also have been teaching for more years. These account for 29 per cent of the variance.

*Job dissatisfaction*

Main-scale teachers' job dissatisfaction had as its predictors similar variables to those of the total sample, in that high pressure from 'management/structure of the school' and 'lack of status/promotion' are of major importance, accounting for 40 per cent of the variance.

*Table 6.11* Who are the vulnerable main-scale teachers?

| Stressors | Individual characteristics of teachers | Outcome |
|---|---|---|
| Ambiguity of role (+) | Time conscious behaviour (+) | Mental ill health |
| Appraisal of teachers (−) | Ambitious/competitive | Job dissatisfaction |
| *Management/structure of the school* (+) | behaviour (−) | Alcohol consumption |
| | Prioritise/objective | Intention to leave |
| *Lack of status/ promotion* (+) | coping (−) | |
| | *Length of time in* | |
| Number of times accepting class of an absent colleague (+) | *teaching career* (+) | |
| | Mental ill health (+)* | |
| | Employee relations | |
| *Pupil/teacher interaction* (+) | satisfaction (−)* | |
| *Job insecurity* (−) | | |

*Notes*: Italic entries predict two or more stress outcomes.
     * Dependent variables linked to intention to leave.

*Alcohol consumption*

As with the other teaching grades, the ability of the study variables to predict high alcohol consumption in main-scale teachers is very poor. Three variables predict 7 per cent of their alcohol consumption – the more often they had 'accepted the class of an absent colleague', the lower their intrinsic job satisfaction, and the lower the pressure from 'appraisal of teachers'.

*Intention to leave*

Seven variables predict the 'intention to leave' of main-scale teachers, accounting for 20 per cent of the variance. As with other groups, mental ill health was the major predictor. In addition, main-scale teachers are more likely to leave if they are less satisfied with their fellow teachers, suffer increased pressure from 'lack of status/promotion' and 'pupil–teacher interaction' and have been teaching for more years.

## SUMMARY

The previous three chapters have presented the results of our study into teacher stress in the UK. In-depth statistical analysis, coupled with a high degree of commitment and openness from the teachers involved, means that we have been able to obtain some very helpful data which illuminate the stressors teachers face and their reactions to those problems. The following, and final, part of the book will bring together these findings in an attempt to make some recommendations for managing stress in teachers.

# Part III
# Recommendations

*Had I been present at the Creation, I would have given some useful hints*
*for the better ordering of the Universe.*

(Alfonso the Great)

# Part III
## Recommendations

# 7 What can be done about teacher stress?

The purpose of this final part and chapter of the book is to present recommendations for actions that may be taken by individual teachers, managers of schools and educational policy makers to reduce the negative stress manifestations highlighted by the study described in Part II. As the previous chapter summarised, teachers in the UK are generally experiencing low job satisfaction and poor mental well-being and are displaying a number of behavioural manifestations of stress (e.g. alcohol abuse and withdrawal behaviours). The costs of these outcomes are high for the teachers and the schools within which they teach, suggesting a need for intervention. This chapter will suggest ways of dealing with stress by:

- describing the ways in which stress management may be approached;
- briefly outlining the areas that are a cause for concern in the light of the results;
- providing recommendations for the alleviation of stress in teachers, drawing upon the concerns described in terms of strategies for (a) the teachers themselves, (b) managers of schools, and (c) the education sector generally.

## A MULTI-DIMENSIONAL APPROACH TO TEACHER STRESS ALLEVIATION

When deciding how to manage stress, two approaches may be taken: a *'preventative approach'* (i.e. aimed at preventing the stressor from inflicting pressure or strain by eliminating or neutralising its effect), and a *'curative'* approach, whereby stress is dissipated or relieved *after* it has been experienced. One has to decide the level at which the intervention is to take place: the individual level (e.g. relaxation techniques); the organisational level (e.g role issues, participation, person/environment fit); or the individual/ organisational interface (e.g. organisational structure, selection, placement, training, physical and environmental aspects of the job) (De Frank and Cooper 1987). Table 7.1 shows these three levels of intervention with examples of the possible outcomes that may result. Whichever level is

*Table 7.1* Levels of stress management and outcomes

| Interventions | Outcomes |
| --- | --- |
| *Focus on individual* | *Focus on individual* |
| Relaxation techniques | Mood states (anxiety, depression) |
| Cognitive coping strategies | Psychosomatic complaints |
| Biofeedback | Subjectively experienced stress |
| Meditation | Physiological parameters (blood |
| Exercise | pressure, catecholamines, muscle |
| Employee Assistance Programmes | tension) |
| (EAPs) | Sleep disturbances |
| Time management | Life satisfaction |
| *Focus on individual/* | *Focus on individual/* |
| *organisational interface* | *organisational interface* |
| Relationships at work | Job stress |
| Person–environment fit | Job satisfaction |
| Role issues | Burnout |
| Participation and autonomy | Productivity and performance |
| | Absenteeism |
| | Turnover |
| | Heath care utilisation and claims |
| *Focus on organisation* | *Focus on organisation* |
| Organisational structure | Productivity |
| Selection and placement | Turnover |
| Training | Absenteeism |
| Physical and environmental | Health care claims |
| characteristics of the job | Recruitment/retention success |
| Health concerns and resources | |
| Job rotation | |

*Source*: De Frank and Cooper (1987)

taken, there are important implications for the individual (e.g. improved satisfaction and mental well-being), the effects of the individual/organisational interface (e.g. improved attendance and less withdrawal) and the organisation (e.g. improved productivity).

Although opinions vary, there is a general belief, based on research, that if stress management techniques are to really work, then they have to focus on all three of the levels mentioned in Table 7.1. If stress management only focuses on the individual teacher, and expects teachers to inoculate themselves against stress by learning to cope with strain and pressure, many other problems may result in the future (Matteson and Ivancevich 1987). This is highlighted in the work by Sadri *et al.* (1989) who assessed the objectiveness of a counselling service implemented by the Post Office. Results revealed that, although such a counselling service had beneficial effects on levels of anxiety, depression and sickness absence rates, it did not improve the reported levels of job satisfaction or organisational commitment.

In addition, there are a number of types of intervention that may alleviate the stress in teachers that comes from an 'extra-organisational' perspective (i.e. features from outside the school environment that dictate its functioning). This is where teaching is different to many other jobs in that it is directly linked to governmental control. Although the school can be seen to be the 'organisation', we may also need to consider the education system as a whole as the larger organisation. When observing teachers it may be noted that they all talk and understand the same language with regard to their experiences at work. This is related to the fact that most of the problems they face at present are 'extra' rather than 'intra' organisational (i.e policies imposed from outside that affect the way in which they work). Therefore stress management also needs to consider the 'societal or environmental level' where the aim is to alter the environmental factors that influence teachers' working lives. Although it is not possible to have an effect on all of these (e.g. the financial climate), it is possible to influence the media and the societal image of teachers. Whatever suggestions are considered, it is important to be aware that an attempt at alleviating stress at the individual level will not always be effective if the actual problems (e.g. poor conditions and pay) do not alter – so an organisational perspective must be taken in parallel. When responding to the questionnaires used in our study, teachers expressed a desire that stress management should be made a major priority, and that greater awareness of a multi-dimensional approach to stress alleviation should be encouraged.

Taking responsibility for the education of the young within our society will always be a demanding task, and so it is likely that particular pressures and stressors in teaching will always be present. A point for optimism is the recent emphasis upon the need to intervene at the organisational level (Cox *et al.* 1989). Prior to this, the teaching profession has tended to see stress as primarily an individual problem, suggesting coping mechanisms for dealing with stress (i.e. that the individual needs to adapt and change). Consequently, very little attention has been paid to organisational strategies for decreasing the effect of potentially stressful situations. However, it is apparent from this study that many of the sources that lead to stress lie within the organisation.

**Stress among teachers: current causes for concern**

In the past teachers have been reluctant to voice their dissatisfaction with their working environments, but increasing unease has led to industrial action and an increase in the number of teachers leaving the profession. The study questionnaire invited teachers to provide their own suggestions for alleviating stress. These ideas will be incorporated in the following sections alongside theoretical and empirically tested suggestions for the improved management of stress. Teachers were very forthcoming with suggestions and, as can be seen in Table 7.2, the major recommendations are related to physical aspects of the job and the working environment. The table presents the suggestions in order of frequency of mention and concern – and we can see 'improved organisational support' as a major factor (e.g. increased resources, pay, training, smaller classes and physical working conditions). There are also comments with regard to the individual/organisational interface in terms of improved implementation of change, involving teachers in its pace, its extent and the decision-making process. Teachers make few recommendations with regard to interventions at the individual level, which may be seen to reflect a reluctance to attribute blame for the stress to themselves. They do mention, however, the need for stress management programmes (i.e. a counselling service, and stress-breaks in the form of sabbatical leave). This is still talking about a curative approach to problems that have already occurred, rather than ways of making individuals develop a better approach to their surroundings and its stressors.

Therefore, the current piece of research revealed a number of interesting findings that have led to the following conclusions concerning the management of stress.

## STRESS MANAGEMENT AT THE LEVEL OF THE INDIVIDUAL TEACHER

### What can teachers do for themselves?

It has become apparent, while studying teachers and their experience of stress, that the 'individual' facet is of crucial importance. As mentioned previously, teachers rarely consider that they have been responsible for the stress they face, but some are aware that they need to become actively involved in their *own* stress management. One teacher reported:

> During my career, I have been treated once for tension. Since then I have had very high blood pressure due to work and was advised to either change my attitude to work or pack it in – I hope that I have done the former.
>
> (Female secondary teacher)

This book does not want to be limited to the methods of intervention at the individual level, as much literature is available on this type of approach (e.g. Gray and Freeman 1988); the book is rather aimed at all of those involved in the education arena. However, the authors have had a great deal of experience in running stress management workshops and advising on stress management interventions, and believe strongly that there are many things that individual teachers can do for themselves to manage their stress. To ensure that teachers do not feel that this is an acceptance of blame, schools can help teachers to recognise and identify the sources and results of occupational stress by introducing 'whole school' policies of providing educational and counselling support (i.e. 'caring cultures'), and

*Table 7.2* Stress management interventions recommended by teachers

---

- Increased implementation of change
  - fewer initiatives
  - increased information and communication
  - clearer guidelines
  - more teacher involvement in policy making and decision making
- Improved promotion prospects
- Improved professional image
- Increase in organisational support
  - staff
  - resources
  - money
  - time
- Increased pay/allocation of incentive allowances
- Smaller classes
  - reduction in teacher/student ratio
- Less contact time
- Improved training
  - teacher training
  - managerial skills training
  - retraining
- Overall better working conditions
  - quiet rooms to study
  - improved staffrooms
- Stress management
  - stress management workshops
  - sabbatical leave
  - confidential and professional counselling service
- Improved policy on cover/supply
- Decrease in administrative duties/greater secretarial help
- Miscellaneous
  - improved discipline policy, creche facility, proper INSET provision.

---

by providing clear guidelines outlining the harmful effects of stress. Since this particular piece of research was started, and the preliminary results published, many publications have been provided to this end. However, the emphasis needs to be placed on the ability of the individual to control his or her own reactions to stress. It is not unusual for individuals on the receiving end of stress management to adopt the attitude that this approach is introduced as a method of control to keep them quiet, while ignoring the problems that exist in their working environment. Teachers are probably not exempt from this type of attitude. An element of 're-education' needs to take place, but this also emphasises the importance of introducing stress management programmes (SMP) at all levels.

Matteson and Ivancevich (1987) and Romano (1988) have reviewed the major individual stress management techniques, and these may be relevant to teachers.

1  *Exercise*. This may be seen as the contemporary alternative to the 'fight or flight' response to the stressful situation. De Vries (1981; cited in Matteson and Ivancevich 1987) has concluded that significant tranquillising effects can be produced by moderate rhythmic exercise of 5 to 30 minutes' duration, and that anxiety levels may be reduced by routine vigorous exercise. As anxiety is a problem in teachers, this would seem to be a viable method of stress release.

2  *Relaxation training*. This involves a number of methods that teachers could apply both during the school day and at home: breathing exercises, muscle relaxation, meditation, autogenic training (muscle relaxation and meditation) and mental relaxation strategies. The benefits would seem to be reduced levels of anxiety, alcohol consumption and perceived stress, which are all problems experienced by teachers.

3  *Biofeedback*. This involves the voluntary control of bodily functions: brain waves, heart rate, muscle tension, stomach acidity and blood pressure. Its benefits include reduced anxiety, tension, migraine, headaches, stress-related hypertension and also modification of Type A behaviour. Therefore, this may prove useful for teachers as they display many of these behaviours and symptoms of stress.

4  *Cognitive techniques*. The aim is to allow and encourage individuals to reappraise or restructure the stressful situations so that they are no longer stressful – by removing cognitive distortion such as over-generalising, magnifying and personalisation, and introducing assertiveness training. The benefits are that ultimate control may be handed over to the individuals to enable them to control their reactions to stressors. The ultimate benefits reduce particular aspects of Type A behaviour, therefore relevant to this sample, and also reduce blood pressure. In addition this may help teachers to develop mental control over their situations, so reducing ambiguity, etc.

A number of these methods could be acquired by teachers through expert counselling and training, thus learning to alleviate their own stress. The important thing is that as these methods may be carried out with ease and with little disruption to lifestyle, they will not become secondary stressors.

## Managing stress with physical activity

One of the most disturbing findings from this study of teacher stress is that too many teachers are suffering from excessive levels of anxiety and other symptoms of mental ill health. They are also turning to alcohol for stress release, and are suffering from a number of stress-related illnesses. One particular approach to stress management which may develop to alleviate all of these symptoms is the use of physical activity (e.g. aerobic exercise).

The rationale for this is that, if we go back to the 'fight or flight model' in Chapter 1, we can see that physical activity is the natural final phase in the stress response. After preparation for 'fight or flight', after the exposure to stress, we deal with the threat by some form of physical activity. In our working lives, many of the usual innate responses (e.g. attack or run away) are not appropriate and so we may fail to adapt and so build up the potential response (e.g. in the form of hormones etc.). Though the links are not always clear, it is believed that this over-arousal of the sympathetic nervous system and changes in hormonal functioning and/or immune responses, are potential causes in the onset of disease (Hinkle 1987). These responses to stress have been found to be linked, among others, to coronary heart disease (Theorell 1986), peptic and duodenal ulcers (Gilligan *et al.* 1987), cancer (Cooper *et al.* 1986) and mental ill health (Miner and Brewer 1976).

Exercise is therefore beneficial, as it naturally dissipates hormones, glucose, and lipids which would usually be released in the stress response. This is because exercise itself is a stressor – it results in changes in blood flow, oxygen consumption, blood pressure, heart rate, breathing rate and metabolic rate. However, it reduces psychological stress in that it acts as a mental diversion – a release for emotions or physical tensions – and is therefore a 'displacement defence mechanism', a cut-off point to distinguish between work-worrying and home relaxation. It would appear that for this reason it would be particularly beneficial for teachers.

In order to decrease the level of physiological arousal that normally occurs in response to a stress or threat, long-term aerobic exercise may be beneficial as regular exercise develops the same systems that are activated during exposure to stress. Physically fit individuals tend to exhibit lower activation/arousal levels in response to a stress (i.e. less muscular activity, lower resting heart rate, less accumulation of the acid by-products of exercise) than unfit individuals (Ledwidge 1980). The increased hormonal response capacity is associated with a more stress-tolerant and calm temperament – and exercise can extend the capacity of some hormones. It can also help the body to achieve the proper chemical balance needed to respond effectively to stress. However, training that is too intensive may increase susceptibility to illness due to excessive production of chemicals (e.g. cortisol) (Fitzgerald 1988).

Systematic exercise may improve mental function by increasing blood circulation to the brain, which enhances the availability of glucose and ultimately improves oxygen transportation (Ismail and Trachtman 1973) and with exercise certain brain peptides (e.g. endorphines) are released and so some positive psychological benefits may be accrued (e.g. increased calmness and happy state, alleviated symptoms of depression, and a tranquillising effect of moderate rhythmic exercise) (e.g. De Vries 1981). Reduced electrical activity to the muscles during or after exercise may lead to a relaxed state or a reduced anxiety state (De Vries 1968). On a more psychological note, during exercise, personal reflection may take place especially throughout exercise that is repetitive in nature, e.g. similar to a meditative stance.

It is worth noting that correlations between increased fitness and psychological benefits cannot always be seen. Mood changes may be caused by improvements in self-efficacy and mastery with exercise, and the achievement of moderate targets or goals has a positive effect on self-esteem and possibly self-image. In addition, activity *per se* may change one's lifestyle patterns and so buffer the effects of stress (e.g. social support, less bad behaviour, and the presence of significant others). Teachers, therefore, would do well to take part in some form of physical activity in an attempt to manage stress for all the positive reasons noted above.

## Modifying Type A behaviour

Our research has discovered that teachers have a tendency to exhibit Type A behaviour, which has implications for the experience of stress. There needs to be a greater awareness of how to modify the behaviours that are associated with Type A, and those that have been shown to be detrimental to teachers in this study.

Many researchers have conducted studies into the modification of Type A behaviour. It may be that it is rather premature to attempt to modify Type A when there is not yet full agreement among researchers as to what it is, or indeed how to measure it. However, a number of the recommendations that will be put forward here will reflect those mentioned in the previous section. A number of studies testing the feasibility of modifying Type A have been completed (e.g. the Recurrent Coronary Prevention Project (RCPP)) (Friedman *et al.* 1986). The methods that these studies have employed will not be considered here, but rather a number of pointers will be made which provide ideas of how to modify Type A behaviour. If it is the case that teachers as a group exhibit high levels of Type A behaviour, then they are at risk. A recommendation is that, as part of the stress management workshops provided in schools (or indeed 'off their own bat'), teachers are given a measure of Type A to self-administer, and are then provided with suggestions with which to modify that behaviour. It is important, however, that when administering the test, teachers are made aware of the differing features that have been identified within Type A, so that they can be attacked specifically (e.g. time conscious behaviour). Price (1988) describes four specific treatment approaches that can be considered: (1) reducing hostility, (2) increasing relaxation, (3) improving physical exercise, and (4) reducing the psychomotor characteristics of Type A. These can all be seen to be relevant to teachers and be realistic possibilities for action.

## Reducing hostility

This treatment approach is based upon the idea that the particular component of Type A that has the most toxic effect is that of hostility (e.g. Mathews and Haynes 1986), suggesting that methods should be developed that measure this characteristic. It has been suggested that hostility occurs when individuals are exposed to time pressures, when in competitive situations, when their self-esteem is threatened, etc. As these would seem to be features that are relevant to teachers, they should be considered – stress management needs to train teachers to cope with such pressures so that hostility may be reduced, or indeed prevented (i.e. lifestyle modification).

## Increasing the relaxation response

Systematic relaxation training (Bernstein and Borkovec 1973) should be used with Type A individuals: (1) because their hard-driving behaviour makes it difficult for them to relax and (2) they seem to be constantly 'mobilised as if their well-being were constantly threatened, resulting in chronic sympathetic nervous system arousal' (Price 1988). Progressive muscle relaxation has been shown to reduce factors associated with sympathetic arousal such as accelerated heart rate and elevated blood pressure (e.g. Johnston 1985). The problem with relaxation is that it has not been found to have major effects on the reduction of Type A behaviour (e.g. Jenni and Wollersheim 1979) and yet it may have more to do with the fact that few people ever practise it consistently to feel the benefit (Price 1988). Therefore, it could be encouraged, but teachers need to be aware that they have to make this an everyday feature. This could prove to be beneficial to teachers as they have been found to exhibit stress-related physiological outcomes in other research by the authors (Travers and Cooper 1994).

## Increasing physical exercise

A systematic exercise programme may benefit Type A teachers, in conjunction with the lifestyle modification programme. This is helpful in relation to coronary risk as it has been found to reduce heart rate, blood pressure, and high (though not low) scores on the Jenkins activity scale (Blumenthal *et al.* 1980). This is relevant because Type A individuals seldom take part in regular exercise, although it may have a calming effect. This study did not ask respondents to indicate whether or not they took regular exercise, but it is suggested that this could be implemented into stress management workshops alongside the Type A profile examination.

## Modifying behavioural indicators that predict high risk

Certain studies have highlighted a number of behavioural indicators of coronary risk that are characteristic of Type A (e.g. the number of self-references (e.g. Scherwitz *et al.* 1986). Therefore one alternative approach is to teach Type A teachers to modulate these characteristics (e.g. reduce the speed with which they speak and reduce self-references, etc.). Some might argue that this is removing the symptom and not the underlying behaviours, but it is worth considering.

*Suggested solutions*

A major problem with these approaches to modifying Type A behaviour is the fact that it may not be beneficial to teach Type A teachers to stop doing particular behaviours, if their overall life strategy stays the same. For example, teachers who learn how to slow their pace of life and relax in the lunch hour may suffer more if they accept the same number of commitments, but subsequently do not manage to finish them. Therefore it may be important to change the Type A 'cognitions'. If Type A individuals have their 'cognitive/emotional' make-up changed, then they have a better chance of maintaining and practising their new-found styles of behaviour. The study revealed that teachers often perceive that they have few prospects outside of teaching (e.g. they believe they are occupationally immobile and cannot meet the requirements of the new curriculum and fear appraisal). Price (1988) argues that although Type A individuals often attempt to project a social image of self-confidence, they have the self-belief that 'I am not good enough yet' and that the only way to succeed is to try harder and do more. What is suggested is that these possible cognitions are investigated in teachers and attempts should be made to reduce them through more positive thinking and feedback groups. Teachers report that, in teaching at present, feedback for good work is not forthcoming and this may be exacerbating these Type A cognitions of self-doubt.

**Time management techniques**

> Just at this moment somehow or other, they began to run . . . the Queen kept crying 'Faster!' but Alice felt she could not go faster, though she had no breath to say so. . . . The most curious part of the thing was, that the trees and the other things round them never changed places at all; however fast they went, they never seemed to pass anything . . . they went so fast that at last they seemed to skim through the air, hardly touching the ground with their feet, till suddenly . . . they stopped.
>
> Alice looked round her in great surprise. 'Why, I do believe we've been under this tree all the time! Everything's just as it was!'
>
> 'Of course it is', said the Queen . . . 'here, you see, it takes all the running you can do, to keep in the same place. If you want to get somewhere else, you must run twice as fast as that.'
>
> (Lewis Carroll, *Through the Looking Glass*)

It would appear that one of the most overwhelming characteristics of this sample is the role of 'time conscious behaviour' in the outcome of mental ill health. It may therefore be beneficial for teachers to be encouraged to improve their time management skills both in and out of work, as they seem to allow teaching to encroach into their home life:

> Many of us feel strong desires to take part in recreational and other interests outside the home, increasingly school is taking over a vast amount of our lives and WE ARE UNABLE TO – strong cause of stress may be that many of us have noticed our social life (entertaining, etc.) has dropped off dramatically over the past three years.
>
> (Female secondary teacher)

Time management has been found to be positively related to most stress outcomes and should include the recognition of 'time robbers' both in and out of work (Mulligan 1989). There are many potential benefits of time management techniques, for example:

- increased efficiency and effectiveness;
- higher productivity;
- increased leisure time (working more effectively means that teachers may be able to make more time for themselves);
- enhanced job satisfaction;
- reduced stress;
- more opportunity to switch off after hours (teachers completing more of their workload during the day makes it easier for them to relax at night);
- more room for forward planning and for long-term solutions (teachers who are not struggling to keep up with themselves have space in which to look ahead);
- higher creativity (creativity flourishes best if one can free time to sit and think).

Teachers need to be able to identify priority areas in their lives and therefore plan time accordingly. As one teacher advises:

> Do not let yourself be pressurised into attending weekend courses, etc., which are *not* directed time, do only one INSET course per term. When asked to do a particular (extra) job say to your superior 'yes I'll do it, if you give me the time'. Avoid Saturday work if possible, ... make sure at least 20 minutes in the lunch hour is FREE – pamper yourself. Never work right through.
>
> (Female secondary teacher)

If teachers examine their current time management problems, it will help them put into perspective the way pressure affects them and help them to manage it effectively. Particularly in the light of the high levels of Type A in teaching, it is very important for them to recognise and accept the role that their own personality may have on their attitudes towards time in general.

Throughout observations, interviews and analysis it became clear that a major problem for teachers is that they rarely have 'breathing space' during the school day and therefore lack time to replenish their energies. Time allocated to them, i.e. lunch and break times, are rarely uninterrupted. The inability to eat in comfort and to relax is inevitably going to be detrimental to the individual and needs to be investigated. One teacher remarked:

> I don't get a minute's break during the course of the school day. Today was a typical lunch time, when I've got all the kids back into school, I run upstairs, grab a cup of coffee and, if I'm lucky, get about 2 or 3 minutes to drink the cup of coffee and sit down.
>
> (Male head of department, inner-city secondary school)

It is suggested that teachers within schools should make an attempt to return to the staffroom for a short period after school has finished, to chat about problems that may have occurred during the day. This may help to provide an element of breathing space, an attempt to reduce tension to prevent them from taking their problems home. Judging by problems that teachers face, and the contribution those problems make to the experience of stress, the previously mentioned methods of alleviating stress should prove popular and beneficial.

## STRESS MANAGEMENT AT THE SCHOOL LEVEL

This section aims to preset some ideas for managing stress by those who manage the schools in which teachers teach.

### Counselling and curative strategies

One of the major points to come out of this study is that the profession needs the introduction of a counselling service to enable staff to become involved in attempts to reduce the high levels of mental ill health that are prevalent in teachers.

A large proportion of the suggestions made by teachers involved the implementation of some form of counselling service both within and outside schools. One teacher stated the need for:

> First rate professional counselling from inspectorate with the right kind of background to earn my respect.
>
> (Female secondary teacher)

In addition to such a service, staff support groups were considered a real possibility. Teachers tend to turn to fellow colleagues when suffering from stress, and this could be expanded upon by the encouragement of the 'formalisation' of such groups and networks. These are procedures that may be implemented rather rapidly in schools.

The above comments lead to the conclusion that stress management workshops and counselling should be compulsory features in the education service so that a proper understanding of the problems, from both individual and organisational levels, may be acquired, and ways of attacking these problems discovered.

Perhaps the best way to solve stress, from the organisational level, is by a problem-solving approach, whereby two main stages can be identified.

1 *Diagnosis*. This involves identifying the sources of stress in the particular working environment, so that adequate interventions can be planned and directed as effectively as possible. This study has highlighted that stress levels and types may be dependent upon the type of school, and so further research needs to examine the possibility of a teacher stress questionnaire that is standardised and may be used as a diagnostic tool, easily administered, at the individual or school levels.

2 *Intervention*. Once the sources of stress have been identified, planned intervention needs to take place. The picture that has been presented concerning teacher stress is very complex. Many sources and reactions to stress have been identified, but it is clear that many stress-inducing influences have gone undetected. However, in the light of the findings, a number of areas that merit further attention will be discussed (i.e. the management of change, improved management, increased organisational support (e.g. resources), improved training).

## Improved organisational support

Findings from the study suggest that problems are emerging from the poor provision of resources in a large number of Britain's schools. Organisational support in schools needs to be increased in terms of staffing levels, resources and time. This is a problem with change in that often teachers are not provided with the resources to meet the new requirements. The issue of lack of resources is a difficult one to address as it is dependent upon many other factors (i.e. governmental budget) and so from a psychological intervention perspective it is rather out of bounds. However, it is a feature of the working environment with which teachers are experiencing problems, and as this will have important psychological and behavioural implications, it cannot be ignored. Teachers believe that they are being prevented from doing a good job and having their workload increased due to the lack of resources in the schools. This suggests that more money, resources and staff are needed as one male secondary teacher requested 'more department money for equipment, materials, etc., for pupils and for me. You end up being out of pocket. It makes me angry.' It would appear that in many departments, particularly in the arts, teachers often have to buy basic materials themselves in order to teach the children the requirements of the curriculum. Teachers would also like more 'support staff' in the classroom as class sizes are very large, and also secretarial support to help with excessive administrative duties required from assessments and profiles. This would help clarify the role of the teacher, as presently they believe that they are largely administrators.

Another important factor is increased availability of time to get prepared in school, as teachers are most often forced to take work home with them. One female secondary teacher made the suggestion of 'a week in school with no pupils to provide time to organise departments/materials/ order stock/read newly published materials and to catch up on changes in exams/assessments/national curriculum, etc.'

This lack of resources is indeed an element in the reduction of job satisfaction, as one female secondary teacher explained that 'most teachers want to teach well, but with too little money . . . and lack of space/equipment, job satisfaction is at an all time low'.

The lack of administrative staff is particularly a problem for teachers in senior management. As one female primary headteacher explained: 'Limited secretarial help is a major problem in primary schools. I have to do much of the admin myself.' And one teacher said he was aware that: 'all this naturally requires greater financial commitment on the part of the central and local government, but as someone once said "If you think education is cheap, try ignorance".'

Therefore it would seem that there definitely needs to be a greater influx of resources if the teachers are expected to carry out their job effectively. Three of these issues in particular will be addressed: resources, staffing levels and working conditions.

### Resources

The teachers expressed the need for both quantitative and qualitative improvements in terms of resources (i.e. they need *more* resources and they need *better* resources). Teachers claim that spending on education has decreased, whereas the government suggests otherwise; whatever the case, this is a feature that not only causes problems for the teachers and the pupils, but is also given as a reason for teachers wanting to leave the profession. In addition to an increase in resources, teachers need to be helped to use these resources to the best effect (i.e. by retraining, etc.), and we shall discuss that issue in subsequent sections.

### Staffing levels

The problem of staff shortages was identified as a serious source of stress by most of the respondents, more specifically as resulting from the need to cover for staff and the lack of administrative support. Often reports in the media and from government have questioned the standard of teaching provided; if there are doubts (and these are a reality), it may be a result of the lack of *quantity* of staff available in schools, rather than the *quality* of teachers already in teaching positions. Decisions about the optimum number of staff needed in schools are questionable; this is a complicated matter and has to take into account not only the available quality of staff but also the requirements of the pupils.

Though the study highlighted potential 'black spots' where added staff are needed (i.e. administrative staff, in class support), it is not just a question of inadequate numbers. The workload facing teachers, though not necessarily unpredictable, may be cyclic (e.g. end of term examinations). It is the case that there are specific and stressful times during the school year when extra staffing levels would be particularly beneficial. This suggests that some form of 'quantification of demands' needs to be developed. Supply teachers are available, but teachers complain of the policies that prevent the use of supply teachers until a current teacher has been absent for three days. A further problem arises from recruitment: as the popularity of teaching as a profession has waned, so too has its attraction for young graduates entering the job market. This will be discussed further in sections on promotional improvements.

Another area for consideration is the provision of better supportive services within schools, so that teachers can devote their energy.towards the professional task of teaching. Teachers are trained to be educators and yet a vast proportion of their day is spent performing mundane administrative tasks, or acting the role of custodian and remediator. This does not make sense economically or professionally. If teachers are a scarce resource, they should be fully utilised without being wasted on jobs that clerical staff could perform. These administrative duties have become much heavier with the increased need for assessments of pupils. Teachers need to be able to argue this latter point in their defence, by explaining to the local managers of schools that, as a matter of 'financial logic', they should have access to and be provided with better supportive services.

*Working conditions*

Included in lack of organisational support is the issue of poor working conditions. Teachers describe poor working conditions as being a source of stress and dissatisfaction, both in terms of the actual state of Britain's schools and the rigid bureaucracies in which some teachers work. Many teachers have the experience of teaching at 'split site' schools, where travel is limited and time pressure becomes a problem. It is also linked to the problem of 'lack of status' in that teachers often find themselves in schools with far from desirable staff facilities (e.g. no clean staffrooms, no quiet rooms in which to work and relax).

Teachers experience an intensive work situation and there is a need for constant attention to be given to the pupils. Teachers rarely obtain a clear 'break' during the school day (i.e. free time to themselves), and there are very few areas of retreat during these breaks. Most schools should therefore attempt to provide a rest area convenient to the work situation, but far enough away to be free from interruption. Teachers need to be able to 'switch off'; it is not enough to 'switch off' only after school hours. The cost benefits of this are that for a smaller influx of funds, working conditions could improve and stress and job dissatisfaction reduced, therefore improving the teachers' performance and reducing turnover. This feature of 'relaxation rooms' is also very important for teachers if the findings concerning Type A personalities and the intervention and treatment of Type A are considered.

**Less contact time and administrative duties**

The second part of the study found that many teachers are exhibiting signs of fatigue, and this needs to be addressed as it has serious implications for motivation, performance and the onset of illness. One of the ways in which this could be alleviated is the improved allocation of time throughout the school day for breaks and meals. It is clear that this is often a problem due to the very 'caretaking nature' of the job, and the staff shortages that are apparent, but it is crucial that something be done about this problem, e.g. as one teacher explained: 'More spare time during the day for personal admin tasks, i.e. guaranteed non-contact time including casual enquiries from pupils.' This is especially important, as extra demands have been placed upon the teachers that force them to either work at home, or allow the work to build up undone, resulting in even more stress. This is especially the case in the primary sector, as one teacher explained to us:

> Current feeling of pressure focused on one main area – how to find time to prepare adequately and maintain 'class file' preparing for the National Curriculum. The relentless need to have everything down on paper in a blow by blow account when I naturally function better on an ad hoc basis within a broad framework of planning. I need a secretary!

**Re-imposition of sanctions for basic behavioural problems**

There is a need for stronger measures in dealing with disruptive pupils. As one teacher said:

> There must be ways to remove the constantly disruptive pupils. We cannot be expected to deliver the goods and be zoo keepers at the same time and then be criticised for failing to reach the highest standards.

Teachers believe that what is needed is a truthful acceptance of the high rates of disruption in state-aided schools and realisation that there is a lack of outside support service.

**Improved management of schools**

The management of schools needs to be improved as poor management is resulting in very low levels of job satisfaction among teachers. This is a problem for the teachers who are being managed and for those teachers who are attempting to manage with little or no experience. Therefore, steps need to be taken to ensure that the management and structure of Britain's schools are improved. Torrington and Weightman (1989) discuss the issue of management in schools, and the results of a study undertaken by them revealed that:

1 staff in schools are a resource that is generally taken for granted and under-utilised to an extent that is unusual in employing organisations;
2 although schools are effective at creating a culture for people to work together, that is in danger of being eroded as more 'managerial' approaches are introduced. These approaches are often based on an inadequate understanding of management practice in other organisations and an oversimplified view of the similarity between running a school and running a business;
3 there are three different approaches to school organisation and management that appear to enhance school effectiveness: collegial, leadership and prescription. Each is appropriate to a different situation, but conventional wisdom in education is that leadership is the 'right' approach.

Inherent in their findings is the unmistakable power with which headteachers tend to run schools to the point where they remark:

We have been baffled by the universal, unshakeable conviction among everyone we have spoken to about the power of the head teacher, who has organizational dominance to a degree almost unknown in our experience of studying management in a wide range of other undertakings. ... Although appropriate for some circumstances, we find this severely limited for most of the situations which schools now face, and all too often teachers themselves ... perpetuate this dangerous dependence on one person.

(Torrington and Weightman 1989)

The above comments suggest that there is a need for change within the structure of the schools, alongside changes in ideals so that they may adapt to the changing environment in which they find themselves. Therefore, not only do headteachers need better training to deal with their added responsibilities, but so too do other members of the school so that they may adjust to their changing roles.

## STRESS MANAGEMENT FOR TEACHERS AT A MORE GENERAL LEVEL

### Improved training both prior to and during career

A concern of teachers, related to poor management, is the problem of training. They do not feel that there is sufficient training for headteachers and also they do not always feel adequately trained to do the job.

The issue of stress management could be introduced as a continuous assessment approach to management and/or self-development. What is necessary in teacher training is not just training to *do* the job, but training to *stay* in the job or *be* in the job without detriment to the individual.

This study emphasised that management is often a source of stress and dissatisfaction. Improved communication and social support from the headteacher can improve job satisfaction and decrease possible stress effects. Many heads on the large scale study expressed a problem with 'man–management' skills, so some heads may benefit from some managerial skills training. In addition, heads have expressed problems with adjusting to the role of financial managers, so training on the financial aspects of their job could be included.

The types of training that teachers are suggesting are, for example: stress awareness; managerial skills for headteachers (i.e. financial training); a national standard; specific role training and retraining where necessary.

> Prepare students properly for the realities of the profession. This is certain to induce an even greater shortfall in the numbers of teachers and precipitate a more rapid response and appropriate response from H.M. government.

Teachers also expressed concerns over the view that they are expected to be experts in their own particular subject area, but that with the changes in modern technology, for example, they often feel out of touch with what is going on.

> We are expected to be experts, innovative, well trained in too many fields – the conscientious teacher is unable to cope with the sheer volume of material to remain equipped to deal with the changing nature of the job. Some form of frequent sabbatical release could enable staff to update without being made to feel 'guilty' either by leaving classes during INSET or by taking 'unfair' amounts of 'time off' at the expense of other colleagues. Perhaps 5 years on, 1 year off.

The introduction of INSET is seen by teachers as a waste of time as it often fails to address the issues that are in greater need of action and discussion, and so could be made better use of.

> INSET – heed should be paid to teachers' real needs, expertise should also be provided rather than leaving us to sit around (and run around)

in circles trying to sort out problems for ourselves as we were when G.C.S.E. was introduced.

Retraining may take many forms, e.g. the introduction of regular sabbatical to help ease pressures, and to gain worthwhile teaching revision.

Mandatory study/refresher leave to follow-up gaps in professional expertise, or plan and actualise professional development issues, e.g. advice on writing C.V.'s, advice on self-projection.

(Female secondary teacher)

As the issue of poor management and its link to teacher stress was made apparent throughout this study, it is important that headteachers be given the managerial skills training that they require to make them efficient resource managers.

Teachers should be offered managerial skills training courses before being asked to undertake certain positions of responsibility.

(Male secondary teacher)

as

Good management makes a tremendous difference. My current head is well organised, is a good communicator, has a lot of common sense, is a committed educator and takes staff morale very seriously. In my experience there are many heads without these skills and qualities. They seriously affect their staff and children.

(Female primary teacher)

An issue related to most of the above features and recommendations is the role of the teachers within schools. This needs to be more carefully and clearly defined so that teachers do not suffer from role ambiguity, which has been found to be a major source of stress that leads to unfavourable outcomes. If management of the schools in which they teach improves, and there is less emphasis upon the 'non-teaching' aspects of the job (e.g. administration), then teachers might regain a clear conception of what their role actually is.

**Improved promotion opportunities**

Greater promotional opportunities are needed within the profession, as a lack of opportunities is also causing job dissatisfaction. This is especially a problem for women teachers.

Ideally it is necessary to improve the career prospects and number of incentive allowances available in teaching. However, it is suggested that career counselling should be introduced for teachers. This is important, especially for women teachers and those who are older and have been in the profession for many years. Women need to be counselled as to what their actual needs are in teaching, as they do not acquire the same positions of seniority as their male colleagues, and yet appear to regard teaching as a favourable career. A problem reflected in the study is the perception of teachers that no other options are available to them in other forms of employment. Career counselling could enable teachers to evaluate their skills and consider different options outside teaching, or indeed identify areas within teaching where their prospects might be improved.

## Increased support mechanisms both in and out of school

The status of teachers, in terms of both recognition and material benefits, merits attention as this is also causing job dissatisfaction.

One of the major changes that teachers feel has taken place over the last few years is the decline in support from parents. They believe that far from supporting them in their role as teachers, parents blame them for any problems that occur both in the classroom and out of it. Teachers feel that parents do not take a big enough part in the education of their children, as one union administrator explained:

> Parents should have as much of a role – if not more – than teachers in bringing up their children in such a way that they are able to join society. Sadly that is not always the case.
>
> (John Andrews, PAT (Professional Association of Teachers),
> Brace 1990)

In addition, support needs to be provided in the form of increased auxiliary help in the classroom, as the problems of staff shortages and extra large classes makes the job of the teacher difficult.

Parents often complain that their child does not receive enough individual attention in the class, but this would seem to be an impossibility when teachers are often teaching classes of 35 children. One teacher suggested:

> It would improve the situation to bring in people . . . who come in and actually supervise the children between lessons, who actually do a lot of the bits and pieces and the paper work, and perhaps an increase in secretarial staff. This would bridge the gap between the teaching and the rest. Therefore the teaching would be looked on in a different way, because sometimes the teaching time is eroded while you are collecting bits and pieces, and everybody thinks that that's part of your job and so they think that's who you are 'somebody who collects bits of paper and gives bits of notices out'.

## Improvement in financial incentives

Again this is a feature that is beyond the scope of psychological intervention, but this is one that teachers feel very strongly about. There would appear to be a number of features linked to the demand for increased pay:

1 the improvement in status that it brings;
2 comparison of teachers with other occupational groups;
3 the need to survive financially, particularly specific teachers working in London.

One of the major financial problems experienced was expressed by a young male teacher working in a secondary school in inner-city London:

> Not having money for lunch – or worrying you are spending too much on lunch. Having to budget strictly for everyday things, e.g. travel pass, lunch, shoes, clothes, going out, etc., everyday essentials, not to mention rent and bills.

One female teacher suggested that an increase in pay might improve the teachers' status, in that the public at large would then appreciate what teachers do and value their contribution to society. It would also help teachers to improve their own feelings of self-worth, and might also encourage more and better qualified people to enter the profession.

In summary it would seem that teachers view themselves as professionals but do not believe that they accrue the same benefits as other professional groups. As one teacher said: 'absolutely pitiful state of pay in this country for a profession as essential to our society as doctors'. Therefore it seems the attitudes of teachers towards the job of teaching will not change, in terms of stress and job dissatisfaction, until they believe that their pay is fair.

**Adequate implementation of change**

Most of all, there needs to be an improved policy on change. Teachers are unhappy with recent changes that have taken place within education. This is not so much due to the changes themselves, but to the manner in which the changes are implemented. Change should not take place without considering the 'end-user' of the product of that change (i.e. in this case the teacher). Change should be more gradual, whereby new features of the job replace the old, and overlap is avoided.

The first chapter of this book highlighted the great number of changes that have taken place within the schools in the UK. Makin and Cox (1991) make the following observation:

> In recent years the government has been keen to 'devolve' management of schools to the schools themselves. There have been two major ways in which this has been attempted. This devolution of managerial and administrative responsibilities is entirely consistent with the government's strategy in other areas of the 'public sector'. The reasoning

behind it appears to be twofold. One is the judgement that such forms of organization are of themselves desirable, the other reason is that such forms of management are more efficient in their use of resources and that they are more responsive to the needs of the customers and clients.

Although the above statement suggests that the intention of the changes is to improve the education service as a supplier, these changes have had a detrimental effect on those working within schools to the point where the provision of the educational service is affected.

The pace and extent of change was seen to be a major source of stress for a large majority of the teachers in the sample. Teachers are not opposed to change as such, but feel that the way that the changes have been implemented have been the major source of stress for them. This does not necessarily mean that they object to the changes, but they object more to the lack of information regarding these changes, as one teacher explained: 'Pressure continues to come from outside the school – e.g. local authority, uncertainties and lack of up-to-date information concerning takeover of Lambeth in April 1990.'

Change is also a problem in terms of its pace of implementation and the fact that often it is designed by people with little involvement in teaching. Therefore, as one teacher explained:

> Set deadlines for the introduction of the National Curriculum by appropriate bodies deciding what is to be incorporated in the first place, and outlining attainment targets to be introduced, as most colleagues seem to have been left in the dark by the Minister of Education and the DES, etc.
>
> (Male secondary deputy headteacher)

Therefore, it is recommended that change needs to be implemented more carefully in terms of the pace, information required and appropriate change masters. Also it is advised that the actual 'end-users' (i.e. the teachers) need to be involved in the change process.

> At the moment education is not interesting ... I think that the L.M.S. strategy is as far reaching as anything else, and if they had just done that and left it for ten years, I think the stress would've been enough on teachers but they would've delivered it. What teachers are saying is 'what the hell is the worth of doing work on this, it's a waste of time as next year they will change it'.

Makin and Cox (1991) draw upon the similarity between the modifications that are taking place within schools and those that occur within commercial organisations, and try to apply models of the way in which organisations should adapt to these changes to schools. They refer to the model of Lievegoed (1973) who suggested that there are three stages through which an organisation must travel in order to progress through changes. These stages are (1) 'pioneer', (2) 'differentiated' and (3) 'integrated'. The pressure to progress through these stages at great pace comes from increasing size, and Makin and Cox (1991) argue that this is what has happened within education departments in recent years. Devolution has resulted as a way of trying to cope with the newly formed highly centralised bureaucracies. They suggest that before the changes, some small education departments may have been organised in the way of the 'pioneer' (i.e. small with few, short lines of communication) where adaptation to change is fairly rapid. Education departments may now be seen to be at the 'differentiation' stage, where increasing size leads to the development of a hierarchy-based organisation, based upon specialist functions and more complex communication. Coordination is required between different areas and often 'rule books' develop to cope with 'routine interactions'. Though some informal contact and networks may develop, these organisations are seen as bureaucratic, rule bound and slow to develop. One possible way to solve these problems is to set up more independent units, each given responsibility for its own management, which is to a large extent what has happened in schools and local education authorities. This, however, is presuming that each one has the expertise required to do this. A major problem facing schools has been the fact that, though they have the expertise to teach, other skills are less readily available. Headteachers, for example, rarely have the finance, accounting, personnel and purchasing skills to take on the new role that has been bestowed upon them. These added functions appear to mean that senior teachers may not have sufficient time to do the job they were trained for (i.e. to teach). The consequences of this are stress and reduced morale (as highlighted by this particular study). This suggests that it is important for those teaching in schools to be made aware of the implications of these changes on fellow teachers. The research revealed that there is often great cynicism concerning the role of the headteacher within schools, and so improved communication needs to take place so that all levels are aware of the extra and new demands that have been imposed upon them.

These are three general points arising from the findings concerning changes in education.

1 Innovative ideas should be thoroughly tested and objectively validated before being imposed on schools, teachers and pupils.
2 They should only be introduced at the same rate as existing practices are disregarded (i.e. if they are improvements, they should replace, not augment; current practice).
3 The 'change masters' would appear to be out of touch with day-to-day activities at the 'chalk-face' and should spend time in schools to enable them to be in touch with current teaching practices, conditions and expectations.

The general conclusion is that if changes must be made, then they should be introduced at a sensible accommodating pace by those with a full understanding of educational practices from the schools themselves, and with inclusion of the views of the end-users of these new policies. Much recent literature concerning the management of change emphasises the need to include those involved in its actual operation. An additional point is that, in order to implement change successfully, there must be adequate backing in terms of resources in order to ensure its smooth running and changeover.

## Improved professional and public image

The study has revealed that teachers do not believe that they have the correct image and level of status in the public eye. There are two ways that this might be improved. The first is by an *improved public image*, brought about by:

> A cessation of hostilities by press, media, etc., especially when you read about how you should do your job better by people who (a) have never taught and (b) wouldn't survive in a classroom full of today's children for even one minute.
>
> (Male secondary teacher)

Therefore, if the media begin to represent the teaching profession in a more favourable light this might influence the views of the public and help to alleviate stress. This may be done in the following way:

> Have media coverage in all fields, press, radio, TV to show and demonstrate the many, many, things that have been accomplished in education despite the lack of investment from this government.
>
> (Female secondary teacher)

The second would involve an *improved professional image*. It may be that teachers should have better professional representation, e.g. by one union to represent them rather than different unions, often competing with each other. The formation of some form of teaching council may help, and in this way teachers could be accountable to their own kind rather than to the government. By creating more rigid professional qualifications and bodies an improvement in status may result; for example, one male teacher in a secondary school suggested:

> The professionalism, in terms of housing our professional body to validate teacher training and courses – i.e. accountants have ICMA, ACCA, ACA, etc.; doctors have the BMA; lawyers have their Inn of Court and the like; but teachers are trained by government (local or otherwise) and only have their unions. If they want professionalism, then let them give us the power and money and *trust* to manage our own affairs in terms of training. Accountants protect their profession by ensuring that their training is of a high standard.

Therefore this image of teachers and teaching would need to be changed in order to alleviate some of the stress they experience.

A better public image may help parents to understand what actually goes on in schools. Currently, the attention that has been received has taken the angle that parents should be aware of their rights, usually to the detriment of the teacher's image. A more positive image is required so that parental support is encouraged. As one male primary teacher explained:

A better understanding is needed between the school and the parents of the kids that go to that school . . . there was something on the news the other night about schools being blamed for all society's ills. That is perfect, because we are.

and another female primary teacher suggested how this may be done:

The teachers self-image requires enhancement in a national sense. The teacher associations should perhaps jointly aim at bolstering teacher confidence by means of a national advertising campaign stressing the teacher's responsibility at a time of great change and pointing out the government's direct responsibility for much of the current disruptions in schools.

In any event, the social status of teachers needs to be improved because the present level is causing great anxiety for a large number of teachers, as one male teacher explained:

People used to be quite pleased when you said that you were a teacher, but now they're not at all impressed. In general terms, I think that a lot of people tend to think that standards have gone down . . . the various teachers' actions have not helped. I just don't think that they think anything goes on in schools, anything of any value.

## CONCLUSIONS

This study has revealed that the particular strains of day-to-day teaching that may be unavoidable (i.e. pupil behaviour, marking, etc.) are a source of pressure for teachers, but these intrinsic job features are not the major predictors of the negative stress outcomes. There are more 'contemporary' features of the job that are causing these negative outcomes, and these are features of the job that can be tackled in an attempt to reduce stress.

In requesting help in stress management techniques, teachers may feel that they have left themselves wide open to criticism that they are unable to cope with the job, and so when deciding appropriate courses of action, it is very important that blame does not appear to rest upon the individual. However, as the results of this study reveal, teachers exhibit high levels of Type A behaviour, which consequently plays a major part in determining a large proportion of the stress outcomes (i.e. mental ill health). This 'person facet' plays a more important role in the resulting stress manifestations than features of the working environment itself, and so it is vital to approach stress management from the individual level. However, a great deal of the stress that teachers are currently experiencing results from aspects of the work environment (i.e. the way their school is managed and change). Therefore, it is also crucial to approach stress management from the organisational level and social context.

The results of this study should be taken as an indication that all is not well in the teaching profession, but, as Peter Ward of the Health and Safety Executive suggests:

> The first important step is for education sector management to recognise that stress is not an indication of weakness or incompetence.
>
> (Hoyland 1990)

If this approach is taken and the methods for alleviating stress utilised, then it might well be possible to witness an improvement in the experience of teachers at work.

# Appendix 1
# Glossary of terms

## SAMPLES, VARIABLES AND DATA

**Sample**
People or things taken as a small subset that exemplify the larger population.

**Population**
All possible members of a group from which a sample is taken.

**Random sample**
Sample selected in which every member of the target population has an equal chance of being selected. If we draw our subjects without biases as a sample from some particular population, then it is possible for the results to be generalised from the sample to the population as a whole.

**Biased sample**
Sample in which members of a subgroup of the target population are over- or under represented (e.g. far too many headteachers compared to main-scale teachers).

**Variable**
A phenomenon (thing 'out there') that goes through observable changes (e.g. job satisfaction over time).

**Independent variable**
The variable which experimenters are deliberately manipulating to measure its effect on some other variable (e.g. sources of pressure in the questionnaire).

**Dependent variable**
The variable in which we are looking for changes or effects (e.g. mental ill health as a response to sources of pressure).

**Probability ($p$)**
A numerical measure of pure chance: '$p$' has a minimum value of 0 and a maximum value of 1. '0' refers to something that never occurs and '1' refers to something that always occurs.

**Significance levels**
Levels of probability at which it is agreed that our findings support/reject our research questions/hypotheses.

| | |
|---|---|
| **5 per cent ($p \leqslant 0.05$)** | Conventional significance level. |
| **1 per cent ($p \leqslant 0.01$)** | Significance (high) level preferred for greater confidence than the conventional one and which should be set where research is controversial or unique. |
| **Qualitative data** | Data gathered which is not susceptible to, or dealt with by, numerical measurement or summary, e.g. quotes and descriptions of stress. |
| **Quantitative data** | Data gathered which is susceptible to numerical measurement or summary e.g. data gathered from the sources of pressure scale. |
| **Items** | Questions or statements in the scales used within the questionnaire. |
| **Likert scale** | A scale on which a respondent can choose from a dimension of responses, usually coded 'strongly against/disagree' to 'strongly for/agree' and with an additional numerical value of, e.g., 1 to 5. |
| **Content analysis** | Analysis of the content of media sources. We may quantify descriptions through coding, categorisation and rating. For example, quotes made by the teachers to open-ended questions in the survey are examined for themes that may be quantified – e.g. 50 of the teachers mentioned that the 'lack of government appreciation' was a reason why they wanted to leave. |
| **Bi-polar adjectival scale** | Where people's attitudes are measured along a continuum from two extremes, e.g. from 'casual about things' to 'always in a rush' on the Type A scale. |

## DESCRIPTIVE STATISTICS

| | |
|---|---|
| **Descriptive statistics** | Methods for the numerical summary of a set of sample data. |
| **Mean (arithmetic)** | The most commonly used measure of the most typical value. It is the average of a set of scores, obtained by adding all the scores together and dividing by the number of scores. The mean score is usually represented by a symbol $\overline{X}$. |
| **Range** | This is simply the difference between the highest and the lowest scores. |
| **Variance** | The statistical measure of the extent to which data vary, i.e. how a set of scores vary around the mean that has been obtained. This is used when we want to know the variation in a sample from which we have collected data. |

| | |
|---|---|
| **Standard deviation (SD)** | Used to express the measure of variability in the same units as the original data (variance is squared to remove negative values – therefore it is the square root of the variance). It is the most commonly used measure of variability or spread. |
| **Normal distribution** | A continuous distribution giving a bell-shaped curve which is symmetrical about its mid-point and is the result of a variable affected by many random influences e.g. height, weight, etc. |
| **Normative data (norms)** | Data that have been obtained from the general population and have therefore provided a normal distribution with which to compare the extremity of our sample and their results. |
| **Frequency data** | Data presented as numbers of cases in specific categories. The **frequency** distribution shows how often certain values occurred, e.g. the number of teachers who smoke. |

## STATISTICAL TESTS

| | |
|---|---|
| *t*-test | Used when we look at two groups or samples and are trying to see if there is a difference between them that is dependent upon membership of that particular group. For example, if we wanted to compare the mental health of primary teachers with secondary teachers we would collect the data and try to examine the difference between the two sets of mean scores. We would then look at the amount of variability in these scores. The greater the differences in the mean scores, the more confident we would be that primary teachers have poorer mental ill health in general, but the greater the variance within each group, the less confident we would be. The *t*-test takes variance and mean scores into account and provides us with a probability which makes us more confident that the difference between the mean scores is not due to chance, but is likely to be due to differences between the responses of the two groups, i.e. secondary teachers perceive greater stress than primary teachers. |
| **Analysis of variance** | A statistical technique which compares variances within and between samples (e.g. across the three teaching grades) in order to estimate the |

significant differences between the mean scores for each sample.

**Correlation**
The extent to which one variable is related to another, often referring to non-manipulated variables, e.g. the relationship between Type A behavioural style and sources of job pressure.

**Factor analysis**
A statistical technique, using patterns of test or subtest correlations, which provide support for theoretical constructs by locating 'clusters' of items or variables that have been scored by respondents in a similar fashion.

**Multiple regression**
A technique in which the value of one variable is estimated using the correlation with several other variables. This is what we call a multivariate test. For example, if we put sources of pressure, personality and age into a multiple regression calculation we can see which one is most likely to lead to low mental health, and it will also order the contribution and predictability of all the variables.

## OTHER TERMS

**Meaningful factors**
The factors obtained are ones which can be seen to have a theoretical meaning and are also reliable.

**Modify/moderate**
When a relationship between two variables and the impact of the independent variable on the dependent variable is affected by some other variable. For example, sources of pressure in the job may lead to mental ill health but it is likely that this effect will be affected or modified by the type of personality that someone possesses.

**Reliability**
The extent to which findings or measures can be repeated with similar results. This means that if we were to carry out the same test more than once on the same individual we should obtain the same result. For example, consider the reliability of an elastic tape measure. When we test to see if a scale of items is statistically reliable we are measuring to see if all the items are linked, and therefore measuring the same concept. If they are not, the chances of obtaining a similar score on a number of occasions are less likely.

**Validity**
This is the extent to which scales/instruments

measure what they are intended to measure e.g. consider the validity of height as a measure of IQ! Also it is the extent to which a research effect can be trusted, i.e. it is not 'contaminated' by other 'extraneous' variables which have not been measured and so cannot be accounted for.

**Predictive**    This is the extent to which scores on certain measures (e.g. personality type) can predict scores on another measure (e.g. mental ill health) in the future. For example in our study multiple regression aims to predict the stress outcomes from the causes of stress among teachers.

Some books which may prove helpful and on which a number of these definitions are based are:

Bryman, A. and Cramer, D. (1992) *Quantitative Data Analysis for Social Scientists*, Routledge.

Coolican, H. (1994) *Research Methods and Statistics in Psychology*, Hodder & Stoughton.

# Appendix 2
# Survey on stress in teaching

## Introduction

The following questionnaire has been designed to measure both the sources and effects of occupational stress; a topic which has been much researched and for which there are many definitions. Generally speaking, occupational stress is regarded as a response to situations and circumstances that place special demands on the individual.

The sources of stress are multiple, as are the effects. It is not just a function of being "under pressure". The sources may be work related, but home life may also be implicated. The effects in terms of health may not just concern how you feel physically, but how you react and behave; again both in your job and home.

The answers to the questionnaire are **strictly confidential and will remain anonymous**. No names are requested, and there is no way in which any individual can be identified. It has been designed to gather information on groups of individuals.

There are six sections in all. These gather information on the following areas: Background information; Your physical health; Your Behaviour; Your Job Satisfaction; Sources of pressure you face in your job; and, How you cope with stress you experience.

As the questionnaire is being completed in a work context, the results will naturally be used in a work application. The explicit intention of the research project is to indicate the potential sources and effects of stress in those who work in the teaching profession, to the mutual benefit of the individual teachers and the profession as a whole.

**What we would like you to do**

- Answer all the questions-remember the data is anonymous
- Give your first and natural answer
- Work quickly and efficiently through the questions
- Base your answers on how you have felt during the last three months
- If you make a mistake, cross it out and provide your new answer
- Check each section to make sure you have answered all the items
- Place the completed questionnaire in the envelope provided and return to us
- Let us know if you would like details of the research results, or have any comments

Completion of the questionnaire will take approximately 45 mins-1 hour.

Thank you for your co-operation in this research project and for completing the questionnaire.

**Prof. Cary Cooper**
(Prof. of Organisational Psychology)

**Cheryl Travers** MSc
(Researcher in Occupational Psychology)

# Section 1: Background Information

The following questions are concerned with personal and background features concerning yourself and your job as a teacher.

The answers to these questions are crucial to the study and are for the purpose of statistical analysis only.

**THEY WILL REMAIN ANONYMOUS AND STRICTLY CONFIDENTIAL.**

**Please answer by circling the appropriate items, or tick/write in the boxes/spaces provided.**

## Part A: You and Your Family

1) Sex:        Male/Female

2) Age:        ☐ years

3) Where do you teach?

| Scotland | ☐ | North West | ☐ | South East | ☐ | Greater London | ☐ |
| N. Ireland | ☐ | Midlands | ☐ | East Anglia | ☐ | | |
| Wales | ☐ | South West | ☐ | North East | ☐ | | |

4) Marital Status:        Married/single/divorced/separated/
widowed/cohabiting

If married, does your partner work?   Yes/No

If Yes, do they work: Full-time/Part-time/Occasionally?

5) Is your partner a member of the teaching profession?   Yes/No

6) Please give the number of children you have in

Pre-school        ☐

Primary school        ☐

Secondary school        ☐

Tertiary college        ☐

Other ☐ (Please specify)_____

## Part B: Your Education

What is your academic background prior to teaching?

Certificate of education ☐   M.Ed ☐   B.Ed ☐   P.G.C.E. ☐   Ph.D ☐

Other ☐ (please specify)_____

## Part C: Work History

1) How many years have you been in teaching altogether? ☐ years

2) What is your current job title?

   Head ☐ Deputy Head ☐ Head of Department ☐ Promoted teacher ☐
   Main scale teacher ☐ Other ☐ (please specify) _____

3) How many years have you held this position? ☐ years

4) Is there any incentive allowance payable for this post? Yes/No
   If 'yes' which A ☐ B ☐ C ☐ D ☐ E ☐
   Head ☐ Deputy Head ☐

5) Do you work in a

   Nursery unit/school          ☐ Secondary school          ☐
   Primary school               ☐ Sixth-form college        ☐
   Middle School                ☐ Tertiary college          ☐
   Special school               ☐ F.E. college              ☐

6) In what type of area would you class your school?
   Inner-city ☐ Suburban ☐ Town ☐ Rural ☐

7) Is your school in the:    Independent sector ☐ State sector ☐ Voluntary-aided ☐

8) How many teaching staff are there in your school? ☐

9) How many pupils are there in your school? ☐

10) What is the range of class sizes that you teach? _____

11) What is the age range in your class? _____

12) What is the pupil/teacher ratio in your school? _____

13) Are you?  Full-time/part-time/supply

14) Are you responsible for any staff?  Yes/No        If yes, how many? ☐

15) How many hours is the pupil week? ☐ hours

16) How many actual teaching hours do you have with pupils each week? ☐ hours

## Part C: Work History (continued)

17) How many hours on average do you spend on other directed time activities in school? ☐

18) How many hours on average do you spend at home each week on the following?

Marking ☐      Preparation ☐      Assessment ☐

19) How many auxiliary helpers (supporting the work of the teacher in the classroom) are there in your school? ☐

20) How many hours have you had to cover for absent colleagues in the last week? ☐

21) On how many occasions during the last term did you have to accept pupils from the class of an absent colleague? ☐

22) How many days approximately have you been absent from work in the last year? ☐

23) How many of these approximately do you believe were due to stress related causes? ☐

24) Have you had any significant illness/es over the last 12 months? Yes/No

If Yes, which illness/es? _____

25) Are you involved in any extra curricular activities with pupils? Yes/No

If yes how many hours per week? ☐ hours

26) What is your principal subject teaching area? _____

27) Have you actively considered leaving the teaching profession within the last five years? Yes/No

If the answer to the above question is 'Yes', please could you tell us briefly why _____

_____

_____

28) Are you currently seeking          Alternative employment          Yes/No

Premature retirement          Yes/No

If the answer to either of the above is 'Yes', please could you tell us briefly why _____

_____

_____

**Part D: Your Habits**

1) Do you smoke? Yes/No

   If 'Yes' how many per day of the following:  Cigarettes ☐

   Cigars ☐

   Pipe ☐

2) Have you noticed changes in how much you smoke in the last 3 months?
   More than usual/same as usual/less than usual

3) Do you drink alcohol? Yes/No

   If Yes, how many units per week on average do you drink (1 Unit = ½ pint of beer, 1 glass of wine or 1 measure of spirit) ☐

4) Have you ever felt the need to cut down on your drinking? Yes/No

5) Over the last 3 months have you noticed any changes in your drinking habits?
   More than usual/same as usual/less than usual

6) What proportion of your consumption would you say was for stress release?
   Smoking ☐ %     Drinking ☐ %

7) Are you at present taking any prescribed drugs? Yes/No

   If Yes, which of these:     antidepressants     regularly/occasionally/never

   sleeping pills     regularly/occasionally/never

8) How often, on average, do you consume the following:

   coffee ☐
   (cups per day)

   tea ☐
   (cups per day)

## Section 2: Your Physical Health

**Please tick the answer that applies to you.**

1) Do you often feel upset for no obvious reason?    Yes...... No......

2) Are you troubled by dizziness or shortness of breath?

         Never...... Often...... Sometimes......

3) Can you think as quickly as you used to?    Yes....... No......

4) Have you felt as though you might faint?  Frequently...... Occasionally...... Never......

5) Do you often feel sick or have indigestion?    Yes...... No......

6) Do you feel that life is too much effort?  At times...... Often...... Never......

7) Do you feel uneasy and restless?  Frequently...... Sometimes...... Never......

8) Do you sometimes feel tingling or prickling sensations in your body, arms or legs?

         Rarely...... Frequently...... Never......

9) Do you regret much of your past behaviour?    Yes...... No......

10) Do you sometimes feel really panicky?    No...... Yes......

11) Has you appetite got less recently?    No...... Yes......

12) Do you wake unusually early in the morning?    Yes...... No......

13) Would you say you were a worrying person?  Very...... Fairly...... Not at all......

14) Do you feel unduly tired and exhausted?  Often...... Sometimes...... Never......

15) Do you experience long periods of sadness?  Never...... Often...... Sometimes......

16) Do you often feel "strung-up" inside?    Yes...... No......

17) Can you get off to sleep alright at the moment?    No...... Yes......

18) Do you have to make a special effort to face up to a crisis or difficulty?

    Very much so...... Sometimes...... Not more than anyone else......

19) Have you ever had the feeling you were "going to pieces"?  Yes...... No......

20) Do you often suffer from excessive sweating or fluttering of the heart? No...... Yes......

21) Do you find yourself needing to cry?  Frequently...... Sometimes...... Never......

22) Do you have bad dreams which upset you when you wake up?

      Never...... Sometimes...... Frequently......

23) Has your sexual interest altered?    Less...... The same or greater......

24) Have you lost your ability to feel sympathy for other people?  No...... Yes......

## Section 3: Your Behaviour

Could you please circle one number for each of the 14 questions below, which best reflects the way you behave in your everyday life. For example, if you are always on time for appointments, on question 1 you would circle a number between 7 and 11. If you are usually more casual about appointments you would circle one of the lower numbers between numbers 1 and 5.

| | | |
|---|---|---|
| Casual about appointments | 1 2 3 4 5 6 7 8 9 10 11 | Never late |
| Not competitive | 1 2 3 4 5 6 7 8 9 10 11 | Very competitive |
| Good listener | 1 2 3 4 5 6 7 8 9 10 11 | Anticipate what others are going to say (nods, attempts to finish for them) |
| Never feel rushed (even under pressure) | 1 2 3 4 5 6 7 8 9 10 11 | Always rushed |
| Can wait patiently | 1 2 3 4 5 6 7 8 9 10 11 | Impatient while waiting |
| Take things one at a time | 1 2 3 4 5 6 7 8 9 10 11 | Tries to do many things at once, thinks about what will do next |
| Slow, deliberate talker | 1 2 3 4 5 6 7 8 9 10 11 | Emphatic in speech, fast and forceful |
| Cares about satisfying him/ herself no matter what others may think | 1 2 3 4 5 6 7 8 9 10 11 | Wants good job recognised by others |
| Slow doing things | 1 2 3 4 5 6 7 8 9 10 11 | Fast (eating, walking) |
| Easy going | 1 2 3 4 5 6 7 8 9 10 11 | Hard driving (pushing yourself and others) |
| Expresses feelings | 1 2 3 4 5 6 7 8 9 10 11 | Hides feelings |
| Many outside interests | 1 2 3 4 5 6 7 8 9 10 11 | Few interests outside work/home |
| Unambitious | 1 2 3 4 5 6 7 8 9 10 11 | Ambitious |
| Casual | 1 2 3 4 5 6 7 8 9 10 11 | Eager to get things done |

# Section 4: Your Job Satisfaction

This set of items deals with various aspects of your job as a teacher. Please tell us how satisfied or dissatisfied you feel with each of these aspects of your present job. Use the scale below to indicate your feelings.

Please answer by circling the number of your answer against the scale shown.

| | |
|---|---|
| I'm extremely dissatisfied | 1 |
| I'm very dissatisfied | 2 |
| I'm moderately dissatisfied | 3 |
| I'm not sure | 4 |
| I'm moderately satisfied | 5 |
| I'm satisfied | 6 |
| I'm extremely satisfied | 7 |

**Remember:** There are no right or wrong answers. Give your first and natural answer by working quickly, but be accurate, and answer all questions.

1)  The physical working conditions      1 2 3 4 5 6 7

2)  The freedom to choose your own method of working      1 2 3 4 5 6 7

3)  Your fellow teachers      1 2 3 4 5 6 7

4)  The recognition you get for good work      1 2 3 4 5 6 7

5)  Your immediate boss      1 2 3 4 5 6 7

6)  The amount of responsibility you are given      1 2 3 4 5 6 7

7)  Your rate of pay      1 2 3 4 5 6 7

8)  Your opportunity to use your abilities      1 2 3 4 5 6 7

9)  Industrial relations between management and teachers in your school      1 2 3 4 5 6 7

10)  Your chance of promotion      1 2 3 4 5 6 7

11)  The way your school is managed      1 2 3 4 5 6 7

12)  The attention paid to suggestions you make      1 2 3 4 5 6 7

13)  Your hours of work      1 2 3 4 5 6 7

14)  The amount of variety in your job      1 2 3 4 5 6 7

15)  Your job security      1 2 3 4 5 6 7

# Section 5: Sources of Pressure You Face in Your Job

Almost anything can be a source of pressure (to someone) at a given time, and individuals perceive potential sources of pressure differently. The person who says they are "under a tremendous amount of pressure at work at the moment" usually means that they have too much work to do. But that is only half the picture.

The items listed below are those which teachers have expressed as being potential sources of pressure in their role as a teacher.

You are required to rate them in terms of the degree of pressure **you perceive each may place on YOU in YOUR job.**

Please answer by **circling** the number of your answer against the scale shown.

| | |
|---|---|
| Strongly disagree is a source of pressure | 1 |
| Disagree is a source of pressure | 2 |
| Slightly disagree is a source of pressure | 3 |
| Slightly agree is a source of pressure | 4 |
| Agree is a source of pressure | 5 |
| Strongly agree is a source of pressure | 6 |

1) Building and maintaining relationships with pupils          1 2 3 4 5 6

2) Overall lack of resources          1 2 3 4 5 6

3) Relationships with pupils' parents          1 2 3 4 5 6

4) Over-emotional involvement with the pupils          1 2 3 4 5 6

5) Dealing with basic behavioural problems          1 2 3 4 5 6

6) Having to 'cover' in unfamiliar areas of the curriculum          1 2 3 4 5 6

7) The unpredictability of 'cover' periods          1 2 3 4 5 6

8) When 'cover' for absent colleagues leads to 'large' classes          1 2 3 4 5 6

9) Inability to plan ahead due to constant changes          1 2 3 4 5 6

10) Knowing that my absence will create problems for other staff          1 2 3 4 5 6

11) The need for constant decision-making in the classroom          1 2 3 4 5 6

12) The likely introduction of 'teacher appraisal'          1 2 3 4 5 6

13) The hours spent marking at home          1 2 3 4 5 6

**Remember: You are required to rate these items in terms of the degree of pressure you perceive each may place on YOU in YOUR role as a teacher.**

14) The advent of Local Management of Schools     1 2 3 4 5 6

15) Lack of 'non-contact' time     1 2 3 4 5 6

16) Being a 'good' teacher does not necessarily mean promotion     1 2 3 4 5 6

17) Administrative tasks     1 2 3 4 5 6

18) Having to produce 'assessments' of pupils     1 2 3 4 5 6

19) Having to attend parents' evenings     1 2 3 4 5 6

20) Teachers can have little influence over
school decisions as a whole     1 2 3 4 5 6

21) Conflict between my department and others for resources     1 2 3 4 5 6

22) Lack of participation in decision-making in the school     1 2 3 4 5 6

23) The 'hierarchical' nature of the structure of my school     1 2 3 4 5 6

24) Lack of 'social support' from fellow teachers in my school     1 2 3 4 5 6

25) Conflict between the needs of my department/class
and the views of senior management     1 2 3 4 5 6

26) Lack of support from my union     1 2 3 4 5 6

27) The lack of clarity concerning my role within the school     1 2 3 4 5 6

28) The lack of value placed on actual 'teaching' itself     1 2 3 4 5 6

29) Lack of support from the government     1 2 3 4 5 6

30) Verbal aggression from pupils     1 2 3 4 5 6

31) Physical aggression from pupils     1 2 3 4 5 6

32) Lack of parental 'back-up' on matters of discipline     1 2 3 4 5 6

33) Lack of support from the Local Authority     1 2 3 4 5 6

34) Witnessing increasing aggression between pupils     1 2 3 4 5 6

Remember: You are required to rate these items in terms of the degree of pressure you perceive each may place on YOU in YOUR role as a teacher.

35) No recourse to sanctions in the school                        1 2 3 4 5 6

36) Lack of support from the school governors                     1 2 3 4 5 6

37) Duration of the summer holidays                               1 2 3 4 5 6

38) Society's diminishing respect for my profession               1 2 3 4 5 6

39) The number of daily confrontations in the class              1 2 3 4 5 6

40) The size of the classes that I teach                          1 2 3 4 5 6

41) The constant changes taking place
    within the profession                                         1 2 3 4 5 6

42) The move towards a 'National Curriculum'                      1 2 3 4 5 6

43) The lack of information as to how the changes are
    to be implemented                                             1 2 3 4 5 6

44) Having to be a "Jack of all trades, master of none"           1 2 3 4 5 6

45) Intra-staff rivalry i.e. within the school                    1 2 3 4 5 6

46) Academic pressure within the school                           1 2 3 4 5 6

47) Increasing involvement with 'pastoral' issues                 1 2 3 4 5 6

48) High demands from parents for good results                    1 2 3 4 5 6

49) Lack of support from the Head teacher                         1 2 3 4 5 6

50) Feeling that my training is not appropriate                   1 2 3 4 5 6

51) When my performance is assessed by others                     1 2 3 4 5 6

52) Lack of job security within the profession                    1 2 3 4 5 6

53) Teaching those who do not value education                     1 2 3 4 5 6

54) Teaching those who take things for granted                    1 2 3 4 5 6

55) Dealing with children who demand immediate attention          1 2 3 4 5 6

56) Continually having to form new relationships                  1 2 3 4 5 6

Remember: You are required to rate the items in terms of the degree of pressure you perceive each may place on YOU in YOUR role as a teacher.

57) Maintaining discipline     1 2 3 4 5 6

58) When pupils try to 'test' you all the time     1 2 3 4 5 6

59) A salary that is out of proportion to workload     1 2 3 4 5 6

60) Not enough opportunity to make my own decisions     1 2 3 4 5 6

61) Reacting too personally to pupils' criticism     1 2 3 4 5 6

62) My school is too 'traditional' and is slow to move with the times     1 2 3 4 5 6

63) The use of school bells     1 2 3 4 5 6

64) Having to work through breaks and lunch times     1 2 3 4 5 6

65) The amount of noise in the school     1 2 3 4 5 6

66) Having to teach in overcrowded classrooms     1 2 3 4 5 6

67) The number of interruptions in class     1 2 3 4 5 6

68) The constant 'answering back' from pupils     1 2 3 4 5 6

69) The threat of re-deployment     1 2 3 4 5 6

70) The neighbourhood in which my school is based     1 2 3 4 5 6

71) Teaching to exam standard     1 2 3 4 5 6

72) Promotion has lead to too few class contacts with pupils     1 2 3 4 5 6

73) Poor staff-student ratios     1 2 3 4 5 6

74) Poorly defined schemes of work     1 2 3 4 5 6

75) Increasing pressures from school governors     1 2 3 4 5 6

76) Lack of time to resolve problems with individual pupils     1 2 3 4 5 6

77) Lack of consensus among staff on matter of discipline     1 2 3 4 5 6

78) Poor working conditions     1 2 3 4 5 6

79) Having to manage a school on a tight budget     1 2 3 4 5 6

**Remember: You are required to rate the items in terms of the degree of pressure you perceive each may place on YOU in YOUR role as a teacher.**

80) Poor staff communications                                            1 2 3 4 5 6

81) Lack of chances for promotion                                        1 2 3 4 5 6

82) Too little responsibility within the school                          1 2 3 4 5 6

83) Taking work home interferes with family life                         1 2 3 4 5 6

84) Awareness of pupils social and financial deprivation                 1 2 3 4 5 6

85) The unfamiliarity of the demands that I face                         1 2 3 4 5 6

86) The inadequate implementation of change in my school                 1 2 3 4 5 6

87) My staff do not understand the pressures I am under
    as a manager                                                         1 2 3 4 5 6

88) The number of supervisory activities I have to perform at school     1 2 3 4 5 6

89) Unrealistically high expectations of others concerning my role       1 2 3 4 5 6

90) Uncertainty about the degree or area of my responsibility            1 2 3 4 5 6

91) Feeling that apart from teaching I have no other
    employable skills                                                    1 2 3 4 5 6

92) Parental attitudes towards my adherence to union
    policies e.g. strikes                                                1 2 3 4 5 6

93) Lack of clerical assistance                                          1 2 3 4 5 6

94) Vandalism of the school premises                                     1 2 3 4 5 6

95) Lack of auxiliary support                                            1 2 3 4 5 6

96) The integration of pupils with special educational needs            1 2 3 4 5 6

97) Truancy                                                              1 2 3 4 5 6

98) Racial tensions within the school                                    1 2 3 4 5 6

# Section 6: How You Cope with Stress You Experience

Whilst there are variations in the way individuals react to sources of pressure and the effects of stress, generally speaking we all make some attempt at coping with these difficulties, consciously or subconsciously. This final section lists a number of potential coping strategies which you are required to rate in terms of the extent to which you actually use them as ways of coping with stress.

Please answer by circling the number of your answer against the scale shown.

| | |
|---|---|
| Very extensively used by me | 6 |
| Extensively used by me | 5 |
| On balance used by me | 4 |
| On balance not used by me | 3 |
| Seldom used by me | 2 |
| Never used by me | 1 |

1) Deal with the problems immediately as they occur  6 5 4 3 2 1

2) Try to recognise my own limitations  6 5 4 3 2 1

3) "Buy time" and stall the issue  6 5 4 3 2 1

4) Look for ways to make the work more interesting  6 5 4 3 2 1

5) Reorganise my work  6 5 4 3 2 1

6) Seek support and advice from my superiors  6 5 4 3 2 1

7) Resort to hobbies and pastimes  6 5 4 3 2 1

8) Try to deal with the situation objectively in an unemotional way  6 5 4 3 2 1

9) Effective time management  6 5 4 3 2 1

10) Suppress emotions and try not to let the stress show  6 5 4 3 2 1

11) Having a home that is a refuge  6 5 4 3 2 1

12) Talk to understanding friends  6 5 4 3 2 1

13) Deliberately separate "home" and "work"  6 5 4 3 2 1

14) "Stay busy"  6 5 4 3 2 1

15) Plan ahead  6 5 4 3 2 1

16) Not "bottling things up" and being able to release energy  6 5 4 3 2 1

17) Expand interest and activities outside work      6 5 4 3 2 1

18) Have stable relationships      6 5 4 3 2 1

19) Use selective attention (concentrating on specific problems)      6 5 4 3 2 1

20) Use distractions (to take your mind off things)      6 5 4 3 2 1

21) Set priorities and deal with problems accordingly      6 5 4 3 2 1

22) Try to "stand aside" and think through the situation      6 5 4 3 2 1

23) Resort to rules and regulations      6 5 4 3 2 1

24) Delegation      6 5 4 3 2 1

25) Force one's behaviour and lifestyle to slow down      6 5 4 3 2 1

26) Accept the situation and learn to live with it      6 5 4 3 2 1

27) Try to avoid the situation      6 5 4 3 2 1

28) Seek as much social support as possible      6 5 4 3 2 1

Stress can be created by personal or work pressures, or a combination of the two. If you have experienced undue pressure recently, which of the following people did you talk to about the situation.

Please tick the appropriate boxes.

| | |
|---|---|
| SPOUSE/PARTNER | ☐ |
| RELATIVE | ☐ |
| HEADTEACHER | ☐ |
| WORK COLLEAGUE | ☐ |
| FRIEND (OUTSIDE OF WORK) | ☐ |

OTHER ☐ PLEASE SPECIFY _____

FINAL PAGE OVERLEAF

Thank you for completing this questionnaire. It may be that the questions did not fully reflect your situation. We would appreciate any further comments you would care to make. Please include any suggestions you have about ways and means by which the current pressures on teachers could be alleviated.

Please check that you have completed all sections, then return the questionnaire as indicated.

Thank you very much for your time and co-operation.

# Appendix 3
# Sources of pressure tables

*Table A3.1*   Male and female teachers

| | n | Mean | SD | t | p⩽ |
|---|---|---|---|---|---|
| **Management/structure of** | | | | | |
| *the school* | | | | | |
| Male | 1,013 | 32.90 | 9.24 | −3.85 | 0.000 |
| Female | 703 | 34.63 | 9.07 | | |
| | | | | | |
| *Class sizes/overcrowding* | | | | | |
| Male | 1,029 | 10.34 | 4.17 | −3.82 | 0.000 |
| Female | 712 | 11.13 | 4.34 | | |
| | | | | | |
| *Appraisal of teachers* | | | | | |
| Male | 1,027 | 18.56 | 5.23 | −4.86 | 0.000 |
| Female | 708 | 19.79 | 5.11 | | |
| | | | | | |
| *Managerial concerns* | | | | | |
| Male | 968 | 9.41 | 3.72 | 4.47 | 0.000 |
| Female | 616 | 8.54 | 3.83 | | |
| | | | | | |
| *Job insecurity* | | | | | |
| Male | 1,038 | 6.16 | 3.13 | −3.70 | 0.000 |
| Female | 715 | 6.72 | 3.07 | | |

*Table A3.2*   School type

| | n | Mean | SD | t | p⩽ |
|---|---|---|---|---|---|
| *Pupil/teacher interaction* | | | | | |
| Primary | 399 | 40.32 | 12.40 | −2.09 | 0.036 |
| Secondary | 1,180 | 41.75 | 11.65 | | |
| | | | | | |
| *Management/structure of the school* | | | | | |
| Primary | 391 | 31.95 | 9.81 | −4.27 | 0.000 |
| Secondary | 1,178 | 34.33 | 8.73 | | |
| | | | | | |
| *Class sizes/overcrowding* | | | | | |
| Primary | 405 | 12.29 | 4.33 | 7.95 | 0.000 |
| Secondary | 1,190 | 10.42 | 4.00 | | |
| | | | | | |
| *Appraisal of teachers* | | | | | |
| Primary | 407 | 20.42 | 4.65 | 5.76 | 0.000 |
| Secondary | 1,180 | 18.84 | 5.19 | | |
| | | | | | |
| *'Cover'/staff shortages* | | | | | |
| Primary | 378 | 16.28 | 5.34 | −2.33 | 0.020 |
| Secondary | 1,145 | 16.99 | 4.62 | | |

*Table A3.3* Teaching grade

|  | n | Mean | SD | t | p≤ |
|---|---|---|---|---|---|
| *Pupil/teacher interaction* | | | | | |
| Senior | 114 | 39.33 | 13.27 | 3.32 | 0.04 |
| Middle | 751 | 40.57 | 11.80 | | |
| Main scale | 870 | 41.79 | 12.26 | | |
| | | | | | |
| *Management/structure* *of the school* | | | | | |
| Senior | 122 | 27.58 | 9.81 | 27.42 | 0.000 |
| Middle | 760 | 33.35 | 8.92 | | |
| Main scale | 908 | 34.51 | 9.09 | | |
| | | | | | |
| *Class sizes/overcrowding* | | | | | |
| Middle | 760 | 10.28 | 4.08 | 4.97 | 0.007 |
| Main scale | 908 | 10.92 | 4.35 | | |
| Senior | 122 | 10.95 | 4.60 | | |
| | | | | | |
| *Changes taking place within* *education* | | | | | |
| Main scale | 908 | 15.28 | 2.87 | 5.58 | 0.004 |
| Middle | 760 | 15.71 | 2.64 | | |
| Senior | 122 | 15.72 | 2.71 | | |
| | | | | | |
| *Appraisal of teachers* | | | | | |
| Middle | 760 | 18.66 | 5.35 | 4.34 | 0.013 |
| Senior | 122 | 18.83 | 5.67 | | |
| Main scale | 908 | 19.42 | 5.02 | | |
| | | | | | |
| *Managerial concerns* | | | | | |
| Main scale | 908 | 8.33 | 3.68 | 55.18 | 0.000 |
| Middle | 760 | 9.34 | 3.58 | | |
| Senior | 122 | 11.99 | 3.99 | | |
| | | | | | |
| *Lack of status/promotion* | | | | | |
| Senior | 122 | 27.41 | 5.60 | 6.91 | 0.001 |
| Main scale | 908 | 29.25 | 5.43 | | |
| Middle | 760 | 29.34 | 5.05 | | |
| | | | | | |
| *Job insecurity* | | | | | |
| Middle | 760 | 6.00 | 3.08 | 12.84 | 0.000 |
| Senior | 908 | 6.09 | 2.88 | | |
| Main scale | 122 | 6.76 | 3.14 | | |
| | | | | | |
| *Ambiguity of teacher's role* | | | | | |
| Middle | 760 | 19.17 | 5.95 | 5.75 | 0.005 |
| Main scale | 908 | 20.15 | 6.08 | | |
| Senior | 122 | 20.28 | 6.59 | | |

*Table A3.4* Type A (A$_1$) and type B (A$_3$)

|  | n | Mean | SD | t | p≤ |
|---|---|---|---|---|---|
| *Pupil/teacher interaction* | | | | | |
| Type A$_1$ | 511 | 42.57 | 12.12 | 2.64 | 0.008 |
| Type A$_3$ | 468 | 40.51 | 12.31 | | |
| *Management/structure of the school* | | | | | |
| Type A$_1$ | 501 | 34.91 | 9.16 | 4.72 | 0.000 |
| Type A$_3$ | 470 | 32.07 | 9.56 | | |
| *Class sizes/overcrowding* | | | | | |
| Type A$_1$ | 516 | 11.10 | 4.48 | 2.63 | 0.009 |
| Type A$_3$ | 471 | 10.37 | 4.19 | | |
| *Changes taking place with education* | | | | | |
| Type A$_1$ | 525 | 15.76 | 2.70 | 2.52 | 0.012 |
| Type A$_3$ | 478 | 15.30 | 2.98 | | |
| *Appraisal of teachers* | | | | | |
| Type A$_1$ | 512 | 19.85 | 5.33 | 3.63 | 0.000 |
| Type A$_3$ | 474 | 18.64 | 5.09 | | |
| *Management concerns* | | | | | |
| Type A$_1$ | 478 | 9.83 | 4.00 | 6.52 | 0.000 |
| Type A$_3$ | 425 | 8.19 | 3.57 | | |
| *Lack of status/promotion* | | | | | |
| Type A$_1$ | 514 | 30.18 | 5.04 | 5.46 | 0.000 |
| Type A$_3$ | 469 | 28.29 | 5.75 | | |
| *Cover/staff shortages* | | | | | |
| Type A$_1$ | 488 | 17.34 | 4.86 | 2.91 | 0.004 |
| Type A$_3$ | 455 | 16.42 | 4.87 | | |
| *Ambiguity of the teacher's role* | | | | | |
| Type A$_1$ | 513 | 20.64 | 6.17 | 4.69 | 0.000 |
| Type A$_3$ | 464 | 18.80 | 6.07 | | |

# Bibliography

Alschuler, A.S. (ed.) (1980) *Teacher Burnout*, National Education Association.

AMMA (1986) *A Review of the Research into the Primary Causes of Stress Among Teachers*, Assistant Masters and Mistresses Association.

*Appropriation Accounts 1989/90*, Vol. 7: Classes XII and XIII; *Education and Science and Arts and Libraries*, HMSO.

Argyris, C. (1964) *Integrating the Individual and the Organization*, Wiley, New York.

Austin, D.A. (1981) 'The Teacher Burnout Issue', *Journal of Physical Education, Recreation and Dance*, 52 (9): 35–56.

Bacharach, S.B., Bauer, S.C. and Conley, S. (1986) 'Organisational Analysis of Stress: The Case of Elementary and Secondary Schools', *Work and Occupations*, 13 (1): 7–32.

Baron, R.A. (1986) *Behaviour in Organizations*, second edition, Allyn & Bacon, Newton, Mass.

Bayer, E. and Chauvet, N. (1980) 'Libertés et Constraintes de l'Exercice Pedagogique', Faculté de Psychologie et Sciences de l'Education, Géneve.

Becker, H.S. (1960) 'Notes on the Concept of Commitment', *American Journal of Sociology*, 66: 32–40.

Beech, H.R., Burns, L.E. and Sheffield, B.F. (1982) *A Behavioural Approach to the Management of Stress*, Wiley, Chichester.

Beehr, T.A. and Franz, T.M. (1986) 'The Current Debate About the Meaning of Job Stress', *Journal of Organizational Behaviour Management*, 8 (2): 5–18.

Beehr, T.A. and Newman, J.E. (1978) 'Job Stress, Employee Health, and Organizational Effectiveness: A Facet Analysis, Model and Literature Review', *Personnel Psychology*, 31: 665–99.

Begley, D. (1982) 'Burnout Among Special Education Administrators', Paper presented at the Summer Convention of the Council for Exceptional Children, Houston, Texas.

Bentz, W.K., Hollister, W.G. and Edgerton, J.W. (1971) 'An Assessment of the Mental Health of Teachers: A Comparative Analysis', *Psychology in the Schools*, 8: 27–76.

Bernstein, D.A. and Borkovec, T.D. (1973) *Progressive Relaxation Training: A Manual for the Helping Professionals*', Research Press, Champaign, Illinois.

Blackie, P. (1977) 'Not Quite Proper', *Times Educational Supplement*, No. 3259.

Blase, J.J. (1982) 'A Social-Psychological Grounded Theory of Teacher Stress and Burnout', *Educational Administration Quarterly*, 18 (4): 93–113.

Bloch, A. (1978) 'Combat Neurosis in Inter-City Schools', *American Journal of Psychiatry*, 135: 1189–92.

Blumenthal, J.A., McKee, D.C., Haney, T. and Williams, R.B. (1980) 'Task

Incentives, Type A Behavior Pattern, and Verbal Problem-Solving Performance', *Journal of Applied Social Psychology*, 10 (2): 101–14.

Bortner, R.W. (1969) 'A Short Rating Scale as a Potential Measure of Pattern A Behaviour', *Journal of Chronic Diseases*, 22: 87–91.

Bortner, R.W. and Rosenman, R.H. (1967) 'The Measurement of Pattern A Behaviour', *Journal of Chronic Disorders*, 20: 525–33.

Brace, A. (1990) 'Thugs in the Classroom Make 160,000 Teachers Ill', *Today*, 17 November.

Brenner, S.D., Sorbom, D. and Wallius, E. (1985) 'The Stress Chain: A Longitudinal Study of Teacher Stress, Coping and Social Support, *Journal of Occupational Psychology*, 58: 1–14.

Breuse, E. (1984) 'Identificación de las Fuentes de Tensión en el Trabajo Profesional del Enseñiante', in J.M. Esteve (ed.) *Profesores en Conflicto*, Narcea, Madrid.

Bridges, E.M. (1980) 'Job Satisfaction and Teacher Absenteeism', *Education Administration Quarterly*, 16: 41–6.

Brief, A.P., Rude, D.E. and Rabinowitz, S. (1983) 'The Impact of Type A Behaviour Pattern on Subjective Workload and Depression', *Journal of Occupational Behaviour*, 4: 157–64.

Brief, A.P., Schuler, R.S. and Van Sell, M. (1981) *Managing Job Stress*, Little, Brown, Boston.

Bromet, E.J., Dew, M.A., Parkinson, D.K. and Schulberg, H.C. (1988) 'Predictive Effects of Occupational and Marital Stress on the Mental Health of a Male Workforce', *Journal of Organizational Behaviour*, 9 (1): 1–13.

Burke, E. and Dunham, J. (1982) 'Identifying Stress in Language Teaching', *British Journal of Language Teaching*, 20: 149–52.

Burke, R.J., Shearer, J. and Deszca, G. (1984) 'Correlates of Burnout Phases Among Police Officers', *Group and Organizational Studies*, 9: 451–66.

Cannon, W.B. (1935) 'Stressors and Strains of Homeostasi', *American Journal of Medical Science*, 189 (1).

Capel, S.A. (1987) 'The Incidence of and Influences on Stress and Burnout in Secondary Teachers', *British Journal of Educational Psychology*, 57: 279–88.

Caplan, R.D., Cobb, S. and French, J.P.R. (1975) 'Relationships of Cessation of Smoking with Job Stress, Personality and Social Support', *Journal of Applied Psychology*, 60 (2): 211–19.

Caspari, I.E. (1976) *Troublesome Children in Class*, Routledge & Kegan Paul, London.

Catterton, B.L. (1979) '1978–1979 Teaching Stress Events Inventory – Portland Study of Teachers', *Educational Resources Information Centre*, No. 185042.

Chakravorty, B. (1989) 'Mental Health Among Schoolteachers', in M. Cole and S. Walker (eds) *Teaching and Stress*, Open University Press, Milton Keynes.

Chan, K.B. (1977) 'Individual Differences in Reactions to Stress and Their Personality and Situational Determinants: Some Implications for Community Mental Health', *Social Science and Medicine*, 11: 89–103.

Cherniss, C. (1980) *Professional Burn-Out in Human Service Organizations*, Praeger, New York.

Cheshire, T.E. (1976) 'Priorities in Education', *National Westminster Bank Quarterly Review*, November.

Chicago Teachers' Union (1978) *Chicago Union Teacher* (Special Supplement), March.

Cichon, D.J. and Koff, R.H. (1978) 'The Teaching Events Stress Inventory', Paper presented to the American Educational Research Association annual meeting, Educational Research Information Centre, No. 160–2.

Claggett, C.A. (1980) 'Teacher Stress at a Community College. Professional

Burnout in a Bureaucratic Setting', *Educational Resources Information Centre*, No. 195310.
Clare, J. (1990) 'Wage Boost for Teachers Urged to Woo Recruits', *The Daily Telegraph*, 10 May.
Clark, E.H. (1980) 'An Analysis of Occupational Stress Factors as Perceived by Public School Teachers', Unpublished Doctoral Dissertation, Auburn University.
Claxton, G. (1988) *The Less Stress Workshop* (copyright G. Claxton, King's College London).
Coates, T.J. and Thoresen, C.E. (1976) 'Teacher Anxiety: A Review with Recommendations', *Review of Educational Research*, 46 (2): 159–84.
Cobb, S. (1976) 'Social Support as a Moderator of Life Stress', *Psychosomatic Medicine*, 38: 301–14.
Cobb, S. and Kasl, S.V. (1977) *Termination – The Consequences of Job Loss*, H.E.W. Publications, NIOSH, USA, pp. 77–224.
Cole, M. (1985) 'A Crisis of Identity: Teachers in Times of Political and Economical Change', *Coloquio Internacional Sobre Functión Docente y Salud Mental*, Universidad de Salamanca, Salamanca.
Comber, L. and Whitfield, R. (1979) *Action on Indiscipline: A Practical Guide for Teachers*, NASUWT.
Connors, S.A. (1983) 'The School Environment: A Link to Understanding Stress', *Theory in Practice*, 22 (1): 15–20.
Cooke, R. and Kornbluh, H. (1980) 'The General Quality of Teacher Worklife', Paper presented at the Quality of Teacher Worklife Conference, University of Michigan, Ann Arbor.
Cooke, R.A. and Rousseau, D.M. (1984) 'Stress and Strain From Family Roles and Work Role Expectations', *Journal of Applied Psychology*, 69: 252–60.
Cooley, E. and Lavicki, V. (1981) 'Preliminary Investigations of Environmental and Individual Aspects of Burnout in Teachers', Paper presented at Oregon, Education Association, Otter Rock, Oregon.
Cooper, C.L. (1981) *The Stress Check*, Prentice-Hall, Englewood Cliffs, NJ.
—— (1983) 'Identifying Stressors at work: Recent Research Developments', *Journal of Psychosomatic Research*, 47 (5): 369–76.
—— (1985) 'The Stress of Work: An Overview', *Aviation, Space and Environmental Medicine*, July: 627–32.
—— (ed.) (1986a) *Stress Research: Issues for the Eighties*, Wiley, Chichester.
—— (1986b) 'Job Distress: Recent Research and the Emerging Role of the Clinical Occupational Psychologist', *Bulletin of the British Psychological Society*, 39: 325–31.
Cooper, C.L. and Crump, J. (1978) 'Prevention and Coping With Occupational Stress', *Journal of Occupational Medicine*, 20 (6): 420–6.
Cooper, C.L. and Kelly, M. (1993) 'Occupational Stress in Headteachers', *British Journal of Educational Psychology*, 63: 130–143.
Cooper, C.L. and Lewis, S. (1993) *The Workplace Revolution*, Kogan Page, London.
—— (1994) *Managing The New Work Force*, Pfeiffer, San Diego.
Cooper, C.L. and Marshall, J. (1975) 'The Management of Stress', *Personnel Review*, 4 (4): 27–31.
—— (1976) 'Occupational Sources of Stress: A Review of the Literature Relating to Coronary Heart Disease and Mental Ill-Health', *Journal of Occupational Psychology*, 49: 11–28.
—— (1978) 'Sources of Managerial and White Collar Stress', in C.L. Cooper and R.L. Payne (eds) *Stress at Work*, Wiley, Chichester, pp. 81–105.
Cooper, C.L. and Melhuish, A. (1980) 'Occupational Stress and Managers', *Journal of Occupational Medicine*, 22: 588–92.

Cooper, C.L. and Mitchell, S. (1990) 'Nursing the Critically Ill and Dying', *Human Relations*, 43 (4): 297–311.

Cooper, C.L. and Payne, R. (eds) (1988) *Causes, Coping and Consequences of Stress at Work*, Wiley, Chichester and New York.

Cooper, C.L. and Roden, J. (1985) 'Mental Health and Satisfaction Among Tax Officers', *Social Science Medicine*, 21 (17): 747–51.

Cooper, C.L., Cooper, R.D. and Eaker, L.H. (1988a) *Living with Stress*, Penguin Health, London.

Cooper, C.L., Davies-Cooper, R. and Faragher, E.B. (1986) 'A Prospective Study of the Relationship between Breast Cancer and Life Events, Type A Behaviour, Social Support and Coping Skills', *Stress Medicine*, 2: 271–7.

Cooper, C.L., Sloan, S.J. and Williams, S. (1988b) *Occupational Stress Indicator*, NFER Nelson, UK.

Cooper, C.L., Watts, J. and Kelly, M. (1987) 'Job Satisfaction, Mental Health and Job Stressors Among General Dental Practioners in the UK', *General Dental Health Practice*, January: 77–812.

Coughlan, R.J. (1969) 'The Factorial Structure of Teacher Work Values', *American Educational Research Journal*, VI: 169–89.

Cox, T. (1977) 'The Nature and Management of Stress in Schools In Clywd County Council' (ed.), *The Management of Stress in Schools* (Conference Report prepared by Clywd County Council Department of Education).

—— (1978) *Stress*, Macmillan, London.

—— (1985a) 'The Nature and Management of Stress', *Ergonomics*, 23: 1155–63.

—— (1985b) *Stress*, Macmillan, London.

Cox, T., Boot, N., Cox, S., with Harrison, S. (1988) 'Stress in Schools: An Organisational Perspective', *Work and Stress*, 2 (4): 353–62.

Cox, T., Boot, N. and Cox, S. (1989) 'Stress in Schools: A Problem-Solving Approach', in M. Cole and S. Walker (eds) *Teaching and Stress*, Open University Press, Milton Keynes.

Cox, T., Mackay, C.J., Cox, S., Watts, C. and Brockley, T. (1978) 'Stress and Well Being in School Teachers', Paper presented to the Ergonomics Society Conference on Psychophysiological Response to Occupational Stress, Nottingham University, Nottingham, England. (Cited in Litt, M.D. and Turk, D.C. (1985) 'Sources of Stress and Dissatisfaction in Experienced High School Teachers', *Journal of Educational Research*, 78 (3): 178–85.)

Crane, S.J. and Iwanicki, E.F. (1986) 'Perceived Role Conflict, Role Ambiguity and Burnout Among Special Education Teachers', *Remedial and Special Education (RASE)*, 7 (2): 24–31.

Crisp, A.H. (1977) 'Psychoneurosis in the General Population', *Journal of International Medical Research*, 5 (Suppl. 4): 61–80.

Crisp, A.H., Jones, M.G. and Slater, P. (1978a) 'The Middlesex Hospital Questionnaire: A Validity Study', *British Journal of Medical Psychology*, 51: 269–80.

Crisp, A.H., Ralph, P., McGuinness, B. and Harris, G. (1978b) 'Psychoneurotic Profiles in the Adult Population', *British Journal of Medical Psychology*, 51: 293–301.

Crown, S. and Crisp, A.H. (1979) *Manual of the Crown–Crisp Experiential Index*, Hodder & Stoughton, London.

*Daily Express, The* (1991) 'Heads Crack Up as School Stress Takes Heavy Toll', 20 April.

*Daily Telegraph, The* (1990) 'Wage Boost for Teachers Urged to Woo Recruits', 10 May.

Daley, M.R. (1979) 'Burnout: Smouldering Problem in Protective Services', *Social Work*, 24 (5): 375–9.

D'Arienzo, R.V., Muracco, J.C. and Krajewski, R.J. (1982) *Stress in Teaching*, University Press of America Inc.

Davidson, M.J. and Cooper, C.L. (1980a) 'The Extra Pressures on Women Executives', *Personnel Management*, 12 (6): 48–51.

—— (1980b) 'Type A Coronary-Prone Behaviour and Stress in Senior Female Managers and Administrators', *Journal of Occupational Medicine*, 22 (12): 801–5.

—— (1982) *Women and Information Technology*, Wiley, Chichester and New York.

—— (1983) *Stress and the Female Manager*, Martin Robertson, Oxford.

—— (1984) 'Occupational Stress in Female Managers: A Comparative Study', *Journal of Management Studies*, 21 (2): 185–205.

—— (1992) *Shattering the Glass Ceiling: The Woman Manager*, Paul Chapman Publishing, London.

De Frank, R.S. and Cooper, C.L. (1987) 'Worksite Stress Management Interventions: Their Effectiveness and Conceptualisation', *Journal of Managerial Psychology*, 2 (1): 4–10.

Department of Health and Social Security (1981) *Drinking Sensibly*, HMSO, London.

—— (1986) *Employment Gazette*, August.

DES (1973a) *The Supply of Teachers*, Reports in Education, No. 78, DES.

—— (1973b) *Teacher Turnover*, Reports in Education, No. 79, DES.

—— (1976) *Statistics of Education, 1976: Teachers*, 4: 19–38, HMSO, London.

—— (1980) *Education For 16–19 Year Olds*, Macfarlane Report, DES, London.

De Vries, H.A. (1968) 'Immediate and Long-term Affects of Exercise upon Resting Muscle Action Potential', *Journal of Sports Medicine*, 8: 1–11.

—— (1981) 'Tranquillizer Effects of Exercise: A Critical Review', *The Physicians and Sports Medicine*, 9: 47–55.

Dewe, P.J. (1985) 'Coping with Work Stress: An Investigation of Teachers' Actions', *Research in Education*, 33: 27–60.

—— (1986) 'An Investigation into the Causes and Consequences of Teacher Stress', *New Zealand Journal of Educational Studies*, 21 (2): 145–57.

Docking, R.A. (1985) 'Changing Teacher–Pupil Control Ideology and Teacher Anxiety', *Journal of Education for Teaching*, 11: 63–76.

Dunham, J. (1976a) 'Stress Situations and Responses', in NAS/UWT (1976) *Stress in Schools*, Hemel Hempstead.

—— (1976b) 'The Reduction of Stress', in NAS/UWT (1976) *Stress in Schools*, Hemel Hempstead.

—— (1977a) 'The Effects of Disruptive Behaviour on Teachers', *Educational Review*, 29 (3): 181–7.

—— (1977b) 'The Signs, Causes and Reduction of Stress in Teachers', in *The Management of Stress in Schools*, Clwyd County Council.

—— (1978) 'Change and Stress in the Head of Department's Role', *Educational Research*, 21: 44–7.

—— (1980) 'An Exploratory Comparative Study of Staff Stress in English and German Comprehensive Schools', *Educational Review*, 32: 11–20.

—— (1981) 'Disruptive Pupils and Teacher Stress', *Educational Research*, 23: 205–13.

—— (1983) 'Coping with Stress in Schools', *Special Education: Forward Trends*, 10 (2): 6–9.

—— (1984a) 'Teachers-Targets for Tension', *Safety Education*, 162: 11–13.

—— (1984b) *Stress in Teaching*, Croom Helm, Beckenham.

—— (1986) *A Decade of Stress in Teaching Research in the United Kingdom (1976–86)*.

—— (1992) *Stress in Teaching*, Routledge, London.

Dworkin, A.G. (1980) 'The Changing Demography of Public School Teachers: Some Applications for Faculty Turnover in Urban Areas', *Sociology of Education*, 53 (2): 65–73.

—— (1985) 'When Teachers Give Up', *Burnout, Turnover and Their Impact on Children*, Texas Press and Hogg Foundation for Mental Health, Austin, Texas.

—— (1987) *Teacher Burnout in the Public Schools: Structural Cause and Implications for Children*, State University of New York Press, New York.

Education Reform Act (1988) HMSO, London.

Edwards, J.R. and Cooper, C.L. (1990) 'The Person–Environment Fit Approach to Stress: Recurring Problems and Some Suggested Solutions', *Journal of Organizational Behaviour*, 11: 293–307.

Edworthy, A. (1988) 'Teaching Can Damage Your Health', feature on a research report, *Education*, 8 January.

Ellis, A. (1978) 'What People Can Do for Themselves to Cope with Stress', in C.L. Cooper and R. Payne (eds) *Stress at Work*, Wiley, Chichester.

Eskridge, D.H. (1984) 'Variables of Teacher Stress, Symptoms, Causes and Stress Management Techniques', Unpublished Research Study, East Texas State University.

Esteve, J.M. (1984) 'L'image des Enseignants dans Les Moyens de Communication de Masse', *European Journal of Teacher Education*, 7 (2): 203–9.

—— (1989) 'Teacher Burnout and Teacher Stress', in M. Cole and S. Walker (eds) *Teaching and Stress*, Open University Press, Milton Keynes.

Esteve, J.M. and Fracchia, A.F.B. (1986) 'Innoculation against Stress: A Technique for Beginning Teachers', *European Journal of Teacher Education*, 9 (3).

Etzion, D. (1984) 'The Moderating Effect of Social Support on the Relationship of Stress and Burnout', *Journal of Applied Psychology*, 69 (4): 615–22.

Faure, E. (1973) *Aprender a Ser*, Ahariza, Madrid.

Feitler, F.C. and Tokar, E.B. (1981) 'Teacher Stress, Sources, Symptoms and Job Satisfaction', Paper presented at the Annual Meeting of the American Educational Research Association, Los Angeles.

—— (1982) 'Getting a Handle on Teacher Stress: How Bad is the Problem?', *Educational Leadership*, 39 (6).

Fielding, J.E. (1984) 'Health Promotion and Disease Prevention at the Worksite', *Annual Review of Public Health*, 5: 237–65.

Fielding, M. (1982) 'Personality and Situational Correlates of Teacher Stress and Burnout', Doctoral Dissertation, University of Oregon; *Dissertation Abstracts International*, 43/02A.

Fimian, M.J. (1982) 'What is Teacher Stress?', *Clearing House*, 56 (3): 101–5.

—— (1983) 'A Comparison of Occupational Stress Correlates as Reported by Teachers of Mentally Retarded and Nonmentally Retarded Handicapped Students', *Education and Training of the Mentally Retarded*, 18 (1): 62–8.

—— (1984) 'The Development of an Instrument to Measure Occupational Stress in Teachers: The Teacher Stress Inventory', *Journal of Occupational Psychology*, 57 (4): 277–94.

—— (1987) 'Teacher Stress: An Expert Appraisal', *Psychology in the Schools*, 24: 5–14.

Fimian, M.J. and Santoro, T.M. (1981) *Correlates of Occupational Stress as Reported by Full-Time Special Education Teachers. I. Sources of Stress II. Manifestations of Stress*, Educational Information Research Centre, No. 219–543.

—— (1983) 'Sources and Manifestations of Occupational Stress as Reported by Full-Time Special Education Teachers', *Exceptional Children*, 49 (6): 540–3.

*Financial Times*, (1990) 'Policies Urged to Combat Teacher Stress', 17 November.

Fisher, S. (1986) *Stress and Strategy*, Lawrence Erlbaum Associates, London.

Fiske, D. (1978) 'Presidential Address to Society of Education Officers', January.

Fitzgerald, L. (1988) 'Exercise and the Immune System', *Immunology Today*, 9: 337–9.

Fleishut, J. (1985) *A Longitudinal Study of the Origin and Intensity of the Job-related Stress of Elementary School Teachers*, Temple University Press, Ann Arbor.

Fletcher, B. and Payne, R.L. (1980a) 'Stress at Work: A Review and Theoretical Framework, Part I', *Personnel Review*, 9 (1): 19–29.

—— (1980b) 'Stress at Work: A Review and Theoretical Framework, Part II', *Personnel Review*, 9 (2): 5–8.

—— (1982) 'Levels of Reported Stressors and Strains Among School Teachers: Some UK Data', *Educational Review*, 34 (3): 267–78.

Franco, S. and Esteve, J.M. (1987) 'La Profesión Docente: un Estudio Sobre la Salud y el Absentismo del Profesorado'. Unpublished thesis, University of Malaga, Spain.

Freeman, A. (1987) 'Pastoral Care and Teacher Stress', *Pastoral Care in Education*, 5 (1): 22–8.

French, J.R.P. and Caplan, R.D. (1970) 'Psychosocial Factors in Coronary Heart Disease', *Industrial Medicine*, 39: 383–97.

French, J.R.P. and Caplan, R.D. (1973) 'Organisational Stress and Individual Strain', in A.J. Marrow (ed.) *The Failure of Success*, Amacon, New York, pp. 30–66.

French, N.K. (1993) 'Elementary Teacher Stress and Class Size', *Journal of Research and Development in Education*, 26 (2): 66–73.

Friedman, M. and Rosenman, R.H. (1959) *Type A Behavior and Your Heart*, Knopf, New York.

—— (1974) *Type A: Your Behavior and Your Heart*, Knopf, New York.

Friedman, M., Rosenman, R.H. and Carroll, V. (1958) 'Changes in the Serum Cholesterol and Blood Clotting Time in Men Subjected to Cyclic Variation of Occupational Stress', *Circulation*, 17: 852–61.

Friedman, M., Thoresen, C.E., Gill, J.J., Ulmer, D., Powell, L.H., Price, V.A., Browin, B., Thompson, L., Rabin, D.D., Breall, W.S., Bourg, E., Levy, R. and Dixon, T. (1986) 'Alteration of Type A Behaviour and Its Effect on Cardia Recurrences in Post Myocardial Infarction Patients: Summary Results of the Recurrent Coronary Prevention Project', *American Heart Journal*, 112: 653–65.

Freudenberger, H.J. (1974) 'Staff-Burnout', *Journal of Social Issues*, 30 (1): 159–65.

—— (1977) 'Speaking From Experience. Burnout: The Organizational Menace', *Training and Development Journal*, 7: 26–7.

—— (1980) *Burnout: How to Beat the High Cost of Stress*, Bantam Books, New York.

—— (1983) 'Burnout: Contemporary Issues, Trends and Concerns', in B.A. Farber (ed.), *Stress and Burnout in the Human Service Professions*, Pergamon Press, New York.

Galloway, D., Ball, T., Blomfield, D. and Seyd, R. (1982a) *Schools and Disruptive Pupils*, Longman, London.

Galloway, D., Panckhurst, F., Boswell, K., Boswell, C. and Green, K. (1982b) 'Sources of Stress for Class Teachers', *National Education*, 64: 166–9.

—— (1986) 'Sources of Stress for Primary School Headteachers in New Zealand', *British Educational Research Journal*, 12 (3): 281–8.

Ganellen, R.J. and Blaney, P.H. (1984) 'Stress, Externality and Depression', *Journal of Personality*, 52 (4): 326–37.

Gillespie, D.F. (1983) *Understanding and Combatting Burnout*, Vance Bibliographies, Monticello, Illinois.

Gilligan, I., Fung, L., Piper, D.W. and Tennant, C. (1987) 'Life Events, Stress and

Chronic Difficulties in Duodenal Ulcer: A Case Control Study', *Journal of Psychosomatic Research*, 31: 117–23.

Glowinkowski, S.P. and Cooper, C.L. (1985) 'Current Issues in Organisational Stress Research', *Bulletin of the British Psychological Society*, 38: 212–16.

Goble, N.M. and Porter, J.F. (1980) *La Cambiante Función de Profesor*, Narcea, Madrid.

Goldberg, R.J. (1983) 'Stress in the Workplace: An Integrated Approach', *New Directions for Mental Health Services*, 20: 65–74.

Goldberg, D. and Huxley, P. (1980) *Mental Illness in the Community: The Pathway to Psychiatric Care*, Tavistock Publications.

Golembiewski, R.T., Munzenrider, R. and Carter, D. (1983) 'Phases of Progressive Burnout and Their Worksite Covariates', *Journal of Applied Behavioural Sciences*, 19: 461–81.

Goodell, H., Wolf, S. and Rogers, F.B. (1986) 'Historical Perspective, Chapter 2', in Wolf, S. and Finestone, A.J., *Occupational Stress. Health and Performance at Work*, PSG Inc, Littleton, Mass.

Gray, H. and Freeman, A. (1988) *Teaching Without Stress*, P.C.P. Education Series, London.

Gruneberg, M.M. and Oborne, D.J. (1982) *Industrial Productivity. A Psychological Perspective*, Macmillan, London.

*Guardian, The* (1991) 'History Teacher Wounded in Front of Class', 6 March.

Gutek, B.A., Repetti, R.L. and Silver, D.L. (1988) 'Nonwork Roles and Stress at Work', in C.L. Cooper and R. Payne (eds) *Causes, Coping and Consequences of Stress at Work*, Wiley, Chichester.

Hammond, J.M. (1983) 'School Improvement Using a Trainer of trainers Approach: Reducing Teacher Stress', *Journal of Staff Development*, 4 (1): 95–100.

Hargreaves, A. (1988) 'Teaching Quality: A Sociological Analysis', *Journal of Curriculum Studies*, 20 (3): 211–31.

Hargreaves, D. (1978) 'What Teaching Does to Teachers', *New Society*, 9 (43): 540–3.

Hargreaves Report (1984) *Improving Secondary Schools*, ILEA, London.

Harvey, D.F. and Brown, D.R. (1988) 'OD Interpersonal Interventions', in D.F. Harvey and D.R. Brown (eds) *An Experiential Approach to Organizational Development* (3rd edition), Prentice Hall International, Englewood Cliffs, New Jersey.

Hawkes, R.R. and Dedrick, C.V. (1983) 'Teacher Stress: Phase II of a Descriptive Study', *National Association of Secondary School Principals Bulletin*, 67 (461): 78–83.

Hembling, D.W. and Gilliland, B. (1981) 'Is There an Identifiable Stress Cycle in the School Year?' *The Alberta Journal of Educational Research*, 27 (4): 324–30.

Hendrix, W.H., Ovalle, N.K. and Troxler, R.G. (1985) 'Behavioural and Psychological Consequences of Stress and its Antecedent Factors', *Journal of Applied Psychology*, 70 (1): 188–201.

Herd, J.A. (1988) 'Physiological Indices of Job Stress', in J.J. Hurrell Jr, L.R. Murphy, S.L. Sauter and C.L. Cooper (eds) *Occupational Stress: Issues and Developments in Research*, Taylor & Francis, London.

Hewton, E. (1986) *Education in Recession: Crisis in County Hall and Classroom*, Allen & Unwin, London.

Hiebert, B.A. and Farber, I. (1984) 'Teacher Stress: A Literature Survey with a Few Surprises', *Canadian Journal of Education*, 9 (1): 14–27.

Hingley, P. and Cooper, C.L. (1986) *Stress and the Nurse Manager*, Wiley, Chichester.

Hinkle, L.E. (1987) 'Stress and Disease: The Concept After 50 Years', *Social Science and Medicine*, 25 (6): 561–6.

HMI (1986) *Report of Her Majesty's Inspectorate on the Effects of the Education Service in England and Wales of Local Authority Expenditure Policies*, DES, London.

HMSO (1990) *Managing Occupational Stress: A Guide for Managers and Teachers in the Schools Sector*, HMSO.

Holmes, T.H. and Rahe, R.H. (1967) 'The Social Readjustment Rating Scale', *Journal of Psychosomatic Research*, 11: 213–18.

Hoover-Dempsey, K.V. and Kendall, E.D. (1982) 'Stress and Coping Among Teachers: Experience in Search of Theory and Science', *Educational Information Research Service*, No. 241503.

Hoyland, P. (1990) 'Stress Blamed for Teachers' Health Problems', *The Guardian*, 17 November: 6.

Hughes, C. (1990) 'Early Retirement Trend "Inflaming Teacher Shortage"', *The Independent*, 5 November.

Humphrey, M. (1977) 'Review – Eysenck Personality Questionnaire', *Journal of Medical Psychology*, 50: 203–4.

Hurrell, J.J. and Kroes, W.W. (1975) *Stress Awareness*, National Insitute for Occupational Safety and Health, Ohio, Cincinnati.

ILO (1981) *Employment and Conditions of Work of Teachers*, International Labour Organisation, Geneva.

—— (1986) *Psychosocial Factors at Work: Recognition and Control*, Report of the Joint ILO/WHO Committee on Occupational Health, Ninth Session, 1984, International Labour Office, Geneva.

*Independent*, The (1990a) 'Resignations Causing Turbulence in Schools', 18 September.

—— (1990b) 'Cracks Appear at the Chalkface', 18 September.

—— (1990c) 'Early Retirement Trend Inflaming Teacher Shortage', 5 November.

—— (1991) 'Teachers Retiring Because of Stress', 25 January.

Innes, J.M. (1981) 'Social Psychological Approaches to the Study of the Induction and Alleviation of Stress: Influences Upon Health and Illness', in G.M. Stephenson, and J.M. Davies (eds) *Progress in Applied Social Psychology*, Vol. 1, Wiley, Chichester.

*Instructor* (1979) 'Teacher Burnout: How to Cope When the World Goes Black', *Instructor*, 88 (6): 56–62.

Ismail, A.H. and Trachtman, L.E. (1973) 'Jogging the Imagination', *Psychology Today*, 6: 79–82.

Ivancevich, J.M., and Matteson, M.T. (1984) 'A Type A–B Person–Work Environment Interaction Model for Examining Occupational Stress and Consequences', *Human Relations*, 37 (7): 491–513.

Iwanicki, E.F. (1983) 'Towards Understanding and Alleviating Teacher Burnout', *Theory in Practice*, 22 (9): 27–32.

James, P.H. (1980) *The Reorganization of Secondary Education*, NFER, Windsor.

Jenkins, C.D., Rosenman, R.H. and Friedman, M. (1968) 'Replicability of Rating the Coronary-Prone Behaviour Pattern', *British Journal of Preventative and Social Medicine*, 22: 16–22.

Jenni, M.A. and Wollersheim, J.P. (1979) 'Cognitive Therapy, Stress Management Training, and the Type A Behaviour Pattern', *Cognitive Therapy and Research*, 3: 61–73.

Johnston, D.W. (1985) 'Invited Review: Psychological Interventions in Cardiovascular Disease', *Journal of Psychosomatic Research*, 5: 447–56.

Kahn, R.L., Wolfe, D.M., Quinn, R.P., Snoek, J.D. and Rosenthal, R.A. (1964) *Organisational Stress: Studies in Role Conflict and Ambiguity*, Wiley, Chichester.

Kalker, P. (1984) 'Teacher Stress and Burnout: Causes and Coping Strategies', *Contemporary Education*, 56 (1): 16–19.

Kasl, S.V. (1983) 'Pursuing the Link between Stressful Life Experiences and Disease: A Time for Reappraisal', in C.L. Cooper (ed.) *Stress Research: Issues for the Eighties*, Wiley, Chichester.

Kelly, A.V. (1974) *Teaching Mixed Ability Classes*, Harper & Row, London.

Kelly, M.J. (1988) *The Manchester Survey of Occupational Stress in Headteachers and Principals in the United Kingdom*, Manchester Polytechnic.

Kelsall, R.K. (1980) 'Teaching', in R. Silverstone and A. Ward (eds) *Careers of Professional Women*, Croom Helm.

Kinnuen, U. (1988) 'Teacher stress during an Autumn term in Finland: Four types of stress processes', *Work and Stress*, Special Issue: *Stress in the Public Services*, 2 (4): 333–40.

Kinnuen, U. and Leskinen, E. (1989) 'Teacher Stress During a School Year: Covariance and Mean Structure Analyses', *Journal of Occupational Psychology*, 62: 111–22.

Kornhauser, A. (1965) *The Mental Health of the Industrial Worker*, Wiley, New York.

Krause, N. and Stryker, S. (1984) 'Stress of Well-Being: The Buffering Role of Locus of Control Beliefs', *Social Science and Medicine*, 18 (9): 783–90.

Kyriacou, C. (1980a) 'Sources of Stress Among British Teachers: The Contribution of Job Factors and Personality Factors', in C.L. Cooper and J. Marshall (eds) *White Collar and Professional Stress*, Wiley, Chichester.

—— (1980b) 'Occupational Stress Among Schoolteachers: A Research Report', *CORE*, 4 (3).

—— (1980c) 'Stress, Health and Schoolteachers: A Comparison with Other Professions', *Cambridge Journal of Education*, 10: 154–9.

—— (1980d) 'Coping Actions and Occupational Stress Among Schoolteachers', *Research in Education*, 24: 57–61.

—— (1981a) 'Social Support and Occupational Stress Among Schoolteachers', *Educational Studies*, 7 (1): 55–60.

—— (1981b) 'What Can Schools Do to Reduce Occupational Stress Among School Teachers?', Paper presented at the British Educational Research Association National Conference.

—— (1982) 'Reducing Teacher Stress: A Job for Psychologists in Education?', *Education Section Review (BPS)*, 6: 13–15

—— (1986a) 'Teacher Stress and Burnout', Paper delivered at the First International Meeting on Psychological Teacher Education, University of Minho, Portugal.

—— (1986b) *Effective Teaching in Schools*, Blackwell, Oxford.

—— (1987) 'Teacher Stress and Burnout: An International Review', *Educational Research*, 29 (2): 146–52.

—— (1989) 'The Nature and Prevalence of Teacher Stress', in M. Cole and S. Walker (eds) *Teaching and Stress*, Open University Press, Milton Keynes.

Kyriacou, C. and Pratt, J. (1985) 'Teacher Stress and Psychoneurotic Symptoms', *British Journal of Educational Psychology*, 55: 61–4.

Kyriacou, C. and Roe, H. (1988) 'Teachers' Perceptions of Pupils' Behaviour Problems at a Comprehensive School', *British Educational Research Journal*, 14 (2): 167–73.

Kyriacou, C. and Sutcliffe, J. (1977a) 'Teacher Stress: A Review', *Educational Review*, 29: 299–306.

—— (1977b) 'The Prevalence of Stress Among Teachers in Medium-Sized and Mixed Comprehensive Schools', *Research in Education*, 18: 75–9.

—— (1978a) 'Teacher Stress: Prevalence, Sources and Symptoms', *British Journal of Educational Psychology*, 48: 159–67.

—— (1978b) 'A Model of Teacher Stress', *Educational Studies*, 4: 1–6.

—— (1979a) 'Teacher Stress and Satisfaction', *Educational Research*, 21 (2): 89–96.

—— (1979b) 'A Note on Teacher Stress and Locus of Control', *Journal of Occupational Psychology*, 52: 227–8.

Lachman, R. and Aranya, N. (1986) 'Job Related Attitudes and Turnover Intentions Among Professionals in Different Work Settings', *Organization Studies*, 7 (3): 273–93.

Lachman, R. and Diamont, E. (1987) 'Withdrawal and Restraining Factors in Teachers' Turnover Intentions', *Journal of Occupational Behaviour*, 8: 219–32.

Laughlin, A. (1984) 'Teacher Stress in an Australian Setting: The Role of Biographical Mediators', *Educational Studies*, 10 (1): 7–22.

Lawrenson, G.M. and McKinnon, A.J. (1982) 'A Survey of Classroom Teachers of the Emotionally Disturbed: Attrition and Burnout Factors', *Behavioural Disorders*, 8: 41–8.

Lazarus, R.S. (1966) *Psychological Stress and the Coping Process*, McGraw-Hill, New York.

—— (1978) 'The Stress and Coping Paradigm', Paper presented at 'The Critical Evaluation of Behavioural Paradigms for Psychiatric Science' Conference, California.

—— (1981) 'Little Hassles Can Be Hazardous to Health', *Psychology Today*, (July): 58–62.

Lazarus, R.S. and Bilkman, S. (1984) *Stress, Appraisal and Coping*, Springer Publishing, New York.

Ledwidge, R. (1980) 'Run for your Mind: Aerobic-Exercise as a Means of Alleviating Anxiety and Depression', *Canadian Journal of Behavioral Science*, 12: 126–40.

Levinson, H. (1978) 'The abrasive personality', *The Harvard Business Review*, 56 (May–June): 86–94.

Lewin, K., Lippitt, R. and White, R.K. (1939) 'Patterns of Aggressive Behaviour in Experimentally Created Social Climates', *Journal of Social Psychology*, 10: 271–99.

Lewis, S. and Cooper, C.L. (1989) *Career Couples*, Unwin, London.

Lievegoed, B.C.J. (1973) *The Developing Organisation*, Methuen, London.

Lindenthal, J., Myers, J. and Pepper, M.P. (1972) 'Smoking, Psychological Status and Stress', *Social Science and Medicine*, 6: 583–91.

Litt, M.D. and Turk, D.C. (1985) 'Sources of Stress and Dissatisfaction in Experienced High School Teachers', *Journal of Educational Research* 78 (3): 178–85.

Lortie, D.C. (1975) *School Teacher: A Sociological Study*, University of Chicago Press, Chicago.

Lowenstein, L.F. (1991) 'Teacher Stress Leading to Burnout: Its Prevention and Cure', *Education Today*, 41 (2): 12–16.

Maccoby, E. and Jacklin, C. (1974) *The Psychology of Stress Differences*, Oxford University Press, London.

McCrae, R.R., Costa, P.T. and Bosse, R. (1978) 'Anxiety, Extroversion and Smoking', *British Journal of Social and Clinical Psychology*, 17: 269–73.

McGrath, J.E. (ed.) (1974) 'A Conceptual Formulation for Research on Stress', in *Social and Psychological Factors in Stress*, Holt Rienhardt and Winston, New York.

McGuire, W. (1979) 'Teacher Burnout', *Today's Education*, 68.

Mackay, C.J. and Cooper, C.L. (1987) 'Occupational Stress and Health: Some Current Issues', in C.L. Cooper and I.T. Robertson (eds) *International Review of Industrial and Organizational Psychology*, Wiley, Chichester.

McLean, A.A. (1979) *Work Stress*, Addison-Wesley, USA.

McMichael, A.J. (1978) 'Personality, Behavioural and Situational Modifiers of Work Stressors', in C.L. Cooper and R.L. Payne (eds) *Current Concerns in Occupational Stress*, Wiley, Chichester.

Makin, P. and Cox, C. (1991) 'The Management of Schools' (Paper in preparation).
Mancini, V., Wuest, D., Clark, E. and Ridosh, N. (1982) 'A Comparison of the Interaction Patterns and Academic Learning Time of Low-Burnout and High-Burnout Physical Educators', Paper presented at Big Ten Symposium on Research on Teaching, Lafayette, Indiana.
Mancini, V., Wuest, D., Vantine, K. and Clark, E. (1984) 'Use of Instruction and Supervision in Interaction Analysis on Burned Out Teachers: Its Effects on Teaching Behaviours, Level of Burnout and Academic Learning Time', *Journal of Teachers in Physical Education*, 3 (2): 29–46.
Margolis, B.L., Kroes, W.H and Quinn, R.P. (1974) 'Job Stress: An Unlisted Occupational Hazard', *Journal of Occupational Medicine*, 1 (16): 654–61.
Marshall, J. (1977) 'Job Pressures and Satisfactions at Managerial Levels', PhD Thesis, UMIST, Manchester.
Martin, T.N. Jr (1979) 'A Contextual Model of Employee Turnover Intention', *Academy of Management Journal*, 22: 313–24.
Martinez, A. (1984) 'El Perfeccionamiento de la Functión Didáctica Como Vía de Disminución de Tensiones en el Doconte', in J.M. Esteve (ed.) *Profesores en Conflicto*, Narcea, Madrid.
Mathews, K.A. and Haynes, S.G. (1986) 'Type A Behaviour Pattern and Coronary Disease Risk: Update and Critical Evaluation', *American Journal of Epidemiology*, 123: 923–60.
Matteson, M.T. and Ivancevich, J.M. (1987) 'Individual Stress Management Interventions: Evaluation of Techniques', *Journal of Managerial Psychology*, 2 (1): 24–30.
Maxwell, M. (1974) 'Stress in Schools', *Centrepoint*, 7: 6–7.
Meichenbaum, D. (1985) *Stress Innoculation Training*, Pergamon Press, Exeter.
Merazzi, C. (1983) 'Apprendre à Vivre Les Conflicts: Une Tâche de la Formation des Enseignants', *European Journal of Teacher Education*, 6 (2): 101–6.
Miles, R.H. and Perreault, W.D. (1976) 'Organisational Role Conflicts: Its Antecedents and Consequences', *Organisational Behaviour and Human Performance*, 17: 19–44.
Miller, K.I. and Monge, P.R. (1986) 'Participation, Satisfaction and Productivity: A Meta-Analytic Review', *Academy of Management Journal*, 29, (4): 727–53.
Milstein, M.M. and Golaszewski, T.J. (1985) 'Effects of Organisationally-based and Individually-based Stress Management Efforts in Elementary School Settings', *Urban Education*, 19 (4).
Miner, J.B. and Brewer, J.F. (1976) 'Management of Ineffective Performance', in M.D. Dunette (ed.) *Handbook of Industrial and Organizational Psychology*, Rand McNally, Chicago.
Minkler, M. and Biller, R.P. (1979) 'Role Shock: A 1001 for Conceptualizing Stresses accompanying Disruptive Role Transitions', *Human Relations*, 29, (2): 125–40.
Miskel, C. and Heller, L. (1973) 'The Educational Work Components Study; An Adapt Set of Measures for Work Motivation', *Journal of Experimental Education*, 42: 45–50.
Mobley, W.H. (1982) *Employee Turnover: Causes, Consequences and Control*, Addison-Wesley, Reading, Mass.
Moracco, J.C., D'Arienzo, R.V. and Danford, D. (1983) 'Comparison of Perceived Occupational Stress between Teachers who are Constructed and Discontented in their Career Choices', *The Vocational Guidance Quarterly*, pp. 44–51.
Moracco, J.C., Gray, P. and D'Arienzo, R.V. (1981) *Stress in Teaching: A Comparison of Perceived Stress Between Special Education and Regular Teachers*, Educational Information Research Center, Alabama, USA, No. 2028228.

Moss, L. (1981) *Management Stress*, Addison-Wesley, Reading, Mass.

Mowday, R.T., Koberg, C.S. and McArthur, A.W. (1984) 'The Psychology of the Withdrawal Process', *Academy of Management Journal*, 27 (1): 79–94.

MSC (1984) *Training For Jobs*, Cmnd 9135, HMSO, London.

Muchinsky, P.M. (1977) 'Employee Absenteeism: A Review of the Literature', *Journal of Vocational Behaviour*, 10: 316–40.

Mulligan, J. (1989) *The Personal Management Handbook*, Sphere, London.

Mykletun, R.J. (1984) 'Teacher Stress: Perceived and Objective Sources and Quality of Life', *Scandinavian Journal of Educational Research*, 28 (1): 17–45.

Nagy, S. (1982) 'The Relationship of Type A Personalities, Workaholism, Perception of the School Climate and Years of Teaching Experience to Burnout of Elementary and Junior High School Teachers in Northwest Oregon School District', Unpublished Doctoral Dissertation, University of Oregon, Eugene, Oregon.

Nagy, S. (1985) 'Burnout and Selected Variables as Components of Occupational Stress', *Psychological Reports*, 56 (1): 195–200.

NAS/UWT (1976) *Stress in Schools*, National Association of Schoolmasters/Union of Women Teachers.

Needle, R.H., Griffin, T. and Svendsen, R. (1981) 'Occupational Stress: Coping and Health Problems of Teachers', *Journal of Health*, 51 (3): 175–81.

Needle, R.H., Griffin, T., Svendsen, R. and Berney, C. (1980) 'Teacher Stress: Sources and Consequences', *Journal of School Health*, 50 (2): 96–9.

Nelson, D.L. and Quick, J.C. (1985) 'Professional Women: Are Distress and Disease Inevitable?', *Academy of Management Review*, 10 (2): 206–18.

NYSUT (1980) *Disruptive Students Cause Stress*, Information Bulletin, New York State United Teachers.

Nias, J. (1985) 'A More Distant Drummer: Teacher Development as the Development of Self', in L. Barton and J. Walker (eds) *Education and Social Change*, Croom Helm.

O'Connor, K. (1985) 'A Model of Situational Preference amongst Smokers', *Personality and Individual Differences*, 6 (2): 151–60.

Ojanen, S. (1982) *Opettajien Stressi (Teacher Stress)*, Reports from the Department of Education, Series A: 23, University of Tampere, Finland.

Orpen, C. (1978) 'Work and Non-Work Satisfaction: A Causal Correlational Analysis', *Journal of Applied Psychology*, 63: 530–2.

Parber, B.A. (ed.) (1983) *Stress and Burnout in the Human Service Profession*, Pergamon, New York.

Patton, J. and Sutherland, D. (1986) *Survey on Symptoms of Stress Among EIS Members in Clackmannanshire Schools*, Educational Institute of Scotland, Clackmannanshire Branch.

Payne, R., Jick, T.D. and Burke, R.J. (1982) 'Whither Stress Research? An Agenda for the 1980's', *Journal of Occupational Behaviour*, 3: 131–45.

Pearlin, L.I., Menaghan, E.G., Lieberman, M.A. and Mullen, J.T. (1981) 'The Stress Process', *Journal of Health and Social Behaviour*, 22: 337–56.

Pearlin, L.I. and Turner, H.A. (1987) 'The Family as a Context of "The Stress Process"', in S.V. Kasl and C.L. Cooper (eds) *Stress and Health: Issues in Research Methodology*, Wiley, Chichester.

Peston, M. (1982) 'Sir Geoffrey's Framework for Decline', *Times Educational Supplement*, 12 March.

Pettigrew, L.S. and Wolf, G.E. (1981) *Validating Measures of Teacher Stress*, Spencer Foundation, Chicago.

Phillips, A. (1980) 'Survey of Teacher Stress in Secondary Schools in the Local Authority', M.Phil thesis, University of Aston.

Phillips, B.L. and Lee, M. (1980) 'The Changing Role of the American Teacher:

Current and Future Sources of Stress', in C.L. Cooper and J. Marshall (eds) *White Collar and Professional Stress*, Wiley, Chichester.

Phillips, A. and Whitfield, R. (1980) Report of a Pilot Survey of Secondary School Teachers' Working Conditions, Birmingham, University of Aston Department of Education Inquiry.

Pines, A. (1982a) 'Helpers Motivation and the Burnout Syndrome', in T.A. Wills (ed.) *Basic Processes in Helping Relationships*, Academic Press, London and San Diego.

—— (1982b) 'Changing Organizations. Is a Work Environment without Burnout an Impossible Goal?', in W.S. Paine (ed.) *Job Stress and Burnout*, Sage Publications, Beverly Hills, California, 189–211.

Pines, A. and Aronson, E. with Kafry, D. (1981) *Burnout: From Tedium to Personal Growth*, The Free Press, New York.

Plant, M.A. (1979) 'Occupations, Drinking Patterns and Alcohol-related Problems: Conclusions from a Follow-up Study', *British Journal of Addiction*, 74 (3): 267–73.

Porter, L.W. and Steers, R.M. (1973) 'Organisational, Work, and Personal Factors in Employee Turnover and Absenteeism', *Psychological Bulletin*, 80: 151–76.

Pratt, J. (1976) 'Perceived Stress Among Teachers: An Examination of Some Individual and Environmental Factors and Their Relationship to Reported Stress', Unpublished MA thesis, University of Sheffield.

—— (1978) 'Perceived Stress Among Teachers: The Effects of Age and Background of Children Taught', *Educational Review*, 30: 3–14.

Price, V.A. (1988) 'Research and Clinical Issues in Treating Type A Behaviour', in B. Kent Houston and C.R. Snyder (eds) *Type A Behaviour Patterns: Research Theory and Intervention*, Wiley, New York.

Pring, R. (1984) *Personal and Social Education in the Curriculum*, Hodder & Stoughton, London.

Quick, J.D., Horn, R.S. and Quick, J.C. (1986) 'Health Consequences of Stress', *Journal of Behavioural Medicine*, 8 (1): 19–36.

Quick, J.C. and Quick, J.D. (1984a) *Organisational Stress and Preventive Management*, McGraw-Hill, USA.

—— (1984b) 'Preventative Stress Management at the Organisational Level', *Personnel*, September–October: 24–34.

Ranjard, P. (1984) *Les Enseignants Persécutés*, Robert Jauze, Paris.

Ranson, S. (1990) *The Politics of Reorganizing Schools*, Unwin Hyman, London.

Ranson, S., Taylor, B. and Brighouse, T. (1986) *The Revolution in Education and Training*, Longman, Harlow.

Rapoport, R. and Rapoport, R.N. (1971) *Dual Career Families*, Penguin, London.

Romano, J.L. (1988) 'Stress Management Counselling: From Crisis to Prevention', *Counselling Psychology Quarterly*, 1, 2 and 3: 211–19.

Rosenman, R.H. Friedman, M. and Strauss, R. (1964) 'A Predictive Study of C.H.D. The W.C.G.S.', *Journal of the American Medical Association*, 189: 15–22.

Rotter, J.B. (1966) 'Generalised Expectancies for Internal Versus External Control of Reinforcement', *Psychological Monographs*, 80 (1; whole number 609): 1–28.

Rudd, W.D. and Wiseman, S. (1962) 'Sources of Dissatisfaction Among a Group of Teachers', *British Journal of Educational Psychology*, 32 (3): 275–91.

Russek, H.I. (1965) 'Stress, Tobacco, and Coronary Disease in North American Professional Groups', *Journal of the American Medical Association*, 192: 189–94.

Russell, D.W., Altmaier, E. and Van Velzen, D. (1987) 'Job-Related Stress, Social Support and Burnout Among Classroom Teachers', *Journal of Applied Psychology*, 72 (2): 269–74.

Sadri, G., Cooper, C.L. and Allison, T. (1989) 'A Post Office Initiative to Stamp Out Stress', *Personnel Management*, August.

Schein, E.H. (1985) *Organizational Culture and Leadership*, Jossey-Bass, San Francisco.

Scherwitz, L., Graham, L.E., Grandits, K.G., Buehler, J. and Billings, J. (1986) 'Self-involvement and Coronary Heart Disease Incidence in the Multiple Risk Factor Intervention Trail', *Psychosomatic Medicine*, 48: 187–99.

Schonfield, I.S. (1992) 'A Longitudinal Study of Occupational Stressors and Depressive Symptoms in First-Year Female Teachers', *Teaching and Teacher Education*, 8 (2): 151–8.

Schuler, R.S. (1980) 'Definition and Conceptualization of Stress in Organizations', *Organizational Behaviour and Human Performance*, 25: 184–215.

—— (1982) 'An Integrative Transactional Process Model of Stress in Organizations', *Journal of Occupational Behaviour*, 3: 5–20.

Schwab, R.L. (1981) 'The Relationship of Role Conflict, Role Ambiguity, Teacher Background Variables and Perceived Burnout among Teachers', Doctoral Dissertation, University of Connecticut; *Dissertation Abstracts International*, 41 (09–A), (2): 3823–a.

—— (1983) 'Teacher Burnout: Moving Beyond "Psychobabble"', *Theory into Practice*, 22: 21–5.

Schwab, R.L. and Iwanicki, E.F. (1982) 'Perceived Role Conflict, Role Ambiguity and Teacher Burnout', *Education Administrative Quarterly*, 18: 60–74.

Selye, H. (1976a) *The Stress of Life* (revised edition), McGraw-Hill, New York.

—— (1976b) *Stress in Health and Disease*, Lippincott, Philadelphia.

—— (1980) *Selye's Guide to Stress Research, Vol. I*, Van Nostrand Reinhold.

—— (1983) 'The Stress Concept: Past, Present and Future', in C.L. Cooper (ed.) *Stress Research: Issues for the Eighties*, Wiley, Chichester.

Shaw, J.B. and Riskind, J.H. (1983) 'Predicting Job Stress Using Data from the Position Analysis Questionnaire', *Journal of Applied Psychology*, 68: 253–61.

Simpson, J. (1962) 'Sickness Absence in Teachers', *British Journal of Industrial Medicine*, 19: 110–15.

—— (1976) 'Stress: Sickness Absence in Teachers', in NAS/UWT, *Stress in Schools*, pp. 11–17.

Sloan, S.J. and Cooper, C.L. (1987) 'Sources of Stress in the Modern Office', in A. Gale and B. Christie (eds) *Psychophysiology and the Electronic Workplace*, Wiley, Chichester.

Smilansky, J. (1984) 'External and Internal Correlates of Teachers' Satisfaction and Willingness to Report Stress', *British Journal of Educational Psychology*, 54 (1): 84–92.

Smith, J. and Cline, D. (1980) 'Quality Programs', *Pointer*, 24 (2): 80–7.

Smith, M.J., Cohen, B.G., Stammerjohn, L.W. and Happ, A. (1981) 'An Investigation of Health Complaints and Job Stress in Video Display Operations', *Human Factors*, 23: 389–400.

Spanoil, L. and Caputo, G.G. (1979) *Professional Burnout: A Personal Survival Kit*, Human Services Associates, Lexington, Mass.

Sparks, D.C. (1979) 'A Biased Look at Teacher Job Satisfaction', *Clearing House*, 52 (9): 447–9.

—— (1983) 'Practical Solutions for Teacher Stress', *Theory into Practice*, 22 (1): 33–42.

Sparks, D.C. and Hammond, J. (1981) *Managing Teacher Stress and Burnout*, Educational Information Research, Educational Information Research Centre, No. 200252, Washington, DC.

Spencer, D., Steers, R. and Mowday, R. (1983) 'An Empirical Test of the Inclusions of Job Search Linkages in Mobley's Turnover Decision Model', *Journal of Occupational Psychology*, 56: 603–9.

SPSS Inc. (1986) *SPSS User's Guide*, 2nd edition, McGraw-Hill, USA.

Spuck, D.W. (1977) 'Rewards Structure in the Public High School', *Educational Administration Quarterly*, pp. 18–34.

Steers, R. and Mowday, R. (1981) 'Employee Turnover and Post Decision Accommodation Process', in B. Staw and I. Cummings (eds) *Research in Organizational Behavior*, Vol. 3, J.A.I. Press, Greenwich.

Stewart, J.D. (1983) 'Tying Hands in the Town Hall', *Times Educational Supplement*, 9 December.

Sutherland, V.J. and Cooper, C.L. (1986) *Man and Accidents Offshore*, Lloyds of London Press, London.

—— (1988) 'Sources of Work Stress', in J.J. Hurrell, Jr, L.R. Murphy, S.L. Sauter and C.L. Cooper (eds) *Occupational Stress: Issues and Developments in Research*, Taylor & Francis, London.

—— (1991) *Understanding Stress: A Psychological Perspective for Health Professionals*, Chapman & Hall, London.

Tannenbaum, R. and Massarik, F. (1989) 'Participation by Subordinates in the Managerial Decision-Making Process', in M.T. Matteson and J.M. Ivancevich (eds) *Management and Organizational Behavior Characteristics*, Irwin, Homewood, Illinois.

Taylor, J.K. and Dale, I.R. (1971) *A Survey of Teachers in Their First Year of Service*, University of Bristol.

Tellenbeck, S., Brenner, S.O. and Lofgren, H. (1983) 'Teacher Stress: Exploratory Model Building', *Journal of Occupational Psychology*, 56: 19–33.

Terkel, F. (1972) *Working*, Avon Books, New York.

Theorell, T. (1986) 'Characteristics of Employment that Modify the Rise of Coronary Heart Disease', in F. Wolf and A. Sinestone (eds) *Occupational Stress: Health and Performance at Work*, Plenum Press, New York.

Thoits, P.A. (1982) 'Conceptual, Methodological and Theoretical Problems in Studying Social Support as a Buffer Against Life Stress', *Journal of Health and Social Behaviour*, 23: 145–9.

*Times, The* (1990) 'Classroom Stress Taken its Toll on Teachers', 16 November.

Tinning, R.J. and Spry, W.B. (1981) 'The Extent and Significance of Stress Symptoms in Industry – With Examples from the Steel Industry', in E.N. Corlett and J. Richardson (eds) *Stress, Work Design and Productivity*, Wiley, Chichester.

Toffler, A. (1970) *Future Shock*, Pan, London.

Torrington, D. and Weightman, J. (1989) 'The Management of Secondary Schools', *Journal of Management Studies*, 26 (5 September).

Travers, C.J. and Cooper, C.L. (1991) 'Stress and Status in Teaching: An Investigation of Potential Gender-related Relationships', *Women in Management Review and Abstracts*, 6 (4): 16–23.

Travers, C. and Cooper, C.L. (1994) 'Psychophysiological Responses to Teacher Stress: a Move Towards more Objective Methodologies', *European Review of Applied Psychology*, 44 (2): 137–46.

Tunnelcliffe, M.R., Leach, D.J. and Tunnelcliffe, L.P. (1986) 'Relative Efficacy of Using Behavioural Consultation as an Approach to Teacher Stress Management', *Journal of School Psychology*, 24: 123–31.

Van Dijkhuizen, N. and Reiche, H.M.J.K.I. (1980) 'Psychosocial Stress in Industry: A Heartache for Middle Management', Paper presented at the Symposium on Psychosocial Factors in the Pathogenesis of Coronary Heart Disease, Maastricht, March 1979; to be published in *Journal of Psychotherapy and Psychosomatics*.

Wanberg, E.G. (1984) 'The Complex Issue of Teacher Stress and Job Dissatisfaction', *Contemporary Education*, 56 (1): 11–15.

Wanberg, E.G., Metzger, D. and Levitov, J. (1982) 'Working Conditions and Career Options Lead to Elementary Teacher Job Dissatisfaction', *Journal of Teacher Education*, 33 (5): 37–40.

Warnat, W.I. (1980) 'Teacher Stress in the Middle Years: Crises vs Change', *Pointer*, 24 (2): 4–11.

Warr, P., Cook, J. and Wall, T. (1979) 'Scales for the Measurement of Some Work Attitudes and Aspects of Psychological Well-Being', *The Journal of Occupational Psychology*, 52: 129–48.

Watts, M. and Cooper, C.L. (1992) *Relax: Dealing With Stress*, BBC Books.

Weiskopf, P.E. (1980) 'Burnout Among Teachers of Exceptional Children', *Exceptional Children*, 47: 18–23.

Westerhouse, M.A. (1979) 'The effects of tenure, role conflict and role conflict resolution on the work orientation and burnout of teachers', Doctoral dissertation, University of California at Berkeley. *Dissertation Abstracts International*: 41(01A), 8014928, 174.

Wilson, C.F. (1980) *Stress Profile for Teachers: Test Manual and Preliminary Data*, Department of Education, San Diego County, San Diego.

Wolpin, J. and Burke, R.J. (1986) 'Occupational Locking-in: Some Correlates and Consequences', *International Review of Applied Psychology*, 35: 327–46.

Woodhouse, D.A., Hall, E. and Wooster, A.D. (1985) 'Taking Control of Stress in Teaching', *British Journal of Educational Psychology*, 55: 119–23.

Woods, P. (1979) *The Divided School*, Routledge & Kegan Paul, London.

Yerkes, R.M. and Dodson, J.D. (1908) 'The Relation to the Strength of the Stimulus to the Rapidity of Habit Formation', *Journal of Comparative Neurology and Psychology*, 18: 459–82.

Zabel, R. and Zabel, M.K. (1982) 'Factors in Burnout Among Teachers of Exceptional Children', *Exceptional Children*, 49: 261–3.

# Author index

# Subject index